ORAL HISTORIOGRAPHY

DAVID HENIGE

ORAL HISTORIOGRAPHY

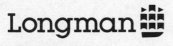

London New York Lagos

Longman Group Limited
Longman House
Burnt Mill, Harlow, Essex, UK

Published in the United States of America
by Longman Inc., New York

Published in Nigeria by
Longman Nigeria Ltd., Ikeja, Lagos

First published 1982

British Library Cataloguing in Publication Data

Henige, David
  Oral historiography.
  1. Oral history
  I. Title
  907.2   D5

    ISBN 0-582-64364-3
    ISBN 0-582-64363-5 Pbk

Library of Congress Cataloging in Publication Data

Henige, David P.
  Oral historiography.

  Bibliography: p.
  Includes index.
  1. Oral history. 2. Historiography. I. Title
D16.14.H46   907′.2   82–168
ISBN 0-582-64364-3   AACR2
ISBN 0-582-64363-5 (pbk.)

Printed in Great Britain by
Butler & Tanner Ltd, Frome and London

For Cindi, Chris, and Brian

CONTENTS

Nothing can stop. Nothing is left of those days but my story and your words.
Nothing remains behind.
[Ute informant, 351, p. 119].

PREFACE

John Stuart Mill once remarked that the friends he valued most were those who were not afraid to criticise and challenge his opinions rather than always being content to agree with them. The helpfulness and interest of friends and colleagues is certainly one of the most gratifying aspects of writing. I have also been fortunate enough to encounter many friendly critics along the way and they have helped give this work a broader perspective than I could possibly have provided alone. Carol Dickerman, Janet Ewald, Steven Feierman, Paul Irwin, Melvin Page, Laura Smail, and John Tosh read parts of earlier drafts that dealt with areas of their own expertise. David Newbury, Donald Wright, Thomas Spear, and an anonymous publisher's reader each read the entire manuscript at one time or another and were able to react to its effect as a whole. I am especially grateful to the first two, who provided the kind of painstaking commentary that is so important to authors, who find it all too easy to lose sight of the trees occasionally for concentrating on the forest, if not from sheer tedium.

I am particularly happy to pay belated thanks to the late Douglas Jones, who often invoked in me the very salutary feeling that, in his self-effacing way, he had forgotten more about African history than I had ever managed to learn. Douglas also possessed a well-developed sense of the incongruous and was very quick to spot the weak or missing links in any argument. I like to think that I have written what follows with the care that I would have if he were still arguing it out with me point by point.

Although he was temporarily spared the reading of this particular manuscript, Joseph Miller has read several others during the past few years and has always proved to be a trenchant, but usually friendly, critic. I have no doubt that, once he has the chance, he will be so on this occasion as well.

Priscilla Neill and the staff of the Interlibrary Loan Department of the Memorial Library, University of Wisconsin, have not only made a specific contribution to this work but have secured for me many hundreds of other items during the past decade. I am sure that I am but one among many who appreciate the actively helpful attitude we have invariably met with when doing business with them. The extent of the bibliography suggests only that my debt is greater than most.

Although he has read most of the present work, the signs of Jan Vansina's influence here are the result of many years of discussion, which have seldom failed to be chastening and stimulating. Equally important is the fact that, even though Jan's early work has stood the test of time remarkably well in a field where progress has been rapid, much of the most searching criticism of its argument has been his own. I have found this particularly exemplary, as I have his zest, turbulent energy and insatiable curiosity; his encouragement of new ideas; and his love of stirring things up – all traits that seem generally in short supply, whether within scholarship or outside it. I hope that I have been able to convey some of this in the body of this work.

INTRODUCTION

> What should they know of England who only England know?
> [Kipling, *The English Flag*]

> How can the historian beguile himself into the belief that he need only
> question the natives of a tribe to get at their history?
> [Robert Lowie, 302, p. 163][1]

This book is not intended to be an exhaustive study of the contemporary practice of oral historiography. In a work of this size it would scarcely be possible to do justice to the complexity of this subject; entire books have been devoted to such topics as the art of interviewing, the role of performance, or the effects of life situations on recall, that can be discussed only briefly here. Instead this should be regarded simply as an effort to draw together a few of the many strands relating to the prospects of oral historical research and the problems associated with carrying it out successfully.

Those who practise oral historical research have not always applied the nomenclature of the field with notable consistency and it is especially important to make clear the ways in which we use various terms here. We naturally begin with 'history' itself. It is not at all easy—and it may not be desirable—to attach to this term a single all-purpose definition, since in conception and practice it can assume a host of identities. Should 'history' encompass all that has ever happened anywhere and at any time? In that case historians have set themselves an impossible task. Or does history include only those activities of which traces still survive? In this case historians are obliged to confine themselves to trying to understand what has happened in the past on the basis of knowing only a fraction of it. Or is history no more than the result of whatever questions historians decide to ask of whatever surviving data they use? When this is true historians create history as well as re-create it and appear to refute Aristotle's observation that not even God can change the past. Finally, 'history' is sometimes used to describe the *métier* of historians—that is, they 'do history'.

There is little profit in lingering on this issue lest we begin to see even historians' legitimate goals as confusing and unattainable. Here we need do no more than accept that 'history' is never really quite synonymous with 'the past' but consists of whatever relics of that past survive—whether they be words, artifacts, or the results of natural forces—but with the added proviso that historians do not react to these traces passively but often augment their number. Oral historians are among the greatest of the adders since virtually none of the data they use are accessible before their research. In other words, for them collecting data involves turning data into evidence as well.

'Historiography' is a more straightforward term meaning the study of (literally 'the writing about') the past. In this way historiography as an

---

[1] For ease of reference the bibliography at the back of the book is numbered consecutively. When references are made to a particular work the number of the title precedes the number of the page or pages to be consulted.

activity incorporates *any* form of historical enquiry, including that based on oral sources, from the conception of a problem through to its solution or abandonment. For this reason, and because the term is less likely to be cŏnfused with others of its kind, it is used in the title of this work.

We are left with defining the two styles of oral historiography: 'oral history' and 'oral tradition'. Though quite different—one an activity, the other a genre of source—these terms have frequently been used interchangeably. As normally used nowadays, 'oral history' refers to the study of the recent past by means of life histories or personal recollections, where informants speak about their own experiences. Whether or not this terminology is particularly appropriate, it seems here to stay and is reflected in the titles of several books and journals, as well as the names of several associations devoted to pursuing this aspcct of oral historical research.

'Tradition'—as in 'oral tradition'—also has, or should have, a connotation of its own. In order for anything to be regarded as a tradition, it should be widely practised or understood in a society and it must have been handed down for at least a few generations. The term, however, is all too often misapplied to represent just about anything to which anyone wishes to give legitimacy or added luster. Strictly speaking, oral traditions are those recollections of the past that are commonly or universally known in a given culture. Versions that are not widely known should rightfully be considered as 'testimony' and if they relate to recent events they belong to the realm of oral history. It is with these particular distinctions in mind that I use the terms 'oral history' and 'oral tradition' throughout this work. In contrast, 'oral historian' is used collectively to include anyone who seeks to learn about the past by word of mouth, whether the most recent past or a more remote one.

With matters of definition and usage aside, we can turn to discussing the purpose and scope of this work. Somewhat unaccountably, discussions of fieldwork and the interpretation of oral evidence by historians rarely go beyond the limited and ignoble ends of self-aggrandisement. What we usually encounter are apologies for unduly far-reaching conclusions, and of course these stress only the affirmative features of oral research, sparing their readers any details about the unsatisfying, unproductive, and problematic aspects of fieldwork. In trying to provide answers without raising questions, this attitude contrasts strongly with the practice of anthropologists, who delight in debating among themselves the imponderables and vagaries of fieldwork; the relationships among themselves, their theories, and their informants; and the ability of fieldwork to provide genuine insights into a society's collective mentality, if there is such a thing [e.g. 154; 174; 199; 314; 335; 378; 485]. This absence of introspection and discussion among oral historians is particularly regrettable when we consider that historians' first fieldwork experience often sustains their scholarly activities for many years.

There have been a few studies by historians that attempt to answer the same kinds of questions as those that occupy anthropologists [e.g. 253; 377]. Of these perhaps the most thought-provoking is Paul Irwin's recent discussion of his research in Liptako [253]. Most readers should come away from Irwin's study with a richer appreciation of the unavoidable contretemps of fieldwork—the unpredictability of informants, the tribulations of becoming accepted by a strange society with very little to offer its members in return, the manifold imponderables in dealing with oral sources and materials—rather than with an illusory sense that Irwin has been able to unlock all the doors leading to the Liptako past. Irwin candidly recognises the limits of what he has learned and in the process he teaches the reader a great deal about the roles many parts of the Liptako past play in the cut and thrust of the Liptako present.

The limitless variety of the study of the past, which may well be its main attraction, means that, like any study of historical method, the present work might have been organised in any number of ways, with greater or lesser emphasis on various aspects of collecting information about the past. From these possibilities I have chosen an arrangement designed to stress three things above all else: i) that the success oral historiography presently enjoys is only the latest such episode and that we can learn much from studying work from oral historiography's own chequered past; ii) that pursuing the past through the spoken word is like all other forms of historical research in its mixture of the humdrum with the exciting, the momentary with the momentous, and thought with action; and iii) that if oral historians are to put their present success on a permanent footing they must make their sources available for the use of others. Let me elaborate on each of these points.

The penchant for magnifying the novelty and usefulness of oral historical research—making its practice as much a movement as a scholarly activity—is characteristic of enthusiasms. It is not to demean today's oral historians to point out that they are not the newest form of historian but the oldest. The historian of an oral society in Africa or Oceania can gain as much from reading studies of ancient Greek or early Scandinavian historical works as he can from consulting the latest studies of proper fieldwork technique. Chapter 1 merely draws attention to the range of possibilities in this respect.

Chapters 2 to 6 are the core of the book, but the reader is apt to find that they vary considerably in content and orientation. Can there really be any connection between boiling drinking water properly and deciding which elements of an oral narrative reflect fact and which are a matter of performing style? Why discuss palm wine and Polaroid pictures in the same chapter as profitable use of archives? Does it really make sense to package nuts and bolts with architectural drawings?

These are not unreasonable questions but the answer to each of them is a decided 'yes'. The crucial relationship between collecting evidence and its interpretation is, after all, nowhere more intimate than when the historian uses oral sources. When he is himself responsible for developing a body of data, it is clearly essential that he contemplate every aspect of his work carefully and try to see it in its widest context. All historical enquiry is a mixture of the makeshift, the mundane, and the mystifying. Oral historiography is especially so. Interpretive exercises are far more intricate here because the evidence is more varied, kaleidoscopic, and, above all, consciously reactive. Moreover, it is gathered from living sources in unfamiliar environments and in forms that need to be changed from oral to aural to written states. The historian's progress from the germ of an idea through the collection of data and on to their effective interpretation is one in which all stages, and all parts of every stage, are closely intertwined. None can be omitted and success in each depends on completing previous stages. In this way the particular elucidation of some part of the past of an oral society may well depend on whether the historian was careful to boil his[1] water properly, or bring enough spare parts for his equipment, or was able to fit comfortably into the gift-giving networks of the group he studies.

This peculiarly symbiotic relationship between sources and synthesis makes it all the more important that the historian arrays his sources scrupulously and makes them fully available to anyone with a legitimate interest in the results of his work. The failure by many oral historians to fulfill this obligation should be cause for concern by all who value oral research as one tool for studying the past. The evaluation of data, arguments, and conclusions by one's peers has long been a basic tenet of scholarship, but doing this adequately is simply not possible with the present availability of oral sources. Historians seem to expect that faith alone will serve to grant their work its place in the sun and for the present it may, but if their work is to survive the more rigorous and unsympathetic scrutiny of later generations, they must permit the critics to test, test, and test again. If such testing cannot be done, if the sources are lost forever, it is only to be expected that much of today's work will be rejected on these grounds alone. The chapter on this problem appears last because in the longer view its message may be the most important this work can convey.

Just as Chapter 1 tries to set current oral historical research into a temporal perspective, Chapters 4 to 6 (but especially Chapter 5) seek to demonstrate the value of approaching the study of oral evidence from the widest possible angle. Most historians realise the value of comparison, of course, but it is still rare to find many specialised studies based on oral sources that make use of the results of similar work done elsewhere. This blinkered view is needlessly parochial and even foolhardy and results in historians' advancing arguments that were killed and interred years ago. The use here, however slight, of materials from all corners of the globe is designed to suggest the riches available from the intensive study that has been, and is being, carried out on a variety of oral and literate cultures.

In all societies the past is the subject of continuing debate. At its best, historical study, whether based on written sources or derived from oral evidence, contributes to this debate by giving history a purpose through illuminating some aspect of the past as faithfully as it can. At one level the means to this end are the same: to gather, scrutinise, interpret, and array as many sources and arguments as possible. On another level, though, important differences emerge.

We shall see, for instance, that one of the historian's most difficult problems is that oral evidence changes imperceptibly as time passes. As for the human species, a principle of natural selection tends to operate, by which those traditions that are best able to outlive changing circumstances are those that exist today. But, as with plants and animals, surviving requires that they adapt to whatever changes they encounter. However reluctantly, we must assume that many contemporary versions of traditions are to some extent the

---

[1] Though probably with even less justification than usual, the masculine pronoun is used throughout this work to denote our hypothetical historian; this is to avoid the endless use of semantic abominations that I would not care to inflict on any reader.

debris of an obliterated past, the result of its mental landscape being repeatedly exposed to weathering, its shapes deposited in secondary patterns and shifting with the wind. Inevitably, many traditions cannot be regarded as historical fact. Accepting this will be hardest when there is nowhere else to turn, but this is a pity rather than an argument.

Yet it would certainly be unfair not to point out that oral materials share with written sources the quality of being prisms on the past rather than windows. Any study of the historiography of a particular time and place will show this, but two recent analyses of history textbooks in the United States and Britain demonstrate with unusual aptness how readily truth is subordinated to purpose by reflecting the social, political, and moral order of the day [44; 158]. The difference, of course, is that for written materials it is possible to chart, study, and partly explain the nature of these anomalies. Like fossil remains, previous editions or older textbooks have survived to enable the scholar to understand changes and relate them to each other and to their time, whereas oral tradition destroys at least parts of earlier versions as it replaces them.

Even greater than the differences between written and oral sources are the disparities in understanding and conceiving the past by societies that rely on writing and those that must depend only on the spoken word to carry an ever-growing past continually into an ever-changing present. It is probably impossible for those who take communication by the written word for granted to appreciate how difficult it is for any group of people to retain accurately a range of memories, often of things they never experienced personally or that appear to have no practical value. Electing not to remember an event in oral societies—in other words, forgetting it—means that it is cast into oblivion and not just onto a bookshelf. Few Americans can recite the names of the U.S. Presidents, few Britons can remember the names of all the children of Queen Victoria, and few Frenchmen can provide the names of the months of the revolutionary calendar. But any American, any Briton, or any Frenchman can find this information whenever they need to. In short, members of literate societies can be selective or careless in retaining memories, yet still be able indefinitely to retrieve some of what they have forgotten.

Because members of oral societies do not have this opportunity, the past necessarily assumes a very different role for them. The vague collective memory is formalised, systematised, replenished with details, and shaped into formal traditions time and again. This is enormously significant for oral historians, who sometimes profess to believe that members of oral cultures can and do remember more than literate people, if only because they need to if oral historians are to be successful in their work. Of course this is not often demonstrably true—with members of oral societies facts also fade into fancies. They generally forget about as much as other people and in doing so lose it forever, for without effective mnemonic devices forgetting is a disease without a cure. The study of the implications of this has only recently begun to interest oral historians [e.g. 328; 331; 435; cf. 342].

We close as we began—with a disclaimer. The reader seeking any discussion of historical theory will be disappointed. The concern here is only with the lesser species called method and there is no attempt to take into account the various theories or ideologies now vying for the allegiance of historians. Some of these claim to explain the past (e.g. historical materialism or psychohistory), whereas others try to explain why the past cannot be explained (e.g. structuralism or ritual folkloristics). In order to have any validity beyond rhetoric and persuade the unconverted, these theories must be built on a solid foundation of accepted fact. When the data have not been carefully gathered and critically scrutinised, theorising of this kind is ultimately so much wasted effort [e.g. 240; 450]. Our emphasis then is squarely on accumulating data effectively, testing them thoroughly, and meshing them with other evidence so that they can be widely regarded as reliable.

CHAPTER ONE

PUTTING ORAL HISTORIOGRAPHY IN ITS PLACE

> Every single item of folklore, every folk-tale, every tradition, had its origins in some definite fact in the history of man.
> [George Gomme, 190, p. 8]

> I cannot attach to oral traditions any historical value whatsoever under any conditions whatsoever.
> [Robert Lowie, 301, p. 598]

Growing interest in oral historical research has been one of the most striking features of historical study in our time, as advances in sound technology make such an enterprise economically and technically feasible. But a more important impetus has been the widening definition of historical enquiry. The new interest in Third World history that accompanied decolonisation helped bring this about, as did increasingly intensive study in the traditional fields of history. This combination of circumstances has given to oral historiography its own peculiar character. Ironically, in its multidisciplinary focus it is in the forefront of the discipline, whereas in such other areas as standards of textual analysis and breadth of training, it lags behind.

But if recent circumstances have made the nature of oral historical research what it is, learning about the past from the mouths of men is by no means something new. Literacy and non-literacy, and therefore written and oral sources, have always co-existed to one degree or another and until early modern times this oral method of exploring the past was of central importance in much of the world and even since then it has remained of some importance even in the most literate cultures. Therefore, in this study of collecting and interpreting oral historical materials today, a glimpse of some major uses of oral data in the past will establish to what extent modern views and practices reflect and perpetuate earlier ones as well as how they differ from them.

I

Those who would accept the outlines of the fall of Troy as recounted in the *Iliad* would probably consider Homer to have been the first known oral historian [300]. Others need go forward only a few centuries until they encounter the Greek historians of the fifth century B.C. Only the works of Herodotus and Thucydides have survived intact and the work of both, each in its own way, presaged much later oral historical investigation. Both combined the use of oral tradition with information collected personally from informants. By his own account Herodotus travelled widely throughout Asia

Minor and the Near East collecting stories about the past and investigating monumental remains there, so that much of what he included in his work purported to relate to periods many centuries before his own time [19; 196; 343; 477]. This was particularly true for Egypt, where he was awed by the magnitude and antiquity of the many monuments he found, as well as by the testimony of his sources, who regaled him with stories of the Egyptian conquest of western Asia, the building of the pyramids, and a line of more than 300 rulers—all material he wove into his narrative in the belief that they were largely true [67; 297, pp. 89–111]. Actually, although his informants provided a kernel of accurate information, there were many embellishments, distortions of chronology and sequence, and geographical and climatological absurdities.

The work of Thucydides differed from that of Herodotus, for he chose to write about the Pelopennesiàn war, in which he himself briefly took part. He was thus the first of a series of Greek and Roman historians (Xenophon, Polybius, Sallust, Caesar, Tacitus, Ammianus Marcellinus, and others) who participated in many of the events they wrote about. Thucydides started recording almost as soon as the war began and continued throughout the 27 years it lasted, wandering from one Greek city to another interviewing participants [249; 369]. Using these data helped him to include numerous speeches in his work, about which he admitted that he did not aim for 'strict accuracy' but preferred instead to describe what he felt were 'the sentiments most befitting' the occasions on which the speeches were delivered [145; 386]. By modern standards the use of apparently verbatim discourse in place of admitted paraphrase would be seen as poor method, but later historians have generally held the work of Thucydides in high regard for its impartiality, narrative style, research, and reliability [196]. Whether or not he always recorded his information accurately, he managed to give the impression that he did.

Like Herodotus and Thucydides, later Greek and Roman historians relied on a mixture of sources: oral tradition for such events (or non-events) as the return of the Heraclidae, the rape of the Sabine women, and the Gallic sack of Rome; written records for parts of the lists of Athenian archons, Roman consuls, and other officials; and their own observations and those of others for events near their own time [257; 334; 375; 405; 494]. Likewise, it is now being realised that oral data played a considerable role in the compilation of many historical works of early China [e.g. 11; 175; 264; 265; 496].

A particularly important field for which the importance of oral evidence has been recognised for some time is that of Biblical studies, both Old and New Testament, but especially the latter [e.g. 211, pp. 7–51]. Those books that eventually came to constitute the New Testament were collected and put together in the second and third centuries, while others (the so-called Apocrypha) were rejected and relegated to the status of heretical [212; 444; 490]. In studying how and why this happened, Biblical scholars give weight to the various ways these texts developed and were transmitted during the century or so before this final organisation took place [2; 268; 325]. Moreover, the study of the Gospels and Epistles, including the study of the relationships among them and their variants, now considers the effects of orality on these materials, which were composed over a period of 75 years or more [41; 62; 107; 180; 270; 272; 293; 299; 318]. Many early Christians were not literate enough to rely on the printed word so that word of mouth was necessarily the most effective and popular way of passing on Christian teachings to the first converts and then to succeeding generations until such time as a written canon was developed.

II

In medieval western Europe historians continued to rely on oral sources. An important early group of what we would call traditional historians were the bards and poets of the Celtic world—Wales, Scotland, and especially Ireland [e.g. 455]. Like many historians of today, these people spoke about the past as a way to earn a livelihood and to gain prestige within their own society [247; 305]. The great families of the time employed these bard-historians and expected them to enhance family pride and justify the political and social conditions of the times by finding, one way or another, suitable ancestors and other useful precedents. The view of one of their number that 'the antiquary ought to declare and testify, prove and certify the ancient history and family nobility of the princes and monarchs, by specifying their august and noble ancestors' would fit well with recent descriptions of the functions of West African *griots*, Maori *tohungas*, or Rajput genealogists [40; 421; 502]. The bewilderingly rapid geopolitical changes in the Celtic world ensured these oral historians ample scope to invent the past—indeed many pasts—with remarkable success, as they strove to elevate one ruling family or another to paramount status by providing them with a past suitable to their aspirations of the present [273; 283; 348].

By and large the medieval chroniclers of western Europe depended less than the Celtic bards on oral sources and their own inventive powers, but they did often use either oral tradition or eyewitness testimony [387]. All the major chroniclers of the Middle Ages—Bede, Gregory of Tours, Paulus Diaconus, Isidore of Seville, Widukind, and others—wrote in a world that was largely preliterate. The work of each of them included details on the recent past and like their predecessors among the Greeks, Romans, and early Christians they used their own memories and those of eyewitnesses to incorporate many anecdotes into their accounts.

The first major written source for Norman England is the famous Domesday Book, a survey of landholding compiled in 1086. From its completion it began to be used to settle disputes, determine revenues, and search for ancestors because it provided so thorough a record at a single moment in time. One expert described the Domesday Book as signifying 'an epoch in the use of the written word', and so it did [90; 169, p. 90]. But, like many a printed source, it was based largely and directly on testimony presented orally at several local hearings at which the data were gathered [168].

The Norman period was also characterised by a large number of chroniclers, mostly monks, who wrote the history of their own times or of their own diocese or religious house, as well as the lives of holy men. William of Malmesbury (d. 1143) wrote a history of England largely concerned with the century before his death [148; 195, pp. 166–85]. For this he relied on earlier available manuscripts, but he also travelled throughout the country inspecting ruins and interviewing numerous, though unspecified, informants. In regard to these last he confessed that he was worried about the problem of 'believ[ing] in deeds so far removed from our memory that they . . . are buried through lack of writing' but, despite his doubts, he had much recourse to such informants and was not averse to using the information they provided [493, p. 331].

William's contemporary, Henry of Huntingdon (d. 1155), likewise wrote a history of Norman England and he too depended on oral as well as written sources [361]. When he reached the point of describing events that had occurred about sixty years before he was writing, Henry advised his readers that 'now these things are to be told which we either saw ourself or which we heard from those who saw them' [362, p. 21]. Having alerted his readers, he then mixed documentary evidence with orally-derived materials to present a fuller account of his own times.

A third twelfth-century chronicler, William of Newburgh (d. 1198), differed little from his two predecessors in his use of oral sources. He explicitly cited oral testimony several times, frequently prefacing these occasions with statements that he had heard it 'from those who were there or [who had] heard it from those that were there' [362, p. 61]. Such major chroniclers of medieval England as Roger Wendover, Matthew Paris, Robert of Gloucester, and Peter of Langtoft also depended on oral information and each, interestingly, took care to notify his readers when this was the case [195; 476]. In this they typify, as we will see, many historians whose policy was to use both written and oral sources and to advise their readers, almost sheepishly, that they were doing so. This sense of *faute de mieux* has been a constant companion of oral historical research well into our own times.

Certainly, when we turn to medieval continental Europe we see the English pattern repeated. Long before William of Malmesbury and his colleagues wrote, Charlemagne had ordered that 'the very old heathen songs which tell of deeds and wars of former kings' should be 'collected and written down' [136, p. 101]. Later historians continued to use these kinds of materials (for instance, the *Nibelungenlied* or the *Chanson de Roland*) in both their oral and written forms. Generally speaking, there were two historiographic traditions in Europe during the Middle Ages. Some, like Otto of Freising (d. 1158) attempted to write so-called universal history ('universal' meaning 'western Europe') based almost entirely on written sources: such ancient historians as were available and their own predecessors [216; 355]. Others, like Saxo Grammaticus (d. c. 1220) and Adam of Bremen (d. c. 1076) were content to try to preserve the history of their own locales. Otto claimed to record 'nothing save what I have found in the writings of trustworthy men' in his chronicle of western civilisation [355, p. 96]. But he was willing to lapse from this practice for 'the days still fresh in our memories', for which he relied on information provided by 'credible men or seen or heard by ourselves' [355, p. 417].

Saxo Grammaticus divided his history of the Danes into two roughly equal parts. For much of the first part, a largely legendary account of the period before the ninth century, Saxo depended on information he obtained from visiting Icelanders because they 'account[ed] it a delight to consign to remembrance the history of all nations', by which he meant the devising and perfecting of the sagas [77; 260; 411, p. 5]. At the time Saxo wrote, these had not yet been committed to writing and were still being transmitted orally [462]. For the second part of his work, on the two to three centuries before he wrote, Saxo relied on a few written accounts, runic inscriptions, and oral testimony [410; 411; 428].

Adam of Bremen wrote a history of his own diocese, a popular form of historical endeavour during the Middle Ages. In his discussion of sources we see a by-now familiar pattern. For the earlier period about which he wrote he 'collected some items from scattered records' and 'borrowed much from the histories and charters of the Romans'. However, 'by far the greater part' of his account of the eleventh century was based on 'the tradition of older men who knew the facts'—words today's oral historians often repeat in much the same form [4, p. 5].

III

The monkish chroniclers of western Europe were by no means alone in writing about the past. There existed in the contemporary Islamic world a similar tradition that, if slow in getting started, eventually matched, if not surpassed, that of Europe [400; 401]. Like their European counterparts, Muslim historians worked directly and indirectly with oral data as well as written sources. In fact, in earliest Islamic society orality as such was particularly prized. In Muslim legal procedure, for example, a cardinal principle was that eyewitness evidence was to be preferred to any form of written documentation [412]. Moreover, the collection of *hadiths*, or traditions about Muhammad, was the major historical preoccupation of Muslim scholars during the first two centuries after Muhammad's death [see below, p. 75] and the practice of prefacing each hadith with a chain of narrator-transmitters carried over into later Islamic historiography [371].

During most of this early period all attempts to reconstruct and transmit knowledge about the events of the early years of Islam were based on oral materials. Some of the traditionalists who collected, transmitted, and eventually compiled collections of hadiths went so far as to burn whatever they had written down in order that their content could be passed on only by word of mouth [129]. In due course some scholars began to go beyond mere compilation and tried to use hadiths and other traditions as a basis for presenting a more complete view of the past. The first important historian to attempt a large-scale narrative of Muslim expansion was al-Baladhuri (d. 892), who began by stating that he had 'transmitted, abridged, and pieced together into one whole' the various narratives of 'certain men learned in tradition' [25, p. 5; 426]. In this new departure al-Baladhuri used materials from written compilations but much also came from hadith traditions that were still circulating orally, although by this time the great canonical collections had begun to crystallise in written form.

With the possible exception of Ibn Khaldun, the most influential Muslim historian was al-Tabari (d. 923), who undertook the ambitious project of telling 'all that occurred from Adam until the present time,' largely on the basis of what was or had been oral tradition [443, p. 12]. His account of the world before Muhammad consists of a long series of tales about important figures and events that had become part of the popular memory—Biblical personages, Alexander the Great, a few Roman and Byzantine emperors, and the legendary Persian rulers. He presented these stories in no particular order and they were naturally full of errors, if regarded as history. When al-Tabari reached the Muslim era he began to use written sources more freely and he cited variant traditions, though he did not attempt to reconcile them. For his own times he began to rely directly on eyewitness accounts, often repeating several without stating his own preference, to the point where his work became largely anecdotal [317; 443].

al-Mus^cudi (d. 956) was more or less contemporary with al-Tabari but his conception of history and his notions of research could not have been more different. Unlike al-Tabari, al-Mas^cudi was interested in more than the classic lands of Islam. Some historians, he wrote, were content to 'linger among their own kinsmen' but he, like Herodotus, preferred to travel widely and 'extract every fine nugget from its mine and every valuable object from its place of seclusion' [321, sect. 7]. In order to prise this information loose, al-Mas^cudi worked in ways that will seem familiar. For instance, in several places he organised debates and interviews and included in his work materials that he had gathered from the participants in these sessions [276].

From al-Mas^cudi until the fourteenth century many other Muslim historians produced works that relied in part on oral sources or their own experience. Ibn Miskawayh (d. 1030) wrote a history of the Buwayhid dynasty, which he served in various capacities [277; 278]. Several Muslim historians wrote accounts of the Crusades, complementing and correcting those written by their Christian counterparts like Fulcher of Chartres and William of Tyre [167]. As in Europe there appeared many local histories of important urban centres or the many provincial dynasties of the time. Finally, Rashid al-din (d. 1318) wrote the first truly universal history, incorporating what he could learn about the non-Islamic world from travellers and a few translations of historical sources from those areas [57].

With the fourteenth century came the greatest of the Muslim historians. Ibn Khaldun (d. 1406) wrote two major works: a universal history called *Ibar* and his most famous and influential work, the *Muqaddimah*, intended as an introduction to the *'Ibar* but really an extensive philosophy of historical causation and thought. In the *Muqaddimah* Ibn Khaldun expressed the belief that one must avoid 'blind trust in tradition' and he based most of his work on a wide variety of published sources, from Europe as well as Asia and North Africa [250, i, p. 7]. He originally intended to confine his study to the history of north Africa because he felt that 'second-hand information would not give the essential facts I am after' but in 1382 he moved to Egypt and there encountered a more cosmopolitan group of informants [250, i, p. 65]. These he used to gather information to which he would not otherwise have had access. For instance he spoke of being 'informed by people from China' whom he met in Cairo, but he included little data—much of it inaccurate—about the Far East [156; 157].

The development of Islamic historiography from al-Baladhuri to Ibn Khaldun parallels that in Europe with respect to the attitude toward, and use of, oral sources. Most historians whose work has survived wrote to a tripartite model: early, partly legendary history based on a combination of written records and oral tradition; a middle period derived largely from available written materials; and recent and contemporary history for which they used key informants and sometimes their own experience. Ibn Khaldun's preponderant use of documentary evidence signalled a new departure in which oral data began to be considered inferior to written sources—a change that had occurred in European historical writing somewhat earlier.

IV

By the fourteenth and fifteenth centuries nearly every important town and religious house in western Europe had its own series of historians. One or more participant wrote about every war, and many dynasties (particularly the French and Spanish royal houses) employed court historians or panegyrists to record their own deeds and those of real or imagined ancestors [8; 50; 307]. World history gave way to contemporary history and its corollary, finding glorious roots in the past, that spawned a flourishing industry in antiquarian myth that tried to connect every people in Europe with Troy, Rome or Greece. But many of those who wrote history during this period—Geoffroi de Villehardouin, Philippe de Joinville, Polydore Vergil, and Francesco Guicciardini among others—took part in many of the events they were later to describe and relied on other participants to supplement their own recollections [16; 216]. So, whereas many of their predecessors had resembled Herodotus in their use of historical data, the work of these historians more closely resembled that of Thucydides.

In turn these historians served as sources for those who followed in the seventeenth and eighteenth centuries and who at last began to rely more and more on public records and on the collected editions of earlier historical writing [95]. Even though he actively participated in the Puritan Revolution, Lord Clarendon based his massive history of it more on available documents than on his own experience and memory. As a result his account, though still partisan, at least included evidence drawn from both sides. About the same time Clarendon was writing, the creation of the post of Historiographer Royal in France made possible increasing access to official records there, although sycophancy rather than critical acumen characterised many of the incumbents [124; 135; 320; 382].

By the end of the seventeenth century it had become rare for historians in Europe to collect or consult oral data at all. Instead it was a time when compilers first collected editions of primary sources consisting of such established texts as charters, registers, treaties, early lives of saints, and early chronicles. Large collections of these were published in England, France, and Italy and, as if by sheer weight, these forced themselves on the attention of historians, who soon began to pride themselves in their commitment to these documents—'the primary sources' *par excellence*. The principle that the work of writing history necessarily meant consulting these sources, and only them, can be dated from this time.

V

Yet using oral sources was not completely out of everyone's mind. One group of historians, though not averse to using documents, also relied very heavily on a body of materials that once had been entirely oral—the saga literature of

Iceland and other Scandinavian countries. Indeed, the history of saga research in Scandinavia serves as an embodiment of the changes in attitude that took place towards the value of oral sources [14].

The sagas had been written down beginning in the twelfth and thirteenth centuries, but since they often recounted events alleged to have taken place several centuries earlier, those who defended their accuracy and historical value were forced to claim a long period of oral transmission and were therefore committed to an advocacy of the ability of tradition to be remembered accurately for many generations [37; 87; 88]. Moreover, Scandinavian historians habitually undertook the study of the sagas in an atmosphere of competing nationalisms. The major sagas related events from early Iceland and Norway. From the thirteenth century Iceland was a part of Norway but Norway itself was united in a subordinate way to Denmark from the fourteenth century and then from 1814 to 1905 with Sweden. While Norway was attached to Denmark, Sweden claimed it, and of course many Norwegians preferred independence from both, a sentiment that was particularly marked in the nineteenth century.

All of this meant that Icelandic, Norwegian, Danish, and Swedish scholars were all intent on outdoing one another, partly by developing (like the rest of Europe) glamorous but imaginary pasts reaching back to Trojan or Biblical roots or even to Atlantis [137; 201]. This required using the sagas, which purported to relate the history of large parts of Scandinavia well before historical times. Thormod Torfaeus (1636–1719), one of the most notable defenders of the sagas as history, advanced what was to become a familiar argument. In early times, said Torfaeus, 'people retained lays and stories far better than now'. Because of this greater capacity and will to remember, the sagas were able to be 'transmitted orally from parents and grandparents; sons and grandsons retained them by memory and passed them on in the same way to their descendants, until finally they reached those who rescued them from oblivion with the aid of letters' [14, pp. 6–7].

What Torfaeus and others only implied, later historians were to claim more explicitly. In the nineteenth century intellectual romanticism combined with a growing sense of nationalism in Norway and Iceland to lead historians to trust both the content of the sagas and the ability of generation after generation to hand them down unchanged. In Norway important historians such as Peter Munch and Rudolf Keyser wrote on this issue at great length and persuasiveness. In doing so they pushed Torfaeus' belief in the capabilities of the human memory even farther, declaring, for instance, that in order for the various sagas 'to be transmitted from mouth to mouth without omitting even peripheral details it was necessary to reduce them to a particular form that was thenceforth [orally] maintained continuously' while admitting unimportant modifications. This remarkable ability explains their 'otherwise inexplicable preservation' from preliterate times. In short, these historians believed that a saga was 'a detailed narrative, preserved in a specific form, and produced by oral transmission' [15, p. 235]. Of course they had no idea what forms the oral versions of the sagas might have taken at any given time but they were convinced that these had undergone no significant changes during their long oral stage. They were as certain that no changes took place when they were finally written done. On the contrary, the copyists merely 'moved the pen', committing to changeless written form what had already existed in unchanging oral form [147].

Naturally this line of argument was delightfully reassuring to those who wanted to believe in a very ancient and advanced system of government in early Scandinavia as portrayed in many of the sagas. But this view of oral tradition was actually more credulous than those held by such historians as Snorri Sturluson (d. 1241), who had originally transcribed the sagas and who was willing to admit that he did not 'know whether these accounts are true', but only that 'old and learned men consider them to be so' [431, p. 3]. Nevertheless, the views of Munch, Keyser, and others were so in tune with the tenor of the times that they at first swept all before them. But this school of thought was unable to survive the more critical spirit of the late nineteenth century, even in Norway.

This new spirit was in part actuated by its own nationalistic motives, but it proved scarcely less telling for that. By the turn of this century most scholars realised that the debate over the accuracy of saga materials had reached an impasse: neither party could prove specific arguments one way or the other. This feeling has contributed to the prevailing state of the issue, in which the sagas are treated as literary rather than historical in nature. In emphasising the creative and functional aspects of the sagas and, by implication, of their oral antecedents, critics have discarded views that stress any rigidly unchanging characteristics of their oral-to-oral and oral-to-written transmission [14; 262]. Instead they favour the notion that there is often an identifiable historical core in some sagas, but this was much adapted during the period of orality; that when the sagas were written down further artistic licence occurred; and that their chronology is worthless. One modern student of the sagas sums up this view by observing that 'the historical content of the sagas today is valued at not much above nil' [14, p. 55].

VI

The virtual abandonment of oral sources by historians left the moral philosophers and folklorists as the only ones with an interest in, and therefore a willingness to debate about, oral tradition. Neither group was much interested in the past in the same ways as historians are. Rather than trying to identify events and patterns, causes and effects, the moral philosophers of the eighteenth century were most concerned with the nature of man and society in the broadest possible sense. They accepted the argument that particular past events in oral societies were usually unknowable but did not regard this as a disadvantage. The folklorists (then usually called antiquaries) were interested in the oral aspects of literate societies: dances, dress, folktales, and customs. Each group preferred to concentrate on 'rude' or 'primitive' societies, believing that these mirrored the past more closely because they had changed the least, perhaps not at all, over long periods of time. To do this they needed to deal with the problem of the transmission of knowledge and custom in cultures that had no writing [122; 204].

The moral philosophers came first. In the eighteenth century Adam Ferguson and David Hume, members of the Scottish school of moral philosophy, each considered the role of tradition in oral societies. Neither rated it very highly in terms of accuracy. Ferguson was sceptical of oral sources, worrying that, while 'at first they contained some resemblance of truth, they still vary with the imagination of those by whom they are transmitted, and in every generation receive a different form'. Such 'traditionary tales', he went on, are not 'like light reflected from a mirror . . . but like rays that come broken and dispersed from an opaque surface, only give the colours and features of the body from which they last reflected'. Under these circumstances oral tradition ought never to be cited in 'matters of fact relating to the history of mankind', but only to 'ascertain what were the conceptions and sentiments of the age in which they were composed' [152, pp. 112–17]. Ferguson failed to explain how, if tradition changed 'in every generation', it could yet tell us something about the collective mentality of the times and places in which it originated.

Historian as well as philosopher, David Hume concerned himself with the issue of oral data only reluctantly and because he became embroiled in the debate over the authenticity of the so-called Ossianic poems. James Macpherson brought these to the attention of the public in 1760, claiming that he had only translated ancient materials that had originally been composed in the third century and been handed down virtually intact ever since. Stumbling across them in the Scottish highlands, Macpherson had recorded and published them [226]. At first Hume was disposed to accept Macpherson's claims but soon decided he could not credit such a long and uncontaminated transmission. He wrote (but did not publish, the issue being sensitive for Scottish nationalists) a brief treatise in which he discussed the problem. There Hume took a strong position against the authenticity of the poems. Much of his argument sprang from the undeniably modern ring of the poems and some other anachronisms, but he also pointed out how quickly traditions became distorted in the retelling. He went so far as to argue that 'the very name' of Caesar 'would at present be totally forgotten . . . without the help of books'. More tellingly, he asked a question that is even nowadays very much to the point: 'Where have these wonderful traditions skulked during so many centuries' only to be resurrected by Macpherson, he wondered. His question was only intended to be rhetorical of course. He believed that three generations was the longest a tradition could pass 'uncorrupted' in an oral society [74, pp. 471–77].

Led by such men as Andrew Lang and Sidney Hartland in Great Britain and Augustin Thierry and Jules Michelet in France, the study of folklore began to assume its own identity in the nineteenth century [122; 388]. At about the same time, anthropology emerged as a separate discipline. It was inevitable that each would develop points of view regarding the value of oral data. Two expressions of such views appeared in 1914 and 1915, which epitomised much of the feeling of the time. A prominent folklorist voiced one; an influential anthropologist the other.

In 1914 Sidney Hartland reviewed recent publications on the Kuba and the Ganda by Emil Torday and John Roscoe respectively. The authors' excessive freedom with oral evidence alarmed Hartland. He seemed particularly distressed by the king list and resulting chronology that Torday had constructed for the Kuba. He was willing to concede that sometimes tradition had historical value but he held that when anyone attempted to

'calculate the actual dates of events as far back as fifteen hundred years' solely
on the basis of tradition (as Torday had done) it was time to protest [213, p.
429; cf. 471]. Hartland reflected the views of many folklorists of the time when
he argued that 'imagination reconstitutes [the past] not as it was but as a
defective memory' based on how things should have been [213; 430].

The following year a much harsher criticism of oral tradition appeared.
Reacting to an essay on the value of American Indian origin traditions, the
young but already influential anthropologist Robert Lowie pronounced that
he could 'not attach to oral traditions any value whatsoever under any
circumstances whatsoever' because 'we cannot know them to be true' [301, p.
598]. To this uncompromising statement came several brief but spirited
rejoinders. Lowie was surprised but not discomfited by these and simply
pushed his argument along even farther, certainly too far. He was willing to
admit that on rare occasions linguistic, archeological, or ethnographic data
seemed to confirm traditions but to him this was simply irrelevant—confirmation was not really necessary. He concluded that, 'if primitive notions tally
with ours, so much the better for them, not for ours' [302, p. 163].

Lowie went on to argue that it would be imprudent to accept traditions or
any part of them simply because they were plausible—that is, not obviously
mythical—and cited several examples of Indian traditions to emphasise that
the seductively plausible could be as incorrect as the obviously implausible.
He decided that oral tradition tends to remember only the insignificant and
fails to record 'the most momentous happenings'. Unfortunately for his
argument his examples of 'momentous' occasions were confined to early visits
by Europeans [302, pp. 161–67].

Several of Lowie's subsidiary observations were sensible and he put his
finger on a serious weakness of most oral evidence—the inability to support it
independently and thus to accept it without lingering doubts, but of course this
characteristic is shared by a great deal of written data as well. But it was
Lowie's unabashed certitude and unedifying blend of deliberate and reflexive
cultural superiority, which at least now seem so out of place in a trained
anthropologist, that make even his best arguments seem no more than
unwitting reflections of the most insensitive cultural attitudes of his time.

Writing in 1920 the British anthropologist W. H. R. Rivers took an
opposite position. For Rivers, 'where native traditions seem to record
historical events, the conclusions drawn from them are in agreement with
those reached through other lines of evidence'. Though Rivers believed that
traditions should be used for corroboration rather than as principal sources, he
believed, in clear contrast to Lowie, that it was sometimes possible to use oral
materials in the same way as other kinds of data [391].

VII

Rivers' defence of oral evidence probably fell largely on deaf ears since his
anthropologist colleagues were seldom enough interested in the past to care
one way or another. However, the almost complete lack of historians who were
interested in probing the past of oral societies seemed to confirm Lowie's low
regard for the sources such societies produce. Historians accepted without
noticeable demur the scholarly division of labour then (and in some places

still) in force: primitive (i.e. oral) cultures were to be the focus of anthropological study, while historians were to be content—in fact felt obliged—to concern themselves with investigating only the past of the political elites in literate societies. In their attitude historians faithfully mirrored the then-dominant view as put forward by the immensely influential Lord Acton. Incredible as it now seems, Acton had persuaded himself, and many of his colleagues, that all the past worth knowing was knowable—in fact was close to being known. He was certain that 'nearly all the evidence that ever will appear is accessible' with the opening of several major European archives to scholarly research [3, p. 315]. Armed—or rather disarmed—with this point of view, few historians had any interest in struggling with the difficult, and to them unreliable, sources that were available about oral societies. There were no lessons to be learned from doing this, no morals for the edification of leaders and readers alike, no rewards in the esteem of their fellows.

A good measure of the indifference with which most historians regarded the practice of oral historiography—a phrase most would have considered a contradiction in terms—is the way authors of the major handbooks of historical method have treated the subject. Of the dozen or so most widely used that appeared during the first seventy years of this century, only that of Ernst Bernheim devoted explicit attention to traditional materials. In his *Lehrbuch der historischen Methode und der Geschichtsphilosophie* Bernheim divided all historical sources into two classes: 'traces' (documents, artifacts, and the like) and 'tradition' (that which has been 'transmitted and processed by human minds'). Because tradition was not direct evidence of past events it was 'opaque' and often garbled and fragmentary and should, if possible, be used only in conjunction with or as a supplement to written sources. Despite these reservations Bernheim believed that oral data had a place in the work of historians. If they happened to be available, historians should try to use them. Maybe—he was not so explicit here—historians should actually seek them out [38, pp. 444–49].

In contrast, the authors of other handbooks remained firmly within the tradition that defined 'documents' very narrowly: they had to be written. As a result they either ignored tradition as a source entirely [e.g. 92; 139; 290; 389] or mentioned it only to indicate its unusefulness to historians [177; 209; 263]. Manuals written or revised after about 1970 did sometimes mention oral evidence [e.g. 28; 420] but generally referred only to the work of contemporary collectors of oral history in literate societies and were more interested in technique than interpretation. None of the works (including those of Bernheim and his successor Bauer [31]) offered guidance on the problems of conducting fieldwork. This was left to the social scientists, whose theory and practice of applied field research do not always appeal to historians.

VIII

While western historians were resolutely ignoring the possibilities to investigate oral societies, some members of these societies were researching their own past, just as if this activity had not been condemned as worthless by those who were presumed to know better. This work began around the turn of this century and continued until it was overtaken in the 1950s and 1960s by the work of professional historians. These traditional historians regarded what they were doing as history no less seriously than did Acton and his colleagues and much of their work has withstood the later scrutiny of trained historians.

Most of this indigenous historical writing took place in Africa and Oceania. An intensive historiographic tradition began in Uganda around 1900 and still flourishes. The most important traditional historian there was Apolo Kaggwa. The extent of his writing and his prominent position in the local political structure ensured that his views were influential both when he wrote and later. And there were many others similar to Kaggwa in other parts of Africa: Yaro Dyao among the Wolof; C. C. Reindorf and several others in the Gold Coast; J. H. Soga among the southeastern Nguni; John Nyakatura in Bunyoro; Alexis Kagame in Rwanda; and among the Yoruba, where the most intensive activity occurred in all of Africa, Samuel Johnson and countless others [291; 366; 463].

In Oceania this work was most conspicuous among the Maoris and in Hawaii. In the latter, oral traditional historical writing began to appear as early as the 1830s when native Hawaiians began to write accounts of their past at the request of missionaries [155]. Public interest among the Maoris in their past was somewhat later in coming but in this century, especially, many Maoris have published genealogies and other traditional materials, notably in *The Journal of the Polynesian Society*. The most influential Maori student of the past was Peter Buck (Te Rangi Hiroa), a trained anthropologist who published several books and numerous articles. Unlike most of the others mentioned here, Buck was fully aware of the debate over the authenticity of oral tradition and he took the position that once 'the overlying strata of popular exaggeration and modern interpretation' had been peeled away, Maori traditions were 'as thorough and as accurate an account of the history of the past as any unwritten record can hope to be'. Perhaps this seemed somewhat faint praise because Buck added that in some cases 'the ancient writings of a cultured barbarian' were to be preferred to 'the inaccurate writings of a globe-trotting European', whose observations during brief visits were often held by historians to be more useful than any amount of local historical production [70, p. 182].

Buck, Kaggwa, and the others mentioned here tried to write 'Western-style' history while affirming the capacity of materials created in an oral style to support this enterprise. In their work they were often (in fact usually) influenced by missionaries—many were themselves clergymen. As a result outside sources, particularly the Bible, frequently affected their work. Despite this, the local history-writing produced under these circumstances has proven to be indispensable in more recent work on these societies.

IX

Meanwhile some folklorists and anthropologists were engaged in a second round of controversy over the historical worth of oral data. By the 1950s many anthropologists had begun to agree with Rivers that traditions recounted in oral societies could have historical value, while the majority of folklorists, caught up in theory and taxonomy, remained disinclined to accept this. Some folklorists adopted a new approach: all 'myth' (in which they included oral tradition) ultimately sprang from ritual rather than from actual events. The major proponent of this argument was Lord Raglan and his views on the matter were as uncompromising as those of Lowie. 'Tradition never preserves historical facts,' he declared flatly, but only whatever odd and insignificant event ritual considerations might require [379, p. 137]. He went on to argue that 'without precise chronology there can be no history' and since he was certain that 'the savage has no written chronology', he 'can have no history'. In fact, Raglan concluded, since interest in the past 'is solely induced by books', members of oral societies can have no interest in their own history at all. As a result, the events of the past in these societies are 'completely lost' [379, pp. 3–9].

To many of course this view seemed little short of nonsensical. It was absurd, these argued, that without ritual nothing of the past could be remembered and they rejected this ahistorical theorising entirely. First such historically-minded anthropologists as E. E. Evans-Pritchard and then the first trained historians to regard the oral past as fit for study began to view oral materials with a friendly eye.

X

This interest in oral tradition by scholars who were actually trained as historians was a new departure but it was more than just an accident. These belated stirrings of interest stemmed in part from the colonial experience. The sustained and intimate contacts of colonial officials with oral societies over half the earth brought the need to understand better how these societies operated, including how they saw and used their past. To be sure, local officials had long been dealing with oral historical materials, using them to adjudicate disputes or to impose administrative structures designed to facilitate the task of ruling. Many such officials, among them George Grey and Percy Smith in New Zealand, H. R. Palmer in Nigeria, and James Stuart in Natal, would have considered themselves historians, though they lacked the training that most historians undergo.

The first group of professional historians to study oral cultures in the late 1940s and 1950s had not been trained in African history or Oceanic history or American Indian history—there were, after all, no such fields—but in medieval and modern history (and particularly in diplomatic or imperial history) or occasionally in anthropology. Some developed interest in their new subject through their work in colonies on the road to independence, where they taught in newly-established institutes of higher education and engaged in an enterprise more or less new to the work of historians. It was called fieldwork.

These pioneers recruited and trained others and as this process was repeated, the numbers in the field grew. Indeed they grew at a more rapid rate than the numbers in any other field of history at the time. In the early 1960s two very different stimuli helped produce a rise in interest, most obviously among Africanists, but also among Oceanists and American Indian scholars (who developed a somewhat different approach called ethnohistory [94; 365; 418;435]). One of these stimuli was a warning that it was not possible to do oral historiography; the other an extended defence of the potential historical value of oral traditions and other kinds of oral data about the past.

The warning emanated from a latter-day intellectual heir of Lord Acton, still firmly fettered within the documentary-archival tradition. Aroused and alarmed by the blossoming interest in oral societies, Hugh Trevor-Roper decided that the time had come to nip this blossom before it could propagate itself further. In an argument that since has achieved a kind of burlesque notoriety, Trevor-Roper created an occasion to try to revitalise the flagging interest in European history, his own field. Pronouncing that in such places as Africa only the activities of the colonisers could possibly be fit subjects for proper history, Trevor-Roper declared that 'the rest is darkness . . . and darkness is not the subject of history'. Studying the past was, after all, serious business, Trevor-Roper pointed out. We study it 'in order to discover how we have come to where we are'. It would hardly be appropriate then (in his most memorable phrase) to 'amuse ourselves with the unrewarding gyrations of barbarous tribes in picturesque but irrelevant corners of the globe'. [459, p. 971].

Although he could clearly turn a felicitous phrase, Trevor-Roper proved a poor psychologist, finding that heavy-handed and gratuitous declamations about areas in which he was largely untutored served only to intensify interest in Third World history. His words took on a life of their own but the sentiments they expressed had a briefer existence. It is true that from time to time Africanists in particular are fond of repeating Trevor-Roper's phrases, perhaps to remind themselves that they have not yet carried everything before them, but otherwise the words have acquired the same kind of droll irony as those Neville Chamberlain uttered in 1938.

If the influence of Trevor-Roper's observations was more memorable in its mode than its message, the second impetus was neither negative nor inconsequential. This was the appearance of Jan Vansina's primer on oral tradition (in which he included oral history as well), first in French in 1961 and then in English four years later. Somewhat in the nature of a manifesto—although the author thought of it as 'no more than an introduction'—*Oral Tradition* has been phenomenally influential; references to it can be found not only in the footnotes of the writings of Africanists but in those of most other kinds of oral historians as well as anthropologists and folklorists. Trained both as a medievalist and an anthropologist, Vansina brought to his work a salutary respect for evidence and a first-hand appreciation of the peculiar challenges of fieldwork. Despite its pioneering character and despite the great amount of work done since its appearance—including second thoughts of the author—*Oral Tradition* remains the single most useful tool for historians who use oral sources, serving both to guide and justify their work.

The arguments of Vansina might have been like the seeds scattered on the rock, though, had there not already been a rapidly growing interest in exploring oral societies. The reasons for this continuing growth were several. In some cases it was simply a matter of wanting to press down new paths rather than treading and retreading old ones in the hunt for the tiny area yet unexplored, the minor source yet untapped, the minor figure yet unscrutinised, or the new microtechnique yet untried. In other cases it was simply a reflection of the times. History, like the Third World, needed to be decolonised, to be rescued from the tyranny of official documentation, to be allowed to study all facets of the past. In some cases, too, the greater availability of funds for fieldwork drew the interest of young scholars who otherwise might not have been able to bear the financial burdens of extended graduate training. Whatever the reasons, the 1960s and 1970s marked a peak in the self-conscious and scholarly pursuit of oral historiography [109]. Some decline in the rate of increase has already set in and this conforms to the earlier patterns with respect to the use of oral evidence that we have discussed in this chapter. Nevertheless, the development of a force of trained and enthusiastic practitioners supported by a growing body of data and at least the beginnings of a critical literature suggests that, despite the reservations of some [e.g. 339] this time oral historiography is here to stay.

For the moment, the interpretation of oral tradition remains in a state of considerable flux. The idea that traditions are enough like written documents that they can, for example, be subjected to tests that can determine an authentically original core, has given way in most quarters to the realisation that the study and understanding of oral historical materials is far more troublesome and demanding. Among other things, studies on memory have thrown doubt on the possibility that so-called fixed texts can be transmitted over several generations. Taking their cue from anthropologists and litterateurs, historians are also becoming aware of the effects that performance often has on the transmission of data orally. Above all, perhaps, the accumulation of many fieldwork experiences has shown the inescapably 'transactional' nature of collecting oral data—that is, it has reminded us that person-to-person contact itself affects very much the nature of the material gathered. These, as well as other, considerations help to explain both the interest in and challenge of oral historical research today.

CHAPTER TWO

BEFORE THE FIELD: APPROACHING ORAL DATA

What could we have accomplished—having no idea of the language or expertise therein?
      [Fr Jérôme Lalemant, 259, xviii, p. 9]

It is thrifty today to prepare for the wants of tomorrow.
      [Aesop, *The Ant and the Grasshopper*]

Having placed contemporary oral historiography in a context of previous work in the field, we can turn to the main focus of this work, the ways and means to collect and interpret oral data so that they will be able to withstand the ravages of time. Certainly the historian who expects his work to survive and serve as a source of information and inspiration for later generations of scholars must realise that above all else he must regard himself as the servant, and not the master, of any evidence he may uncover. This is no less true for oral historians than for those who continue to rely more conventionally on written documentation. But, like all good servants, historians can improve their lot by making the most of their masters' good and bad characteristics. The purpose of this and the following three chapters is to discuss the means by which oral historians can establish the most profitable relationship with their data.

Like any other scholarly enterprise, oral historical research is a tripartite affair: preparation, collection, and interpretation. But since it is often carried out in an alien culture using a strange language and complicated equipment, the preparation stage will probably be more extended, diversified, and challenging. In dealing with it then, it is necessary to take a programmatic approach that encompasses not only an intellectual point of view but a series of more mundane activities that will be needed to put the historian's aims into effect.

Perhaps it is best to begin by pointing out that the historian who uses oral sources should view his business and go about it in ways that are not very different from those of all other historians. Similarity in style and substance appears in the very first task any historian undertakes: identifying a problem to which he proposes to give his attention. For today's historian of oral cultures this choice remains far wider and more interesting than for most of his colleagues because so much remains to be done, both to secure the basic data and to organise them into wider interpretative and analytical studies. In defining his research undertaking, the intending historian will confront several issues. Is the problem really a significant one whose study will contribute not only to informing its own context but also to illuminating other problems? Has the work been done before? If it has, why does it need to be done again? Does there seem to be enough solid evidence, or the prospect of securing it, to allow the research to succeed?

Although each of these considerations is important, only the last will be dealt with here. After all, there is little point in deciding, for example, that the political structure or economic activities of a Saharan oasis in the third century are worth researching if there could never be enough evidence to determine what these might have been. Nor would wondering about dynastic marriage patterns in ancient South India be more than idle when the sum of the available evidence is a handful of inscriptions. In other words, from the very start of his research the historian is governed in what he can do by the amount and quality of the evidence he believes he can uncover. This constraint should not be considered nihilistic. It is perfectly legitimate to make one or even several false starts in hopes of uncovering sufficient material on a particular topic and often enough the historian will succeed, sometimes to his own surprise.

Nonetheless, it is important to recognise at an early point when a particular line of investigation must be abandoned for lack of sound data. Too often historians become their own worst enemies by failing to realise that it is not always possible to complete what they have begun, to find the sources they were certain existed, to answer all the questions they have raised. Unpalatable though it may be, the likelihood of abandoning an inquiry is especially great in oral research, but since oral historians create (or fail to create, as the case may be) much of the data with which they work, their reluctance to admit failure is all the greater because they may see it to be as much a personal failure as the failure of the past to ensure its own survival through recollection.

Ironically then, many abortive efforts to tackle a particular historical problem are actually failures to recognise the need to search widely enough for data, including those that appear useless or irrelevant at first glance. Since this has often been true for oral historians, there is special relevance to discussing ways to avoid this.

First steps and second thoughts
Once the historian decides he has a topic worth pursuing he will try to develop a research strategy designed to make best use of his ideas and the evidence as he then knows it. In nearly every case he will find it imprudent to rush to the field with tape recorder in one eager hand and notebook in the other and begin to record testimony. On the contrary, he will need first to acquire background knowledge that is as broad and deep as he can make it. He may have come across his topic in a secondary work or a primary source, he may have chanced upon it in conversation, he may be trying to fit it into a larger research project, or he may simply have heard someone discuss a matter that excited his interest. Whatever the case, only by reading all the relevant literature at his disposal can he begin to understand whether his idea is at once significant and practicable.

Without a sure grasp of the literature it will be impossible to proceed to a successful conclusion. Unaware of what has already been done, the historian may proceed to re-invent the wheel and at that will seldom make it round. For many topics, of course, there will be little or no direct historical evidence so that, unless some indirect data happen to exist, relating perhaps to archaeology or linguistics, there is no way the historian can test any oral data he collects. Though at first this may seem attractive, in the long run it is a severe handicap. The constant balancing and comparing of sources—challenged or unchallenged, primary or secondary—remains the only way any scholar can hope to achieve a synthesis that will stand the test of time and criticism.

Any historian begins to form a preliminary view and sense of his research objective with the very first allusion that comes his way, but these will—or at least should—constantly be reshaped and redefined as he acquires more evidence or devises new ways to look at old evidence. It may well be that, as he gathers data from a variety of sources, the historian realises that his first impressions were not entirely correct as to facts or conclusions—may in fact have been entirely wrong. In all walks of life first impressions seldom stand the test of time and experience well. When this is true it may prove desirable to abandon the research. Assuming, however, that all goes well in this respect, the historian must then turn his attention towards collecting oral testimony, although he is still a long way from asking questions of informants. Among the things he must do beforehand are:

1 secure research clearance in the host country and other countries where materials are located; become acquainted with the logistical facts of life in areas where work is planned; learn at least the rudiments of any local languages; examine health problems; and begin to consider the matter of interpreters;
2 become aware of potentially useful documentary materials, since archival research is usually a part of the process generally called fieldwork;
3 develop a research schedule that, at least at this early stage, seems best adapted to make the most efficient use of the allotted time as it may need to be divided among archival research, on-site preparations, interviewing, and transcribing;
4 develop a preliminary list of topics to explore and questions to ask in what seem effective ways.

As we will see, this preliminary guide will change during fieldwork, sometimes almost embarrassingly. At this point, though, it is useful to crystallise ideas, even unformed ones.

Affiliation and research clearance

It may seem odd to suggest that one of the first requirements of research preparation is to learn about affiliation and clearance procedures. Surely, the historian may think, there will be time enough for this later. Yet the experiences of many researchers in recent years indicates that it is by no means pointless to begin learning about this as soon as possible. It usually takes a long time, longer than most researchers think reasonable or necessary.

Whenever and wherever history has been written, much of it has been written by outsiders and, for the moment at least, this is nowhere more true than in oral historical research in the Third World. The advice given below is thus more essential for historians from the West than for researchers who already reside in the area of proposed study. There was a time when little more than a sense of commitment and adventure was necessary to conduct fieldwork in another culture but this is no longer true. Many countries have now established their own priorities with regard to which types of research will be favoured, whom they allow to conduct it, and on what terms it will be done [e.g. 269; 340]. Consequently, historians who prefer to decide ultimately for themselves what they want to investigate are finding it harder to conduct work in the areas of their choice. Worse still, it is often impossible to know until the last moment whether a particular government will authorise the projected research and on what terms. This forces historians either to limit themselves to studying their own societies or to accept constraints that so far have not generally been the lot of their colleagues.

Yet if they feel victimised, it is most often only by bad timing. It is hard to disagree that national governments have the right (some might even say the duty) to exercise some control over scholarly research conducted within their jurisdiction and most governments can cite all too many examples of what has happened when scholars have been given a free hand. It is inevitable that a scholar's sense of what needs to be done will differ from those of government authorities. He is trying to fit his work into the state of his discipline and his own personal goals, whereas national governments are trying to co-ordinate many requests to conduct fieldwork in order best to serve what they see as national interests. So there is likely to be some need to compromise, at least on the historian's part. Bearing this in mind from the first will help smooth the long road ahead.

As a precaution, many oral historians will want to prepare a back-up research programme that could be implemented if it proves impossible to proceed with the primary research. Many times, of course, the work of preparing such contingency plans will be wasted if the first-choice host country is willing to grant research permission on terms the historian is willing to accept. Still, having such an alternative plan in reserve can sometimes save time, money, and grief. It could mean the difference between securing funding and losing it, and therefore between carrying out fieldwork and being forced to abandon it.

Chances of carrying out the preferred research will be improved if the historian acts early and decisively in preparing his ground. This may mean a good deal of correspondence, seemingly endless referrals and worrying hesitations, and even apparent refusals along the way. Dealing with these has simply become part of playing the game of oral research successfully. There is no ideal formula for winning this game (and sometimes it is lost) because no two sets of conditions are ever alike, but it seems reasonable to suggest the value of certain approaches.

The researcher will need to learn details about officials to whom to write for advice and assistance. It is crucial to write early and, if necessary, often and in a courteous but clear fashion. The prudent historian will write to just about everyone imaginable: embassies and consulates, government offices in the host country, and teaching departments and research institutes there. He will also discuss his project with other scholars who have had research experience in the country. Although the sources listed below usually include the names of the incumbents when they were published, it may be best to address the envelope to the office and the enclosed letter to the named individual. Doing this could avoid letters being delayed or not delivered at all because they are mistaken for personal letters addressed to someone no longer in office.

For those in the West, learning about host country diplomatic representation should not be difficult since most governments publish directories with this information. One may consult *The Diplomatic List* (quarterly), *Foreign Consular Offices in the United States* (quarterly), or *Employees of Diplomatic Missions* (quarterly) for details on foreign representatives in the United States and *Key Officers of Foreign Service Posts* (three times a year) for information on American diplomats abroad. For Great Britain see *The Diplomatic Service List* for British missions overseas and *The Stateman's Year Book* for addresses of embassies in the United Kingdom, while *The Year Book of the Commonwealth* provides additional details for members. For other European countries the latest edition of *The Europa Year Book* will be useful. For other areas of interest to oral historians see *The Middle East and North Africa Year Book*, *Africa South of the Sahara*, and *Pacific Islands Year Book*. Many countries also publish diplomatic press directories.

One can secure the addresses of government offices in the host country either from diplomatic representatives of that country or from such sources as *Africa South of the Sahara* or the country's national yearbook. A great deal of data on research institutes is to be found in *The World of Learning*, published in two large volumes each year, but more specialised tools are also available. Among these are *Commonwealth Universities Year Book*, *Directory of African Universities*, *Southeast Asian Institutes of Higher Learning*, *Internationales Universitäts-Handbuch/World Guide to Universities* (4 vols., Munich, 1976), and *Répertoire international des universités partiellement ou entièrement de langue française* (Montreal, 1976).

Naturally enough, scholars tend to learn about others of similar interests by reading, attending conferences, and word of mouth, but these means are not systematic nor are they likely to be comprehensive. Membership lists of such professional organisations as the African Studies Association, American Historical Association, American Anthropological Association, African Studies Association of the United Kingdom, Royal Anthropological Institute, and the Middle East Studies Association (to name only a few) can provide many names but few enlightening details. Of greater value are such tools as *International Directory of Third World Scholars and Specialists* (Waltham, Mass., Crossroads Press, 1981) or *Directory of Third World Studies in the United States* (Waltham, Mass., Crossroads Press, 1981). There are no similar lists for the United Kingdom or France although some universities and research centres issue directories of local area studies specialists from time to time, as do such centres as the Afrika Studiecentrum in Leiden or the Frobenius Institut in Frankfurt. General directories of scholars can also be helpful. Among these are *National Faculty Directory* and the *Directory of American Scholars* for the United States; the *Academic Who's Who* for Britain; *Répertoire national des chercheurs* for France; and *Vademecum deutscher Lehr- und Forschungstätten* for Germany.

Besides such formal and out-datable sources, it is possible to learn about research in progress, recent scholarly travels, and similar activities from newsletters and other publications of organisations and institutes—for example, *African Research and Documentation*, the organ of the A.S.A.U.K. The historian may wish to consider joining those that seems particularly relevant.

It is easy to imagine that the intending field researcher will write 30 or 40 or even more letters during this stage of his preparation and yet acquire only a tentative grasp of affiliation and clearance procedures, which seem to have endless permutations from one country to another or even from one day to the next. Of course, copies of all letters and replies should be kept as it might be necessary to send these along with further letters of enquiry in order to keep things moving. Doing this may also help to keep clear in the researcher's mind just where he stands (or appears to stand) at any particular moment.

The historian should begin these activities in earnest as soon as he develops a practical research proposal. This normally happens at least a year before fieldwork is scheduled since such proposals are needed to apply for funding. Copies of any proposal should naturally accompany any letters and progress, or lack of it, should be monitored closely so that polite but increasingly insistent follow-up letters can be written if needed. No historian should ever feel that his failure to secure needed clearance resulted, even partly, from his own inertia.

Whenever all this seems to be a slightly disreputable activity, far removed from the loftier reaches of scholarly research, the historian need only remind himself that proficiency at this stage has often meant the difference between effective and ineffective research, or between research and no research at all. If the demands of constant corresponding take time away from background reading and language training, it is only because the purposes for which these latter tasks are undertaken depend entirely on success in the former.

Language training

Oral historians who carry out research within their own group or a group that speaks a mutually intelligible language will have few problems in coping with the chief instrument of their research, the spoken word. Commonly, though, oral research is conducted in societies whose members speak a language quite different from the researcher's mother tongue, adding one more responsibility to the already heavy load the historian must bear.

Linguistic competence can reach various levels: with the necessary time and ability the historian can learn the new language so thoroughly that he can deal with informants directly; or he may spend less time and acquire only a nodding acquaintance with the new language in the hope that interpreters and cumulative exposure will eventually permit acceptable levels of communication; finally, he may spend no time at all learning the language beforehand and be prepared to rely entirely on interpreters or other bilingual members of the society.

Of course, little can be said in favour of the last alternative; it is no more than the counsel of despair. In adopting it the historian abandons the chance to do effective research because he will not be able to interact with his sources in ways that would permit him to gain an adequate appreciation of their testimony. Should it prove necessary to operate on this basis, even temporarily, the historian is responsible for making this clear in any publications resulting from that phase of his fieldwork.

All would presumably agree that in principle the first alternative is to be preferred but this will nearly always be the counsel of perfection. Just as it is often impossible to spend a year or more interviewing in the field, so it is difficult to gain truly sufficient knowledge of the local language before undertaking fieldwork. Inadequate time, lack of funds, or unsuitable instruction may, one or all, prevent the historian from meeting the most desirable standards.

So we again are left with a compromise—to try to acquire as deep an acquaintance as possible with the relevant language before leaving for the field. This of course is the counsel of expediency, a common attribute of most scholarly research. In American universities several years of classroom instruction in a particular vernacular is usually required; in fact the granting of scholarships depends on receiving this training. But the number of languages available, and so the level one can reach in them, is often restricted in order to attract a certain level of student interest. This means that only those languages are taught that either by heritage or as lingua franca are spoken widely. The researcher who plans to work among a group that does not speak one of this limited number of languages will derive little benefit (scholarship funds aside, of course) from such instruction. It should be pointed out too, indeed emphasised, that even the best classroom instruction will be deficient when measured against actual field use. Languages in all oral cultures are far more in flux and subject to dialectal deviation than we could ever deduce from the ways they are taught in the classroom.

As a result, the researcher will almost certainly require extended private instruction and study. Sometimes this can be done through individual tutoring, either by a member of the teaching department or, better, a native speaker. Using a native speaker can help to demonstrate the 'give and take' that is part of using any language in the field, where good grammar, careful intonation, and formal vocabulary continually give way to the need to be understood.

Staying healthy

Discussions of fieldwork rarely give attention to the problems of illness, but not many fieldworkers have been able to avoid entirely the loss of time, energy, and spirit resulting from becoming ill, sometimes critically, while in the field. Outside their normal disease environment, perhaps for the first time ever, they will find themselves suddenly susceptible to a host of illnesses that will be painful and debilitating should they fall victim. Avoiding this will require planning, since there is more to staying healthy than undergoing the required inoculations or scrupulously taking the prescribed medicines. A good deal of common sense and anticipation is also required. Attention to health matters should not wait until it is time to visit the doctor or buy the medicine but should be one of those considerations, like research clearance, that is attended to almost immediately, lest unexpected problems cause later delays.

No researcher should leave for the field without acquainting himself with relevant literature of health care in the tropics or without taking a medical kit along. The best introduction to self-care is David Werner, *Where There is No Doctor. A Village Health Care Handbook*. This was published in 1977 and is available in the United States from The Hesperian Foundation, P.O. Box 1692, Palo Alto, California 94302, while in the United Kingodm it can be secured from Teaching Aids at Low Cost, Institute of Child Health, 30 Guilford St., London WC1N 1EH. In addition, the Ross Institute of the University of London School of Hygiene and Tropical Medicine has issued several bulletins that deal with the prevention and treatment of various tropical diseases.

The historian's medical kit should include a variety of items in addition to the obligatory chloroquine sulphate anti-malarial tablets. Among these should be an anti-lice treatment such as Lindane; a bactricin ointment for minor skin infections; one or more kinds of insect repellent, either in spray or ointment form; and, if possible, such prescription drugs as penicillin tablets and doxycycline. If the historian wears glasses he would be well advised to take along a spare pair that is photosensitive, as well as his prescription.

Once the field is reached, an early visit to the nurse on the staff of his embassy could be helpful in acquainting him with the local disease situation, the best available treatment centres, local brand names of the best medicines, and the like. While in the field certain precautions will also be necessary with regard to treating food and water. If at all possible, drinking and cooking water should be filtered, using a Steracyl filter, which sterilises water electrically. Barring this, all water should be brought to a hard boil. Any fruits and vegetables that can be peeled should be, and should not be boiled after being peeled but eaten as they are. It is not enough to wash leafy vegetables in some kind of iodine solution; only boiling will rid these of dysentery-causing amoebas. The researcher should avoid standing in fresh water for fear of contracting bilharzia.

If it proves necessary to fumigate his living quarters, the historian should seal up the areas to be treated and then use something like a Gammexane burner, which should usually be available locally. This emits an acrid smoke that penetrates anywhere insects can propagate and it serves as a residual insecticide for up to six months.

A severe case of diarrhoea can be fatal if it is not treated immediately. While the historian should naturally seek professional treatment, he should in the meantime replace his bodily fluids as much as he can with a mixture of salt and sugar added to water. He should enquire into the best recipe for this as soon as he arrives in the field, either from the embassy nurse or local dispensaries.

Of course, other measures may be needed in a particular locality or season. By arming himself with self-help guides, familiarising himself with the basic literature of specific diseases, and learning local treatment norms and the location of medical facilities, the historian can learn what these might be and supplement the procedures above with them as needed. Doing everything that we have mentioned here will by no means ensure the historian's well-being but not doing them is likely to ensure that he spends some of his time in the field doing nothing more than trying to regain his health.

Tracking down archives

We began this chapter by pointing out that few oral historians will want to concentrate on oral sources without reference to whatever written or artefactual evidence might exist. It is hard to imagine any topic in the realm of oral historiography for which some relevant materials in public or private archival collections do not exist. The historian is likely to realise this as soon as he begins the background reading necessary to determine whether his projected research is feasible.

A recent bibliographical survey of archival literature, though confined largely to western Europe, can provide a useful starting point for determining what has been written on potentially useful collections [29]. The most heavily exploited collections are those official archives created by the colonial power (if there was one) that governed the area in which the historian is interested. These materials will exist at several levels: the local level for day-to-day records, which probably remained in the former colony after independence; regional archives for such areas as French West Africa or the Federated Malay States, which encompassed several smaller units; and the metropolitan level, where correspondence and other documentation relating to the upper reaches of administration have always been housed and where they remain today.

For oral research, which by definition is local level, other kinds of archival materials will often prove more useful than official administrative materials. Among these are such privately-owned collections as business, missionary, and family records. Quite the largest and most important of these are the archives of the almost innumerable missionary societies that scattered across the entire non-western world, sometimes from before the earliest moments of colonisation. It is safe to say that, *whatever* the research focus of an oral historian happens to be, somewhere in the records of the missionary group(s) that served among the people he is interested in, he will find data of value.

To exploit these materials successfully, the historian must do two things. First he must learn which missionaries were involved, usually by consulting specialised atlases, directories, and encyclopedias devoted to a single society or to missionary efforts generally. To date there has been no attempt to compile a bibliography of such tools, which must number in the hundreds by now, but it should not be hard for the historian with localised interests to track down what he needs to know.

This done, he should begin building a bibliography of published missionary sources of interest. Many of these have appeared in the most obscure places that have never been, and may never be, included in standard indexes and bibliographies. If the missionaries were Catholic the historian will find nearly all he needs to know somewhere in the 30 massive volumes of *Bibliotheca Missionum*, a bibliographical paragon covering Catholic activity in the non-western world from the eleventh century almost to the present [220]. Three volumes deal with matters of general missiology, five with the Americas, two with western Asia, four with China, four with the rest of the Far East, five with South and South east Asia, one with Oceania, and six with Africa. Unfortunately no comparable tool has been developed for Protestant missionary publications, which are more scattered and less well-defined. There were far more societies involved, they did not operate under a single aegis, and many had only an ephemeral, almost anonymous, existence.

Locating missionary archives proper will present few problems since several guides have been prepared. The most substantial of these are the *Guides to the Sources of the History of Africa*, prepared by the International Council on Archives. All volumes, devoted to western European collections, have relevant information but that covering the Holy See is naturally the most useful. Another series sponsored by the ICA called *Guides to the Sources of the History of Nations*, series 3: *North Africa, Asia, and Oceania* has begun to appear.

Besides these, one should consult, among others, Noel Matthews' and Doreen Wainwright's *A Guide to Manuscripts and Documents in the British Isles*

Relating to Africa (London, 1971); the latest *Guidà delle Missioni Cattoliche*, published in Rome by the Congregation for the Propagation of the Faith; the *Handbook of American Resources for African Studies* by Peter Duignan (Palo Alto, 1967), which is soon to be superseded by a volume edited by Jean Meeh Gosebrink; Aloha South's forthcoming guide to non-Federal archives in the United States relating to Africa; and numerous other more particularised surveys [e.g. 83; 251; 380].

Becoming aware of business archives is more difficult, though some progress has been made of late. Like many missionary groups, business firms go into and out of business, sometimes rapidly; merge with or are absorbed by other companies; and change their corporate identities disconcertingly often. Nonetheless, there are several sources that may be used in tracking down business archives. A. G. Hopkins has provided a brief survey of British businesses that operated in Africa and some information can be found in Matthews' and Wainwright's *Guide* [241]. Archival reports have also appeared in *African Research and Documentation*. For French business archives see Bertrand Gille, *Les archives d'enterprises* (Paris, 1958); Erwin K. Welsch, *Libraries and Archives in France: a Handbook* (New York, 1979); and numerous articles in *Gazette des Archives*, which also publishes an annual bibliography on French archives. For Belgium one should consult Françoise Peemans and Patrick Lefevre, *Les sociétés coloniales belges: archives et données bibliographiques (1885–1960)* [*Cahiers* de CEDAF, 4/5, 1980]. For the Germanies see Welsch, *Libraries and Archives in Germany* (Pittsburgh, 1975) as well as *Archivalische Zeitschrift, Der Archivar*, and *Archivmitteilungen*. Rather surprisingly, the ICA *Guides* are almost devoid of information on business archives. However, Volume 27 of *Archivum* is devoted to the archives of trade unions.

Finally, we can mention the work of the Pacific Manuscripts Bureau located at the Research School of Pacific Studies of the Australian National University. The Bureau has so far collected several thousand reels of microfilm that contain very extensive materials from Catholic and Protestant missionary archives and journals, ships' logs, patrol reports, and many other sources for the history of Oceania. These have been deposited in several libraries in Australia and in Hawaii. In addition the Bureau publishes a bulletin called *Pambu* that updates holdings information and from time to time describes certain materials more fully.

Opportunities for access to archival collections will vary. In theory most public archives allow virtually unrestricted access to their holdings to qualified individuals subject only to a closed period, usually thirty years but sometimes longer. To use these archives it will ordinarily be necessary to provide letters of introduction and other forms of identification to attest to the worthy purposes behind the historian's interest. For private archives the situation can be better or worse. For most there is no formal commitment to scholarly activities. They were established to serve a particular clientele and may be privately funded and seem quite disorganised to the outsider. In many cases it may be impossible to use materials in these archives and even when a particular archive does accept researchers it may impose a longer closed period or restrict access to certain kinds of materials. On the other hand the historian may be able to establish a rapport with the custodians of small and specialised depositories that is not possible in larger, institutionalised archives, staffed by helpful but harried personnel or even by machines. Historians who use small archives will probably find most curators co-operative, some actually interested, and a few willing to share their unrivalled knowledge of their holdings or to trot out guides and even materials that the historian would otherwise never know about.

Some oral historians profess to regard archives and informants as oil and water and so do not give thought to the best way to integrate archival and field research. Most, though, will probably regard such a point of view as strange and mistaken and we need not consider it here. In coming to a decision on allocating his research time the historian will probably frame his alternatives in the form of several questions. Should he consult the archives first and then conduct fieldwork based in part on his gleanings from them? Or should he hasten directly to the field, temporarily bypassing the archives to avoid the danger of picking up predispositions by using the materials there? Or should he sandwich an archival visit between two stretches of fieldwork? Or, conversely, should he try to visit the archives both before and after fieldwork?

The best answers to these questions will vary, of course, if only owing to the locations of the archives in relation to the field. All things considered, though the last alternative seems best for most cases. It allows fieldwork to be informed—influenced—by data on persons and events described in archival sources, while at the same time it permits a second look at these sources with the perspective of groups whose collective viewpoint seldom appears in archival materials. Of course it is not always possible to achieve this pleasantly balanced effect because of expense or limited time. If it is not, it seems preferable to visit archives before conducting fieldwork. Consider the very real possibility that after intensive fieldwork the researcher, confident that he now grasps at least the broad outlines of the history of his group, then visits the archives and finds there references to events, individuals, and circumstances about which nothing at all was said during his interviewing. If this happens he has lost, perhaps irretrievably, the opportunity to question his informants about these matters. He must either ignore them—hardly advisable—or confine himself to presenting them without compensating context. He will forever wonder whether they were important only to the makers of the archives or whether, for reasons he can only guess once has has left the field, information about them was suppressed by those people he interviewed.

The research timetable
In addition to juggling visits to archives with visits to the field, the historian will need to deal with other kinds of scheduling problems. More often than not he will be subject to time constraints: the period for which funding has been provided, visa restrictions, his obligations to the teaching calendar of his home institution, seasonal local travel, or personal or family considerations. He must not forget that schedules of various kinds also govern the people among whom he wants to work and he needs to be aware of the rhythm of local activity as it may affect his work. For example, if large numbers of local people engage in migrant labour, he would be foolish to attempt useful fieldwork when they are absent, whether or not he is interested in migrant labour itself. The absence of a large pool of possible informants clearly limits his opportunities for gathering data and could easily cripple his research. To make such a

mistake, either voluntarily or just in ignorance, is not much different from failing to consult a particular book because it is on a library shelf too high to reach easily.

Many aspects of a society's living schedule might be of interest to the historian. The timing of major ritual activities, the sequence and duration of the seasons, or the agricultural/hunting/fishing cycles could all enter into his plans, especially since some of them serve mnemonic functions, if only incidentally. The historian who can spend more than a year in the field obviously runs fewer risks of missing recurring events. Barring this—and it is a rarity—the more the historian learns about seasonal patterns of the people he hopes to study, the more likely he is to plan a schedule that will prove both suitable and workable.

The art of asking

Almost from the moment the historian decides to pursue research he will begin formulating general approaches and broad questions that he hopes will be answered. Although the formal results of this exercise will eventually include specific questions, it should never be considered to be more than a rough guide, fairly broad in its organisation, and subject to continual change. The historian produces this in order to devise a strategy that will enable the sum total of the informants he interviews to provide answers for the sum total of the questions he asks. This will never happen, of course, but it must still remain the historian's goal.

The temptation to develop numerous specific questions long before reaching the field is one that needs to be resisted firmly. While a certain measure of specificity can help shape the historian's own ideas, it can also beguile him into thinking that he actually knows what he wants to find even before he begins interviewing.

Most historians no longer rely on questionnaires as extensively as some of their predecessors did or social scientists still do. Even so, constructing preliminary and tentative questions is a necessary aspect of oral research. In addition to providing some focus and direction, such an activity can later serve as an *aide-mémoire* when interviewing is under way. Most of all, though, the thrust and format of the questions can help the historian diagnose his own thoughts on interviewing and impress on him the need to frame his questions with the greatest care.

The *content* of the questions is of course the substance of interviewing but the *form* of the questions is also important because the way they are phrased will affect the validity of the answers to them. After all, answers are far more than simply the results of questions. Sometimes certain answers are the *inevitable* result of certain kinds of questions, so that to ask the question practically guarantees a specific answer. Most people have heard of 'leading questions'—opposing lawyers often challenge them in courts of law, for instance. A leading question is simply one that suggests by its very phrasing the answer the interrogator hopes to receive. We can see the effects this might have by imagining a series of questions a historian might use to *introduce* the subject of resistance to the imposition of colonial rule to his informants. It might go something like this:

1   When did the Europeans come to this area?

2   What happened when the Europeans came to this area?
3   Did you accept the rule of the Europeans when they came?
4   Why didn't you accept the rule of the Europeans when they came?
5   Which groups among you resisted the Europeans when they came?
6   Why didn't everyone resist the Europeans when they came? Why were
     some of you afraid to do what was right?
7   Isn't it true that nearly everyone in this area bravely resisted the brutal
     Europeans when they came and tried to kill and enslave you?

There is certainly a large amount of caricature in some of these questions but it
is not entirely unthinkable that historians have asked questions very much like
them as they tried too hard to find the answers they wanted to hear. In fact
only the first question fulfills the best canons of historical enquiry; it is the only
one that does not suggest that the historian is trying to orchestrate his
interviews. We can discuss each of the questions in turn.

1   This question is a valid way to introduce the issue of colonial rule.
     Presumably it is no secret that the Europeans did come and this phrasing
     merely draws the informant's attention to that part of the past about
     which the historian now proposes to seek information.
2   As the first question in a sequence this is less desirable because it pushes
     the informant, if only with a slight nudge, down the path the historian
     wants him to go. The informant now realises that the historian is
     interested in what 'happened' even though the informant might not
     otherwise have looked at things quite that way. To him the coming of the
     Europeans might have been an event of no consequence—or even no event
     at all, but just change so slow as to be imperceptible. By beginning with
     this question the historian may lose the opportunity to learn about this
     point of view because he has already introduced his own, different, one
     into the discussion.
3   With this question the historian risks a great deal more. Asking it forces
     the informant to make an accept v. reject division that may not at all have
     been part of his world view or that of his society.
4   By now the historian has lost touch with sound interrogating method.
     Now he is not only setting the intellectual terms of the answer but
     suggesting that he prefers very particular answers. It may be that his
     research has already told the historian that all or part of the group *did*
     resist colonial rule, but at this early point in the interview he is (or should
     be) interested in the perceptions of his informants (and not those of earlier
     writers) about the nature and form of any such resistance. He must first
     establish, rather than presume, that the group actually regarded any
     activity as resistance. In phrasing his question in this way, in effect he
     establishes it for the group.
5   Here the interviewer not only tells the informant—who may not have been
     aware of it—that resistance occurred but that it was, at least according to
     the historian's sources, piecemeal. Moreover, he is advising his informants
     that reactions to colonial rule were divided coherently and in definable
     ways. He encourages the informant to answer in terms of the question's
     rules and not the informant's own.
6   Any historian who begins an interview topic with this question—who in
     fact asks it at any time—is little more than a fraud. In addition to telling his

informant that resistance was definably divided, the historian all too clearly establishes his own views on the merits of resistance, and invites—in fact practically forces—his informants to take the same position. What they give him will be echoes, not answers.

7   If we did not reach True Caricature with the last question, we have with this one. We can only hope that such a question would never be posed by any self-respecting scholar at any time anywhere, although the almost total lack of access to field tapes discussed in Chapter 7 prevents us from knowing whether such hopes are entirely justified. Everything that *can* be wrong with a question *is* wrong with this one—and more.

Discussing the list of hypothetical first questions raises a particular aspect of informant behaviour. Like the historian, most informants hope that interviews will be pleasant and satisfying as well as rewarding. But informants have little vested interest in the historian's Truth—probably are little inclined to learn just what it might be. So, from amiability or apprehension, they are likely to pick up any hints contained in the questions that might help them answer them in a congenial fashion. It is not likely that many informants would nowadays feel as apprehensive at being asked about the past as many must have during the past several centuries. Still, an informant who is asked a question phrased like question 6 might well be concerned that the wrong answer will result in the interviewer's scorn or even public dishonour. Likewise, who knows how many answers informants have given simply from a desire to please, a desire made all too easy by a series of fatally-phrased questions?

Naturally it would be unwise to try to develop beforehand an entire sequence of questions designed to anticipate every eventuality since it is utterly impossible to know what these might be. Having rid himself of any temptation to be his informants' informant, the researcher should be content to provide several lists of very general questions for himself that he hopes can open up lines of enquiry that he can later explore while in the field. One tactic open to him at this point is to test his questions on colleagues and friends—and especially on any available members of the society to be investigated. This will help him to gauge the value of a question as a tool for extracting information without at the same time creating or tailoring it. He should especially seek out advice on whether the questions he has devised tip his hand too much. Such comments and criticisms can help smooth out the rougher edges as well as suggest ways in which the questions or general tenor of the list needs to be changed.

Some tools of the trade

Today's oral historian is the beneficiary (though some might say victim) of some very sophisticated recording equipment—more mobile, durable, inexpensive, and reproductively faithful than ever before. Few would disagree that the popularity of oral research bears a close relationship to the growth of recording technology over the past 30 years. Whether being able to escape from the laborious and inhibiting chore of notetaking during interviews, only to transcribe later on, has been a liberating experience, is questionable. Certainly, though, the new technological opportunities have brought new problems.

The most thorough exposition of field recording and evaluating techniques is probably that of Curtin [111]. Some of Curtin's suggestions were the counsel of perfection, given field constraints, and of course some of his technical advice has been rendered obsolete by advances in the field, but the recording, transcribing, and preservation procedures he recommended remain valid. The speed with which today's technological marvels become tomorrow's scrap heap makes it pointless to do more than urge fieldworkers to become as knowledgeable as they can about both the range of equipment available to them and the likely conditions under which they will do fieldwork. In doing this there are several things to keep in mind.

First, there is no need to aim for superior reproductive fidelity in all cases. If all things were equal, it could simply be suggested that the researcher take to the field only the very best equipment money can buy, but in most cases limited funds make such advice merely fatuous. For studying songs or music, or if there is a particular interest in the spoken aspects of the language *per se*, then probably only the best equipment will do. Generally though, 'making do' is an integral part of field experience and a lesser—though not always inexpensive—piece of equipment will often suffice. Language or ethnomusicological departments, or other researchers who have used similar equipment, can offer advice about the reliability and durability of certain equipment. And of course the historian will want to test any equipment beforehand to be sure that its technical qualities (and his) are up to the necessary mark and that the equipment is likely to be sturdy, reliable, and repairable under field conditions.

Even though reproductive quality is the major consideration in examining the merits of any piece of equipment, matters of durability and repairability should be weighed carefully. The most sophisticated equipment is often also the most delicate and what works best in a sound studio may not stand up well to the rigours of the field, which are likely to include dust, humidity, and constant and rough use. These will probably cause machine breakdown eventually and the availability of parts, or even of a new machine, near his research locale will be something the historian needs to know about. This can never be anticipated accurately, marketing being what it is, but at least he can determine which brands are *not* available in a particular area. If there is any choice at all, the historian should not take any equipment to the field that is not marketed locally. To do so is almost to ensure that at some point microphone and tape recorder will have to be exchanged for pen and paper, perhaps for the duration of the field trip.

In addition, the historian should consider the relative merits of reel and cassette recorders, ease of cleaning, the need for a tape counter, the quality of the microphone, and the availability of batteries. The question of weight should likewise be considered since he is likely to find that what once was acceptably light can become intolerably heavy as time passes and more and more tapes and notes are added to his travelling baggage.

It has often been possible for historians in the field to microfilm privately-owned collections of manuscripts or selected parts of local archives. These are not chances to be missed through failing to bring a good quality 35mm single lens reflex camera, several film cartridges, and possibly a tripod. Though advances in camera technology have not matched those in recording, the availability of a wide range of models at an equally wide range of prices forces the historian not to be content to acquire the first camera that comes to his attention. In deciding, he may be able to find good advice from film processing laboratories, art history departments, and libraries.

Several publications can be helpful in indicating relative costs and merits of the many recorders and cameras now available. Many of these also provide directories of dealers and sometimes bibliographies for those with specialised interests. Among them are *The International Microform Source Book*, *Guide to Micrographic Equipment*, and *All About Microfilm Cameras*. In addition *Reprographics Quarterly* (UK), *Journal of Micrographics* (US), and *Le Courrier de la Microcopie* (France) should repay consultation. Above all, though, the historian should benefit from the good experiences and bad of forerunners in the field.

Before closing this survey of equipment, we need to descend from the lofty reaches of advanced reprography and micrography to the workaday level of the manual typewriter. Although venerable compared to the other equipment mentioned here, no historian should leave for the field without a typewriter that is lightweight, durable, and widely available. Plastic cases are somewhat less hardy than metal ones but are not subject to rust. Thought should be given to adding special keys if this would save time-consuming handwork in the field. There is a very wide range of these available at reasonable cost. Finally, and this is a particularly important point even though saved until last, the historian's typing ability should be equal to the demands put on it. Skill, though not necessarily finesse, in typing should be considered essential for all historians in the same way as bibliographical competence. But, while the latter skill is often aspired to, the former is considered unnecessary, if not demeaning. If the historians needs to take a typing course before he leaves for the field, then he should be willing to take it, for it will repay handsome dividends.

Whenever possible, the historian should take two or more pieces of the same equipment. Such spares should be carefully wrapped and packed, sealed as tightly as possible, and not be disturbed unless the need for them arises. Several different spares of parts particularly subject to wear and tear should be taken and the historian should know how to install them. Typewriter ribbons, spare reels, carbon paper, and capstans are only the most obvious of these.

What seems most striking about the points raised in this chapter is the variety of skills the oral historian needs to acquire even before he can leave for the field. In addition to the bibliographic and linguistic competence we expect from all historians, he needs sociological and technological expertise, without which he cannot hope to succeed. He can to some extent prepare himself in this, but the qualities that will ultimately count most—patience, stamina, tolerance, and restraint—he can acquire, or at least demonstrate, only after he has reached the field.

CHAPTER THREE

IN THE FIELD:
COLLECTING ORAL DATA

You Europeans don't tell us your secrets: why should we tell you
ours?
[B. Gartrell, 174, p. 438]

What I tell you three times is true.
[Carroll, *The Hunting of the Snark*]

Having prepared himself beforehand as well as he can, the historian is finally
ready to leave for the field. Viewed in its widest context, the process we call
'fieldwork' is really only an extension and intensification of the work of
preparing for it, but certainly one with its own particular problems. Before
interviewing begins, after it is finished, and even while it is taking place, there
is much to be done that does not relate directly to working with informants and
this chapter will reflect this.

When he is ready to leave for the field the historian may feel confident that
much of what lies ahead is reasonably straightforward, though arduous. Yet,
no matter how certain he is that he has left no stone unturned in his search for
sources, no matter his presumed mastery of the local language, no matter how
carefully he has designed his research objectives, no matter how thorough his
acquaintance with archival materials, the oral historian will find many
surprises—some pleasant, some unpleasant—during his stay in the field. The
reasons why this is so are not obscure. After all, the most outstanding
characteristic of oral research is its unpredictability. The need to deal
constantly with living sources and with a pertinent past guarantees that no
amount of forethought can anticipate fully what will happen.

There has been, and continues to be, considerable debate over the best
ways to conduct ethnographic interviews—encounters of members of one
culture with those of another, often quite different, culture [e.g. 436]. Some
believe that it is most important to understand the viewpoint of the society of
the interviewees from the 'inside', whereas others argue that a society is best
perceived, described, and understood by a 'disinterested' observer who
normally lives outside it and who is able to see many of its facets at once. Many
historians and anthropologists, who view the first alternative as unattainable
and the second as too clinical, prefer a middle position in which the best of each
of these is blended in one way or another. While the historian must realise that
he can never fully achieve the intellectual perspective of the members of the
society he is studying, he also recognises that only a sensitivity to the
importance of this perspective will enable him to pursue research with any
chance of success.

This tension between the 'possible' and the 'desirable', as well as between numerous and often conflicting forms of 'desirable', is really the essence of oral research through fieldwork—that which makes it challenging yet restricting, an art but also a science. An awareness of this tension should underlie the researcher's every activity, in the field as well as later, when he tries to make the best sense of the data he has accumulated. In urging a constant sense of tension this chapter suggests the opportunities of oral research but also points out some of the pitfalls that may result from too narrowly concentrating on the possible with too little regard for what is impossible. In doing so the chapter inevitably lacks a sense of certitude, a feeling that one way is necessarily always better than any other. Thus it lays a heavier burden on the reader than many manuals, which sometimes seem to regard fieldwork as far more cut and dried than it ever can be.

I

Settling in

By definition fieldwork is conducted away from the researcher's primary residence and so the first step is to secure housing that is both adequate and appropriate. Normally there will be a range of possibilities, especially if the fieldworker is affiliated to local research or governmental organisations. Still, choosing the best housing may not be easy since such factors as cost, location, size and amenities must be considered. The choices are likely to be greatest in a large metropolitan area, where some time will probably be spent on the way to the field locale, but even in the countryside there will frequently be several choices.

At first it may be necessary to secure temporary accommodation near the archives or university but the provident researcher should have investigated the possibility of university-related housing before leaving home. Such housing is usually inexpensive as well as convenient, though it is often removed from the heart of society. If the archives and university are not located near each other (sometimes they may even be in different cities) it may be best to secure housing nearer the archives at first because these are likely to be used more heavily at this time than university facilities.

Once temporary housing is secured it is important to confirm and, if necessary, extend research clearance. Governments often extend this initially only for a very short time pending the arrival of the researcher, who must then exchange it for a formal research visa that permits both a longer stay and greater freedom of local travel. This exchange can be frustrating and time-consuming; it usually constitutes the first confrontation with the local bureaucracy. Local scholars can help by writing favourable appraisals of the intended research that will convince local authorities to grant the additional visa. Or local scholars may simply point out that going to a government office at a certain time of day or a certain day of the week, or that doing business with a particular branch office is the best way to settle matters painlessly.

Help with research clearance is only one advantage of affiliation. It also bestows a certain standing in the most relevant university department or institute. While this permits (though it does not ensure) some oversight by local staff, this is seldom a handicap and formal status does provide access to university libraries and other facilities, as well as to local archives and perhaps other government offices. It may also lead to such bonuses as housing and transportation. Conversely it may involve the researcher in university politics, as various interest groups compete for his loyalty and the prestige they seem to think accrues from his presence. This is one of those points in field research (others will be mentioned later) at which it may be advisable to keep a low profile while trying to understand where one's advantage lies, without ever appearing to be in the least interested.

One effective way to avoid time-consuming squabbles is to head for the archives immediately. While each researcher will have his own archives-interview rhythm, it would be foolish not to conduct at least a brief reconaissance of the local collections before serious interviewing begins. Many historians about to conduct field research have found data in the archives, or met other researchers there, that have prompted them to reorganise their research plans. If nothing else, archival materials generally provide a time-depth not possible through interviewing alone. While the historian can sample more widely in his interviewing and perhaps gain a greater range of public and private opinion, these views are virtually synchronic—that is, they are not influenced by more than a few recent circumstances. Work in the archives, on the other hand, may show in richer detail the effects changing circumstances have on public expressions regarding the past. An awareness of these is important to the researcher, both for framing questions and for judging the answers to them.

While it is possible to anticipate working conditions in major European and American archives, the variations within and among smaller collections near the field are likely to be larger and less predictable. Ultimately this can work to the researcher's advantage if he is able to establish good working relations with curators. If he can convince a curator or archivist that his research is important and that their role in it is essential—as of course it often is—it may be possible to wring concessions quite unknown to workers in larger, more formally conducted archives. For instance, working in storage areas or browsing among parts of the collections not represented in finding guides may be possible.

Archival collections that cater to only a few users may not maintain strict opening hours so that the researcher may be able to work through lunch hours and into the evenings or on weekends if he can demonstrate a need. It is hard to imagine, on the other hand, that even the most urgent need would persuade the keepers of any major archive to extend its working hours. Local rules governing access may also be flexible, particularly with respect to non-sensitive or quasi-published materials. In general, though, the familiarity of the archivist with the materials under his care is the greatest benefit the researcher can expect. For instance, the archivist may know that certain materials are classified in unlikely ways that only he can point out to the interested user.

With such privileges come certain obligations. The first is to respect the materials the historian uses as well as any conditions the archives imposes on their use, even though these may seem unreasonable. Accepting these at first may lead to their relaxation as time passes and the historian gains the interest of the archivist. Moreover, the historian should be willing to prepare a detailed guide to the particular body of materials he uses, with a copy for the local authorities and another to be published later for other workers in the same field. Later on, a copy of any publications based on the use of the archives should be sent back as an expression of gratitude.

At the moment many archives in developing countries do not have photocopying or microfilming facilities. Or, if they do, the charges for such work may be too high for the budgets of most researchers. Under these circumstances custodians may not always object to allowing the researcher to film small runs of material so that he can devote more time to such activities as interviewing and transcribing. Such policies may be quite unofficial and may not be consistently applied so that, despite what he may know about the experience of others, the researcher should prepare for the chance to film some archival materials. We have already discussed these preparations but it might be added here that high quality microfilm is often unavailable in many countries and providing equivalent raw film can be an effective way to secure the privilege of filming.

Preparing for interviewing

However important and useful consulting the local archives may be, it is almost always the case that interviewing is the core of historical field research. The first thing to remember in this regard is that social norms are neither universal nor unchanging and that published ethnographic descriptions of such 'norms' may be mistaken, misconceived, or out-of-date. Here the historian must rely on local contacts to acquaint him with at least the most important current features of the culture to which he is about to attach himself. Whatever the historian's interests may be, understanding *social* norms is particularly important because, whereas consulting written sources is a fairly reclusive activity, consulting with living sources is its opposite. In dealing with written materials there is only one active ingredient, the investigator; the sources themselves are passive and unchangeable. Each and every consultation with an informant, however, is at once a research activity and a social occasion. Here the possible minimum of active ingredients is two (the researcher and the informant), the likely minimum is three (the researcher, the informant, and an interpreter), and the possible maximum is very large (the researcher, several informants, an interpreter, and numerous onlookers).

All this means that 'the social quotient' of oral historiography requires the historian to develop a talent he may not previously have needed to use—the ability to deal effectively with the people of another culture. To do this he needs to operate as much as he can within whatever cultural framework he finds himself. This process will not be an easy one, as the debate we mentioned earlier signifies, and it will proceed in fits and starts, even if the 'alienness' of the historian is at an irreducibly low level. He will commit many a blunder, experience many embarrassing moments, antagonise some informants, and end up the butt of many tall tales. Yet the adaptive process need not occur only through bitter experience. One way to limit the incidence of bad moments, cross-talking, and unnecessary misunderstandings is to ply local scholars with many questions about how best to gain the rudiments of social expertise, if only to learn which kinds of social behaviour are *not* acceptable.

However widely the historian has read in the ethnographic literature, it bears repeating that he would be foolish to rely on it for this kind of help [e.g. 174]. The authors of much of it may have been careful but they often had neither the need nor the desire to understand just what mutually acceptable social norms there were. In any case these will have changed as time passes. Breaches of local conventions—offering cash payments instead of hospitality, not observing other forms of local protocol, failing to display acceptable dining etiquette—can easily lead to reticence, lack of interest, or silent hostility. And the historian may never realise why, because one of the social norms he failed to grasp was that it is impolite to criticise guests!

Interpreters: bridges or dams?

It is all but impossible to undertake orderly and productive field interviewing without using interpreters. A common image of the interpreter is that of a person who translates from one language to another, but this is woefully inadequate in terms of formal field research. Here good interpreters decode actions as well as words, norms as well as sentences, culture as well as language, and this makes it crucial that extremely careful attention be paid to the task of selecting them. Necessarily, most interpreters are people of two cultures, with an often imperfect sense of one or even both. By and large, interpreters who have worked with visiting historians have been schoolteachers or advanced students—people who have begun to turn away from their cultural heritage in favour of new modes of thought they have come to regard as better. So the problem is not that of the interpreter interposing himself between two cultural outlooks so much as the fact that he is facing only one of them himself.

Few historians would choose to use translations of important printed sources except in moments of real need and then they would never attempt to build a crucial argument on anything less than the original source in the original language. Yet countless oral historians work every day with interpreters. Since so much oral historiography is cross-cultural and interlingual it is not possible to change this and so it becomes necessary to know how best to perceive the problem and deal with it. Once the need to use interpreters is accepted, the first issue to address is how to go about choosing them. Here it would be easy to be momentarily overwhelmed by the magnitude of the task and to 'solve' the problem simply by engaging the first plausible candidate(s) for the job or those recommended by local authorities. It seems hardly necessary to emphasise how ill-advised this procedure could be since choosing interpreters has as much to do with the success of a venture in oral research as any other factor.

In fact there are no foolproof ways to go about hiring interpreters; numerous and often conflicting rationales will be involved. It may seem sensible, for example, to choose individuals who profess an interest in the past of their own society. First, such people can better appreciate the historian's own objectives, may even tend to identify with them. But this very sense of identification can often be a serious problem because it can interfere with the interpreter's primary role as neutral intermediary. When a predilection for history has already caused someone to investigate their past, certain predispositions may have resulted. Having come to certain beliefs himself, a potential interpreter could hardly refrain from allowing this to colour the ways he goes about his business—the historian's business. This is particularly true when interpreters have been interested parties in any of the disputes that so characterise societies in flux. It might seem almost unfair to blame interpreters for translating their particular orthodoxy into the testimony of informants but it is scarcely tolerable for all that. The researcher who has not mastered the local language must be aware of the background of each interpreter he uses, with a special eye to any known public positions the interpreter may have taken about local ideas concerning the past.

On the other hand, individuals who have utterly no interest in or knowledge of their own history may be difficult to train since the historian will probably find it hard to convince them that what he wants to know is important. Moreover, such interpreters will probably not be able to help the historian use answers he receives in order to suggest further questions or other possible lines of inquiry. Unencumbered by any partisan interest in their work, these interpreters remain fettered by a lack of any interest at all.

The historian will not usually have a large pool of potential interpreters from which to choose, nor the leisure or knowledge to choose wisely if he did. On balance it is probably a good thing that any candidates for interpreter should have *some* knowledge of local history because, as interpreters, they will influence the historian's choice of informants. At the same time the historian remains responsible for determining that this is really knowledge and not just unsubstantiated opinion turned into voluble assertion. In effect, the historian's instincts for judging the character of people among whom he is working is tested most severely at the very beginning of his research. If he fails this test badly it is hard to imagine that his research will be successful.

The historian may need to fire interpreters as well as hire them so he should always try to employ them on an open-ended basis in the event that he needs to dispense with their services for such reasons as lack of commitment to the project, too much politicking for particular points of view, a crippling sense of deference, undependability, or an unexpected shortage of funds. Sacking an interpreter, even with good cause, could easily antagonise those with kinship or political ties with that individual. It might be imprudent to choose too many interpreters from large or influential interest groups since the historian could run the risk of alienating large numbers of possible sources. Hiring from smaller groups in the population and being explicit about the possible short-term aspects of the job can reduce the risk of damage to the historian's research programme on the one hand and to his conscience on the other.

Normally, of course, interpreters are considered to be employees who must be paid in some way. This can be a problem, where a close knowledge of cultural norms is again important. Some societies expect that such payments be in cash or an equivalent, whereas in other societies any attempt to put the relationship on so obviously an employer-employee basis would be regarded with distaste. In the former case it is important that the historian establish clearcut arrangements in terms of the level and form of wages, the extent of the work expected, the sharing of duties, and the like. In the latter case just the opposite is required—a very inexplicit but spontaneous giving of gifts in a way that expresses gratitude at appropriate times and levels and in ways that somehow avoid being even faintly reminiscent of a business relationship.

Some fieldworkers prefer to work with a single interpreter with whom they can establish a close and harmonious relationship on both a business and personal level. The imperatives of good historical research method, however, probably favour using many interpreters, although this means the historian must spend more of his time training them. Using several interpreters allows the historian to experiment in ways that can serve as checks on the work of any one of them so that, for instance, he can more easily detect a relentlessly partisan attitude on the part of a particular interpreter. Then too, using several interpreters will generally afford easier access to all segments of a society, whereas a single interpreter is unlikely to open many doors to groups with which he has few, or even hostile, relations. Using more than one interpreter also helps prevent problems that arise from such eventualities as an interpreter's illness or moving away. All these are grounds enough for the historian to make a concerted effort to employ several interpreters chosen carefully from throughout the society, even if he eventually learns that for most purposes one or two of them are more valuable than the others. This is no different, of course, than selecting written documentation from a number of good, bad, and indifferent sources.

Interviewing strategies

The best of the local archives gleaned, the knowledge of local scholars effectively plumbed, the best available interpreters engaged, transportation and living accommodations secured (all this only in the best of all possible worlds, of course) the historian is at last poised to begin the core activity of his enterprise—field interviewing. Or rather, he is at least ready to establish himself in the field for it may even yet be somewhat too soon to begin serious interviewing.

Most historians who have done fieldwork have found that it takes many months before they feel at home and their informants begin to deal with them in uninhibited ways. In an ideal world, then, the oral historian should try to live among the people he is studying in a restrained and passive way, merely observing and being observed in turn. In a sense this could be regarded as the most effective preparation possible, but at the same time it is virtually always a luxury that the historian can only wish he could afford. Time, financial constraints and over-anxiety almost always are enough to prevent the historian from truly becoming a part of the society in which he works. We must depart then from this ideal world. Having glimpsed it, we return to the situation most field historians are likely to find themselves in.

Thanks mainly to his use of the local archives, the historian has gained some understanding of the recent history of the people he is studying by the time he conducts his first formal interview. He will also have some idea of the social and political relationships that exist today and at least a glimmering as to how history might have been (and will continue to be) used in sustaining or changing these relationships. He has acquired a little knowledge of the demographic structure of the group, perhaps something as elaborate as a census but more likely just a sense of which groups of people do which things and where and why they do them. Finally he has a sense of the economic changes that have occurred during the past half a century or so, how these were imposed, how they were accepted, and how they have led to other kinds of changes. Armed with this knowledge he can now devise a practical research strategy and at the same time he is allowing himself to become better known. The questionnaire he developed long before will look much different now and may in fact have been scrapped as useless. But the historian will be asking many questions and he must now decide of whom he will ask them.

At least from the time of the early Christians, an explicit preoccupation of oral historians has been to get to the oldest people before it is too late, in the belief that they are likely to know more but die sooner, maybe too soon. Historians who tailor their research to this general rule are likely to be no more than half right: experience has frequently shown that there is little enough reason to believe that the elderly, simply by having lived longer, remember more about the past—certainly not that they habitually remember it better. A well-recognised tendency of advancing age is to idealise the past, to see it largely through that most notorious of prisms, the rose-coloured glass. Indeed, if too many elders are interviewed and proportionately fewer younger individuals, the historian could easily receive a false impression of progressive decay and decline within a society.

Such a perspective on the past might be manifested in two ways. On the one hand the elderly informant may see decline only in terms of his own lifetime—that is, in most cases the colonial period. A popular view of this era is that it was more harmful than beneficial, even when not obviously so. Such a point of view could be reinforced, but by no means corroborated, if inappropriate weight were given to the testimony of the elderly on the grounds of their age alone. While such an interpretation would be based on a body of evidence—the cumulative testimony of many informants—this might be distorted in a systematic, if unintentional, fashion.

On the other hand it is possible that some elderly informants will visualise the entire remembered past of their society as a metaphor for their own lives. In this case they may see the period of origins as a kind of golden age (read: youth), followed by a period of indeterminate length and little interest (read: middle age), and culminating in a depressing period of colonial rule (read: old age). This could help explain why, in so many oral cultures, the time of origins is the time most clearly laden with mythic overtones.

The historian's purpose, of course, is to try to construct as accurate and as complete an interpretation of the past as he can, in the light of the evidence he creates and uses. As in dealing with the written record, this requires mixing many kinds of sources judiciously, each contributing to the final result. In formulating a sound research scheme the historian must deal at this point with groups rather than individuals because he must be selective in his interviewing—far more selective, usually, than the historian who uses only written documents needs to be. This is not only because the number of possible informants is usually very large, but also because each time any informant is questioned he becomes in effect a different source than he has been before or will be afterwards, as we will see later.

It will seldom be possible or desirable to interview everyone in a community because, unlike anthropologists or sociologists, historians are accustomed to dealing at a higher level than the household cluster or small village. In deciding on a provisional list of informants, the historian should try to ensure that they are representative in a number of ways: adults of all ages should be included; members of various social and political groupings should be consulted; members of all definable corporate groups should be interviewed; literate and non-literate members of the community need to be represented; and women as well as men should be used as sources. The historian will determine just who these people turn out to be (and of course each individual will belong to more than one category) but the selection standards he uses should be developed beforehand.

It is important to interview across the entire adult age spectrum, not only because elders (though of course not only elders) can have a particular point of view, but also because in most societies a person's age helps to determine his status and influence and therefore his perceptions of his society, past and present. Persons not (or not yet) in authority are apt to judge the grounds for legitimacy and power, including their historical development, quite differently from those who, by virtue of their higher rank, have more at stake in justifying not only their own positions but the authority structure as a whole and they may do this by seeking validation from the past. By the same token, those who anticipate higher rank with advancing years will hold different ideas about past and present authority patterns and the events relating to them than those of the same age who have no expectation of attaining high enough status to share authority and thereby to legitimise it.

The division and practice of authority naturally varies from one society to another as well as at different levels of the same society. In some there will be royal lineages or clans whose members have the right to govern. Or the right to exercise power may be based on entirely different grounds—for instance, age, wealth, or charismatic attributes. But, whatever circumstances the historian finds himself in, the grounds for distinguishing the 'ins' from the 'outs' should become reasonably clear, given time and a certain acumen. When these grounds are established, the historian should take care to spread his interviewing around so that he affords members of both groups opportunities to present their versions of the past. In such societies, however, as the Yoruba, the Akan, and many groups in Malaysia and Indonesia, offices circulate among competing lineages so that the hierarchical power structure is complicated and fluid. In such cases the historian may never feel certain that he has identified the current 'ins' and 'outs' because, try as he may, he will never learn the perceptions of the people themselves.

There are further problems with the selection of informants. It has been fashionable to divide oral societies into neat packages labelled 'clans' or 'lineages' or 'moieties' or 'phratries' or other imposed analytical categories. Scholars have then placed every individual into one or more of these groupings, combined small packages of individuals into larger parcels, and so on. These schemes have the virtue of tidiness, but they often have the disadvantage of being quite wrong, the imposition of a model from outside that no insider would ever recognise. If the fieldworker has relied on outmoded ethnography of this style in preparing for fieldwork, he will probably expect to find certain relationships that are not really there. In his desire to be representative in his interviewing he may then inadvertently perpetuate a system of classification that has never been valid. If he does, he will attribute to informants certain points of view or standards of credibility that they do not have because they do not play the roles he mistakenly ascribes to them. To prevent this problem the historian must support the choice (or rather the choosing) of informants by a careful analysis of social structure as it actually seems to exist, but at the same time with knowledge of the scope and direction of discernible changes that may have taken place during the time for which contemporary data are available.

Another potential problem concerns the ability of informants to read or write. The effects of newly-acquired literacy, particularly when it is restricted to a small part of a society, has always seriously distorted the portrayal of the past. These effects are considered elsewhere in this work. For the moment it is necessary to stress the importance of distinguishing between literate and non-literate members of a society, if they are to be used as informants. This is complicated by the fact that there are many gradations of literacy, many stages of what we might call para-literacy. Through education (whether formal or not) many potential informants have been exposed to ideas and information that had not been available before. The sum of knowledge possessed by literates is usually greater and always different from that of those who have not yet become fully literate.

The historian then is faced with the task of learning what he can about the educational experiences of his most important informants. He can question them on the matter (preferably after interviewing them) and look into any records of local schools during the colonial and independence periods. These should tell him something about who offered what kinds of instruction. At some point the historian should also try to examine textbooks that were used in these schools in order to learn what might have come to informants by way of these rather than through traditions presumed to have been handed down from the past. To my knowledge, no historian of an oral society has attempted to do this systematically and then to present the results. Perhaps it seems an exercise far removed from collecting and understanding oral materials.

A particularly important oversight in collecting oral data has been the ignoring of women as sources. Unless researchers have been interested in a topic that happens to be relevant to the experience of women (say, the institution of the Queen Mother, women traders, or women's secret societies), they seem to have disregarded them as useful informants, presuming them to be uninterested in and unaware of larger questions relating to political or economic change or structural patterns. In most cases this record of neglect seems to have been unconscious; only that part of a society that happened to be male were considered when researchers established pools of informants. Sometimes it may have resulted because researchers found it convenient to accept whatever informants were proffered by members of the group they were studying on the assumption that these knew best who knew best. In some societies, of course, women are expected to dwell in seclusion, so that male researchers have not been able to consult them even when they wished to.

Even with the recent interest in women's roles and activities, the question of using women as informants on all aspects of the past has not been considered very often or explicitly. A good example of the benefits of doing this is Sosne's discussion of women as past actors and present informants in Shi society [433]. Sosne drew three conclusions from her study. The first is that women have often played important parts in the major events of Shi history, a fact not stressed, or perhaps not even noticed, by previous researchers. Sosne's second point is that women informants are knowledgeable about many aspects of the

Shi past. For our purposes Sosne's third conclusion is the most telling of all: she herself only realised the first two points after spending considerable time in the field interviewing women on a matter not related to earlier Shi history at all.

To all appearances Shi society is, and was, dominated by males both genealogically and structurally—and so historiographically as well. Sosne's study of several neglected aspects of the Shi past, based in part on neglected sources from the Shi present, demonstrates how unwise it would be to eliminate any one segment of society, particularly one so large and influential, no matter how unimportant that group may *seem* to be on the basis of the historian's first awareness of the norms and relationships of his group.

More generally, a lack of awareness of the distribution of historical knowledge within any society requires that the historian, once he gains a preliminary sense of the range and kinds of informants he hopes to use, asks important locals for their advice. He may choose to disregard the advice, but asking for such help can satisfy local protocol, which usually expects that access to individuals be gained through the intermediacy of traditional authorities.

After studying all his options and recognising at least some of his constraints—but also his opportunities—the historian can prepare a preliminary list of informants that, he hopes, reflects most elements of the society. If he is particularly shrewd or lucky, perhaps half the names on this list will prove to be worthwhile informants. The other half either will not be interviewed for various reasons or will prove to be of little value. And many individuals not on this list will end up being interviewed. Indeed, when his fieldwork is completed, the historian is likely to be bemused by *how* much different it proved to be.

The one or the many?
The list of possible informants the historian compiles will probably be a long one. Faced with a limited amount of time and a research plan that probably seems far too ambitious to fit into that time, he will be tempted to find ways to get more done in less time. An expedient that some historians have adopted is to interview many informants at once in groups in the belief that interviewing large numbers of people together can gain the collective wisdom of a group just as easily, and far more quickly, than interviewing its members individually.

Many historians, particularly those who have worked in non-centralised societies, have used, and advocated that others use, the group interview [467; 486; cf. 457]. They argue that there are no appointed traditional historians in such societies because there is no central authority to appoint them and no particular point of view for them to propagate. As a result any remaining knowledge of the past is retained collectively. It was experienced and transmitted collectively and it can therefore (in fact can *only*) be recaptured collectively. Under such circumstances, these historians claim, the group interview is not only more practical but more effective because it reflects the ways that knowledge was learned over the generations.

For historians interested in compiling masses of indifferent data this line of reasoning will seem appealing. Tape recorder in hand, it will be possible to interview all acceptable informants in an entire society in almost no time at all, allowing the historian to seek new worlds to interview collectively. The historian who prefers, however, to try to eliminate distortion that might be introduced into testimony by the personal factor will find insuperable drawbacks in using the collective approach as the sole, or even primary method of interviewing, especially as it may prevent the weighing of conflicting evidence.

The principal problem in dealing with informants together relates to what psychologists call 'small group dynamics'. By experience and experiment they have discovered that whenever a group of people congregates, certain things will happen between and among its members. One of the most predictable is that the more aggressive, forceful, or articulate members will dominate discussion, while those individuals of a more quiet and reticent temperament will contribute little or nothing, preferring not to draw attention to themselves. It is by no means those who are most knowledgeable who dominate discussion, for there is no evidence that strength of public personality is related to breadth of knowledge.

Besides personality reasons why the opinions of a single person or a small group will dominate a larger group, there are often more structural reasons why this will occur. Even in the most apparently egalitarian societies there are those who, by virtue of birth, wealth, marriage connections, or innate ability influence the lives and attitudes of their neighbours more than others do. Although the signs of such influences may be few—no regalia, no titles, no ritual deference—it is no less significant. Worse still, the subtle nature of this influence may cause the unwary researcher to overlook it and convince himself that, as in any society, it is just a matter of some people knowing more than others. If he does this he may come away from a group interview with a mistaken impression about who his best informants are likely to be.

These particular problems are usually absent from the private interview, depending somewhat on the status and role of interpreters and whether or not there are bystanders. Here at least, the informant is usually freed from the constraints imposed by the opinions of his peers or superiors. Someone who cannot express himself in assembly will often be more forthcoming when dealing only with the historian. In this regard the historian should be careful not to confuse diffidence with ignorance; sometimes it may take many interviews to draw out a particular informant. At times like these the social skills of the oral historian come into play most clearly, for he cannot abandon a potentially useful informant simply on the grounds that getting his testimony is too troublesome.

If, from the viewpoint of sound method, the private interview is to be preferred to interviewing whole groups in a circus-like atmosphere, the historian might still be well-advised to use group interviews sparingly and purposefully. There is often useful knowledge (though less often historical facts) to be gained from watching members of a group discussing the past. In many cases the historian's best strategy would be to arrange both group and single interviews in each locality, beginning with a group interview that would provide a chance to introduce himself and his research aims. At such a meeting the historian can also discuss how he intends to carry out his plans as well as to seek help from those assembled. Even without asking specific questions he can use the occasion to sense the play of interpersonal relationships within the group [49; 188; 252]. He will probably find it easy to single out the most vocal members of the community, though he is unlikely yet to understand whose verbosity will be useful and whose will not.

If gathering people together in this way can be a revealing experience, it can be a monitory one as well. The historian should always seek advice before trying it; in fact he should never attempt it himself but should leave it to local authorities to arrange. In many communities, for instance, the idea of everyone—men, women, and children alike—meeting together is unthinkable. It would defy local norms of social avoidance and the historian foolish enough to ignore these conventions could well find his sources turned hostile.

There are other risks as well, once such a meeting has been agreed on. The historian may be bombarded on all sides with information, an embarrassment of riches if his knowledge of the language is inadequate to the occasion, as it is very likely to be. He may then find himself obliged to allow his interpreter to decide which of many possible comments he responds to, allowing the interpreter in effect to do the historian's work. This could be a very bad beginning indeed and if it happens frequently it may become a practice from which the historian never recovers and from which he never realises he is suffering.

Above all the historian should carefully avoid—as far as he can with his limited knowledge—particularly sensitive issues at this first meeting, such as land rights, disputed genealogical relationships, or interdicted rituals. At best he will get a surfeit of contradictory information to begin wondering about. At worst the people will think that his inquisitiveness is likely to create social friction they would prefer to do without and simply decide by common consent not to discuss certain matters with him, even privately.

Nevertheless, a few good things *can* come from a shrewdly orchestrated opening group interview, especially if the historian is not able to spend several months quietly observing and absorbing before he begins interviewing. Any hints he can gather about the place of power and authority in the community should help him later, particularly if the alternative is to depend on old ethnographic wisdom. He will also have the opportunity to learn a bit about the social aptitudes of the informants he believes are knowledgeable. However, the greatest benefit from beginning the research programme with a few group interviews and following them with private sessions is that this allows for some interesting and useful diagnosis and comparison. Knowing what certain informants say (or do not say) in company and how this differs from what they say privately can be illuminating, if sometimes disconcerting. But, however discomfiting it may be, the need to control information this way is crucial to the oral historian's work. After all, the gap between public posture and private feeling can be so large as to be indefinable. When this appears to be the case with some informants the historian must try to learn why.

How many and how often?

It is common for oral historians to interview key informants several times. In fact many historians have been no more than transcribers of the words of another and even today it happens that the evidence of a few informants dominates a researcher's interviewing to the point that they might rightfully be considered almost as co-authors. Should the historian sedulously deny himself opportunities to use the apparent expertise of one or two informants to the fullest extent? Not necessarily, but in doing so he needs to be very cautious. The role of the so-called encyclopedic informant has come under fire from critics who worry that the historian who relies on these semi-professional informants risks abandoning his function as interpreter in favour of that of recorder [188; 214; 367]. Often this is a legitimate concern, especially if the historian confines himself to gathering the encyclopedic informant's testimony without bothering to measure it against that of other sources he has used less intensively. Or, worse still, he avoids using other sources at all, content to let his major informants answer his questions [e.g. 500]. Misconceptions about matters as diverse as the existence of a creator god in Maori beliefs and the origins of American baseball can be traced to placing too much faith in a single informant [372, pp. 8–11; 419, pp. 8–12].

When the historian encounters a particularly knowledgeable informant he may wish to record, transcribe, edit, and publish a specific body of information the latter has provided. If he does, he should clearly indicate that he is the editor and the informant the author. Although they could be valuable additions to the literature, attempts to annotate major oral texts have been infrequent. It seems that most historians prefer to incorporate the testimony of such informants into their own work, usually in ways that defy attempts to distinguish the original testimony from later synthesis. The historian who is willing to rely, even if only (or apparently) through force of circumstances, on a few informants is likely, of course, to interpret the past he is studying in a short-sighted and unrepresentative way. He satisfies himself with doing little more than canonising and publicising one particular personal version of the past and disguising it as conventional historical scholarship. Historians would be better advised to speculate—to themselves and in print when it seems necessary—why such informants have arisen and what their impact, and that of any predecessors, might have been on a group's recollection of its past.

In oral cultures that have recognised central institutions there are sometimes official historians responsible for defining the remembrance of the past. Sometimes these people hold office by virtue of birth, sometimes by appointment, sometimes by self-appointment. In ancient Norway and Iceland the skalds performed similar duties; among the Rajputs of western India there are persons responsible for establishing and maintaining the genealogies of prominent families; in parts of Oceania specialists preserve lengthy genealogies tracing the leading families back to gods; while in West Africa *griots* serve rulers and other wealthy patrons by reciting genealogies and devising incomparable deeds for supposed ancestors [40; 421; 502].

Persons in these categories are natural targets for historians, who are likely to have their interest rewarded with an impressive quantity of information: no self-respecting *griot* or Maori *tohunga* would be satisfied with a recitation of less than several hours. Nor would informants of this type be content to provide an account that failed to specify clearly that the line of their patrons is of greater antiquity, wealth, social staus, power and generosity than any others within their range. Oral historiography in early colonial times relied almost completely on such informants. They were the people who were in contact with colonial officials and with the first wave of historians. Both groups tended to ignore evidence outside royal. courts for the past of centralised societies and any evidence at all about the history of non-centralised groups. Today's historians have generally come to realise that official histories of this nature are useful diagnostic tools for the present but of limited value for understanding what happened in the past. Court historians were the encyclopedic informants of yesterday; their successors, untitled and unpaid though many of them may be, are just as likely to serve up an undifferentiated and idiosyncratic vision of the past.

Even those historians—by now the great majority—who have not relied on too few informants have found it useful to interview some informants more than once, in some cases many times. In doing this they have generally asked different questions each time, hoping to secure as much of the informants' knowledge as possible as it was exhibited from one interview to the next. By itself this is not enough. Instead, every oral historian should take pains to check his data constantly by asking the same questions of the same informants two or three times, as widely separated as possible. This procedure should be applied most rigorously to the very informants who seem most knowledgeable since the historian is most likely to use their testimony. Like any other scholar, the oral historian must inhibit his own will to believe by testing most often and carefully that which he would most like to accept.

Oral historians often do not recognise the pernicious influence of this 'will to believe', even though a great deal of their work testifies to its powerful presence. The career of Christopher Columbus illustrates especially well the good and bad points of this attitude. Columbus' obstinate belief in a spherical world led him eventually to the western hemisphere. At the same time his passionate desire to discover a new and better route to the Indies convinced him that he had actually found lands in the Far East. His failure during any of his voyages to find significant wealth, large numbers of people, or complex societies failed to shake his deep-rooted convictions; he died protesting more strongly than ever that he had found 'the Indies'. A less compelling will to believe would have allowed Columbus to accept the evidence of his own eyes long before that, but today the memories of his navigational skills and correct assessment of the earth's shape are tarnished by the memory of his untenable and ultimately fatuous beliefs about the societies he encountered.

Controlling a very natural will to believe is especially important to the historian who collects and uses oral materials. More than any other historian he can so easily affect the creation and use of these materials. At the same time he is less able than those who use only written sources to verify any of what he chooses to accept as true.

Nonetheless, there is little evidence to date that oral historians have recognised the need to be unusually careful in questioning their informants in ways that would risk damaging their credibility. The best way to do this, of course, is to use informants to check themselves. A fine example of this procedure has recently appeared. In his work on the FulBe of Liptako, Paul Irwin discusses at length and with engaging, if sobering, candour his disenchantment at finding that the same informants often provided inconsistent information when asked the same questions a second or third time. Irwin then discusses his increasing awareness that it was hopeless to expect to secure much indisputable data about many aspects of Liptako history. This prompted him to make a second trip to the field designed primarily to test more fully the consistency (and therefore the accuracy) of some of the evidence he had collected earlier. The results of this exercise persuaded Irwin to abandon his earlier purpose of writing a straightforward factual account of Liptako history and instead to deal with the more interesting question of this pattern of fragmentary and contradictory recollection. The result is a fascinating discussion of how political, social, and economic interests (as well as faulty memories) explain why he could not examine Liptako history in ways he could have done in a society for which written documentation is available. But, and this is the relevant point here, he may never have realised the character of his sources had he not been careful to structure his interviewing to open diagnostic paths that would otherwise have been closed [253].

To this argument oral historians might respond (and some have) that oral data have certain special characteristics that should exempt them from these kinds of controls. Unlike written sources, they say, oral sources are not always immutable; they change because the spoken word has no perpetuity. Strangely, instead of regarding this as a handicap, they see it simply as a reason to apply a different set of standards to their study. It is true of course that different historians often make quite different use of and draw markedly different conclusions from the same written materials, but in these cases every historian knows that he is consulting the same sources and that he can see just what others have seen and will continue to see. Irwin's experience, the undisclosed experiences of others, together with common sense, all tell us that for oral historians this kind of confidence would be absurd. Because this is true, no oral historian can be remiss in taking every pain to ensure that he uses his informants well, exploits their knowledge and attitudes exhaustively, and understands their limitations—even if doing this sometimes tries their patience by seemingly insistent repetition.

Eavesdropping on the past

We have already pointed out the dangers of coming to the field armed not only with a series of questions but also with the feeling that asking questions is the best, if not only, way to learn. Certainly a great deal is to be learned through interviewing, but answers are always responses or reactions, to some extent tailored to the question itself. This means that the interview is not necessarily the most unfettered way to transmit knowledge. Fortunately there are other avenues open to the historian. The most important of these is simply the habit of listening. Much can be learned about the past in everyday social discourse. Even the best-prepared historian comes to the field in some measure ignorant. He may think that he has a grasp of the important historical issues and proceeds to test this assumption by asking questions that themselves spring from the original—and possibly incorrect—assumption! Since many historians will not feel obliged to go beyond the limits they have set for themselves the assumption seems to be proved correct.

Of course, this would all be sadly pointless and can be largely avoided if the historian is constantly alert for what we might call 'evidence in spite of itself'. His very presence in the community will certainly serve to incite in its members a greater interest in the past. But this may be expressed most extensively among themselves rather than in direct response to questioning.

This is especially true of issues (land rights, 'collaboration' with the colonial authorities, symbolic behaviour, etc.) that are the subject of continuing dispute or of real or feigned embarrassment. The historian is unlikely to gain as much information in formal interviews about such matters as he would like. But by keeping his ears open—eavesdropping on the past, if you will—he may not only become aware of whole areas of the local past previously unknown to him, but he can learn a lot about present attitudes as well.

How should the historian feel about listening and taking mental notes when he appears not to be interested? Should he feel sheepish and slightly clandestine about turning people's friendliness or communal intercourse to his own advantage? Or should he feel that, if he has been welcomed into the community, it is perfectly fair for him to learn about that community in the same way its members derive their knowledge—informally, casually, routinely? Here again are questions easily asked but not so easily answered. At times the historian will feel a sense of guilt at having learned something he thinks he was not supposed to. At other times, as he becomes more accepted in the community, he will feel delighted at the chance to listen and learn.

Silent observation aside, there will be many times when the historian will feel obliged to take the long way around to his intended destination. Sensitive topics that seldom yield to frontal assault may succumb to a cleverly executed flank attack. During his interviewing and unofficial listening, the historian needs always to be alert to such exposed flanks. For example, if he knows that a punitive expedition was once sent to suppress what the colonial officials called 'cannibalism' or 'human sacrifice', he may prefer to approach the subject, perhaps still a sensitive one, obliquely by asking about specific local or colonial authorities who participated in the campaign or by asking about sites connected with the forces' activities. If these ploys fail, he may try even more insidious methods. He may refer favourably, and apparently at random, to individuals he knows had an unpopular role in the expedition. The need to correct his views may then force informants to present their society's side of the argument.

In some cases these invisible lines of enquiry will be more effective in opening vistas on the past than even the best-designed formal approaches. It will frequently be necessary to cast aside anticipated methods and preconceptions in favour of insights gained while actually in the field.

II

Situations often arise in the field that historians need to anticipate by preparing a range of possible responses. Being ready for these occasions saves moments of embarrassment for both the historian and his informants and thereby helps preserve the friendly relations on which oral historiography necessarily depends. Naturally each of the points mentioned here will vary in its local occurrence so the discussion attempts to avoid particular circumstances in favour of a series of broad questions.

Information at any price?
Presumably the historian in the field sees value in his work. But should he really *expect* the people among whom he is working to be as willing to share

their time with him as he is to share his with them? Of course the short, simple answer to this is 'no'. In most cases the historian imposes himself on people who must continue to lead productive daily lives while he himself is likely to be subsidised for the very purpose of meddling. Although many oral historians have found the interest and enthusiasm their informants show in the historians' work one of its most rewarding aspects, they also realise that they often fail to reach informants who do not care to contribute their own time to fulfilling the historian's ends. While this makes good sense to the informants, it probably distresses the historian, who may begin to turn over in his mind ways to reward willing informants and to seduce reluctant ones.

One answer that will quickly occur to him is to pay informants, either in cash or goods, for their time. After all, the principle of fair payment for services rendered is an honourable one and eminently reasonable on the face of it. But here again, as has frequently been true, the face is not the best aspect of the question to address. Serious consequences can result from a policy of paying informants in any systematic way. By far the greatest danger is that some informants will become entrepreneurs and regard the interview as a market transaction with *pro rata* monetary rewards—the more time and information they offer, the happier their information seems to make the historian, the more he will pay them.

It is not hard to see where this kind of thinking can lead. When Emil Torday was collecting data from the Kuba early in this century, he unwisely promised informants a small fixed sum for the name of every Kuba ruler they could supply. The response was overwhelming and, to Torday, apparently gratifying. No fewer than 121 names were incorporated into the list of rulers he eventually constructed. In retrospect this extraordinary outpuring is bemusing, particularly since only eighteen names in Torday's list were actually Kuba rulers [471]. Yet his scheme of Kuba historical dating survived for nearly 50 years and still lives on in isolated pockets of credulity.

It would be unfair to blame Kuba informants or Torday's interpreters for this fascinating example of overkill. They were really only reacting in a business-like manner to Torday's business-like tactics. They must have felt that if Torday was not only willing to believe anything he was told, but actually to pay for being duped, then it would be foolish for them to display a more delicate regard for accuracy. In fact it may even be unfair to condemn Torday too readily for his belief that money could buy anything, even forgotten memories. His was a time when there dwelt within many investigators of oral societies a strange mixture of contempt for the behaviour and capacity of 'primitive' races and an indomitable belief in their mnemonic abilities.

This should no longer be true. Today any assumption that most informants not only will co-operate eagerly with peripatetic historians but will share with them the same or even higher standards of accuracy is no less naive. Indeed, it has been contradicted many times by the experiences of those who have been victimised by responses not very different from those of the inhabitants of Rabelais' Satinland, who were trained to sell their services only to the highest bidder [234]. As likely as not, interpreters and informants will absorb the historian's sense of urgency to secure data at whatever cost. The historian who operates on a 'pay-as-you-go' basis is likely to be met by a 'give-as-you-pay' attitude. When this happens he may pay a great deal for very little.

Fortunately there are other, better, ways the historian can express his appreciation for the help informants give him, and every historian who relies on interviewing *should* feel the need to repay his informants for their time, patience, and information. But this should never, never be done on a strictly *pro rata* basis. One of the historian's first concerns will be to learn local customs with respect to gift-giving since witlessly contravening these can only harm his chances for a fruitful venture. There will probably be several avenues open to him. For example, he may take along an instant developing camera and provide informants with pictures of themselves and their families. Or he may use local products—beer, palm wine, cloth, salt, aspirin—for this purpose, or provide occasional transportation or porterage.

Protocol as well as expediency is involved in this. The historian will have acquainted himself with the former in his background reading as well as enquiries in the field; the latter is learned only by experience. This applies to both informants and hosts, should the historian find himself a guest while travelling around. With regard to informants, it will usually be best to distribute gifts of roughly equal value (not necessarily the same as cost) to all informants, regardless of how useful they prove to be. If each interview session is treated as an occasion for some kind of token exchange, then the most helpful informants, by virtue of being interviewed several times, will be rewarded accordingly.

Is it really oral tradition?

What should the historian do if, in reply to a question, an informant pulls out some kind of printed source or directs the historian to consult such a source? The materials the informant consults can range from the Bible to books on general or local history, sessional papers and other government publications, newspaper clippings, or even the dissertation or publications of a recent predecessor. At first the historian may be perplexed by this inescapable hint that oral tradition is not always oral. However, this situation is occurring more frequently as the proliferation of work on oral societies combines with widespread rises in literacy levels. When this happens, the historian should be willing to welcome the chance to probe the historical consciousness of the informant and the ways in which this has been formed.

Presumably the historian will be familiar with the source to which the informant refers, knows what it contains and how the data were collected, and whether the conclusions are persuasive. Armed with this knowledge he can question the informant thoroughly. How did he become aware of the source? Did he or other members of the society contribute to the research on which it is based and, if so, how? Why does he believe it contains the truth? What does he like about the source? Can he provide information beyond what is to be found there? Has he discussed the contents of the source with other members of the community?

Whatever the answers to these questions happen to be, they can direct the historian towards other avenues to explore and he should not think that this detracts from his principal task of collecting new data. For instance, he must certainly ask other informants about the source—their opinion as to its validity, whether there are other versions of its contents in circulation, or whether these have been driven out by the appearance of the printed version. He can also try to learn if the owner of the source has used it to consolidate his position as a student of the past, that is, whether it has been used as a tool as well as a source.

The sum of the answers that will emerge will naturally vary from one case to another but they should provide some insight into the origins and nature of historical study in the group. All things considered, the historian should take the initiative by asking at an early stage (after allowing some time for informants to produce them spontaneously) whether any other printed historical sources circulate, who owns them, and how they have been used in discussions about the past.

Just mistaken or lying?

Most researchers realise that, one way or another, their informants have embellished a great deal of their information; that some informants are mistaken about some things; that informants who cannot answer some questions will still provide some reply to avoid being rude or humiliated; and that much unconscious manipulation occurs to shield the past from the unholy designs of the present. Few historians, though, seem to consider that their informants may deliberately and gratuitously lie. Accepting this would be to admit that they have not been able to persuade some informants that co-operation offers more benefits than drawbacks and that there has been in effect a serious failure in public relations.

Despite this, it is clear that deliberate lying is an art-form that is not entirely unknown to informants. In a recent discussion of lying informants Salamone quoted a Tiv informant who seemed not at all ashamed to admit that he and other Tiv informants customarily lied to outsiders who want to know 'personal things' about them [407]. Certainly the sense of privacy in a small-scale oral society is likely to be of quite a different character than in that of most historians, who by vocation are committed to what many might view as unwarranted prying. Rather than express this feeling bluntly and create possible embarrassment, informants are more likely to offer some kind of answer, not one intended to provide factual information but only to allay the historian's curiosity and to send him away feeling satisfied rather than determined to find another informant willing to discuss the unwelcome subject.

Naturally the effects of deliberate lies can be manifold. They often pass undetected, either because the historian does not cross-check the accounts of each informant, or because members of a group have all agreed to tell the same lie, or because the teller of the lie is the one person privy to the details the historian is after. Just as no story can be written about solving the perfect murder, no more can be said about the undetected lie.

Individual lies or patterns of lying that are discovered can at least help the historian learn about which aspects of the past (or present) there is dispute or a sense of avoidance or defensiveness. A single informant may express this (about his genealogical affiliations), or a group of informants (about their role in selecting rulers), or the entire group (about practices held repugnant by outsiders but still practised). Such examples as these would fall into the category of expected lies; that is, the historian should realise that subjects like these offer attractive, sometimes irresistible, opportunities for lying.

Other lies, however, may be wholly unwarranted or idiosyncratic and therefore nearly impossible to anticipate. Orality is no safeguard against those astute pathological liars found in most communities, but the historian can unmask these fairly easily since they seldom attempt to lie with much finesse. However, other apparently motiveless, lying will probably be more difficult to detect and understand [363]. Why should a wealthy man claim poverty when wealth is esteemed in his society? Perhaps in order to avoid paying taxes or to escape social obligations to share wealth. Denial of eligibility to high office may spring from fears that holding the office will result in assassination, dissipation of wealth through institutionalised largesse, or a need to enforce unpopular laws. Denial that a group came from place X despite strong evidence to that effect may stem from apprehension that dormant rivalries will be revived. And so it goes. The best way the historian can recognise that what seems to be ignorance or modesty is really useful lying is to ask his questions widely and be closely familiar with background materials in which the same stories may have appeared and for much the same reasons.

Coping with lies is one of the fieldworker's greatest problems. Sometimes he must call his informant's credibility into open question; most often he will silently devise ways to put it to profit. But even then the dilemma remains. Even when lying is admitted or deduced, the historian cannot be certain that it will stop. Worse yet, when it is not admitted, he may never be sure that it has begun.

How long and how obtrusive?

We have already mentioned that the historian should expect less interest in his work among informants than he himself has. This lack of interest may express itself generally but it may also be manifested during interviews so that it is important to learn the signs of incipient boredom or fatigue. One problem the historian faces in drawing up an interview schedule is deciding how much time to set aside for each interview session. In a way he is measuring his enthusiasm and stamina against those of his informants and this is an unfair battle. If he decides that long interviews (two or three hours or even more) suit his schedule best, he may find that he has a lot of spare time between unexpectedly shortened interviews since this is probably too long a period to spend questioning an informant at a single stretch. On the other hand, if he schedules short sessions (say, an hour), he may find that he is often behind schedule because informants want to talk longer. And being behind schedule is a form of discourtesy he will wish to avoid.

To begin with, at least, it is probably best to try fairly short sessions in the hope of keeping informant interest up while at the same time sampling a wider range of informants. As he learns which informants are likely to talk at greater length, the historian can adjust his schedule accordingly. Obviously it is far better to have to ask an informant if he can return another time than to find it necessary to ask him if he is still awake. In any case, any unanticipated time between interviews is not really spare time since the historian can use it to translate and transcribe.

During interviews the historian will often have to deal with interruptions:

family emergencies, visits from neighbours, meals, social occasions. He will quickly learn that on these occasions a willing self-effacement is necessary and he should always be prepared to break off an interview if he senses that his informant needs to, or simply wants to, do something else for the moment. One of the historian's objectives will be to achieve a balanced reputation for diligence combined with self-denying good humour and unfailing courtesy. It is not hard to understand, after all, that a disgruntled informant will be of little help to him and could in fact make it very hard to interview others successfully.

Getting along with local officials

A researcher working in an alien society faces a certain number of political as well as cultural hurdles. His interest in a particular group may seem perfectly innocuous to him—a chance to engage an interesting intellectual issue, no more—but it may be viewed with suspicion and scepticism by the local authorities, who may impose constraints to a degree that may be unfamiliar and unwanted. This may happen first at the research clearance stage, when officials scrutinise proposals and suggest changes, sometimes major ones. Even researchers who feel obliged to accept such changes may find on reaching the host country that research priorities, or the officials who determine them, have changed so that still further modifications may be necessary. Or it may be that certain areas of the country are regarded as closed to outsiders, even harmless scholars.

If the historian is fortunate enough to reach the desired locale of his research and with his plans relatively unscathed, he may still find local-level officials maintaining a lively, and perhaps unwelcome, interest in his comings and goings. In addition then to coping with informants, interpreters, neighbours, and illness, the oral historian might be forced to explain and justify his aims to local officials, even though he has received research permission at higher levels. It would be pointless to suggest here just how this might be done: circumstances, personalities, and opportunities are almost endless and the means to cope with them range from the comic to the illegal. What can be said with reasonable assurance is that local protocol norms should be learned quickly and then honoured carefully, continually, and (but only sometimes) visibly.

Whatever the historian decides is the best long-term policy to adopt with local officials, he must begin his relationship with them by presenting his credentials. Doing this may not ingratiate him with these officials, but failing to do it creates the risk of being told to discontinue his research simply because he has ignored official sensibilities. Stopping research plans in their tracks has become fairly common, even routine, in places. Sometimes nothing the researcher does can prevent this but he certainly owes it to himself to be sure that the fault lies not with him.

In addition to explaining his purpose, displaying authorisations and testimonials, and presenting a tentative schedule of activities, the historian will want to inquire about local-level archives since these are often under the control of the chief executive officer of the area. This done, the historian may find that a wide range of choices are available as far as his future behaviour towards officialdom is concerned. If he senses a lack of interest, or even latent hostility, by officials he may find it wise to maintain a low profile, confining himself to working with informants and leaving official contacts (save using any local archives) to a later stage in his research or to times when officials are absent. On balance a lack of interest by local bureaucracy is probably a good thing, since keen interest could have unpleasant implications. If officials are drawn from the local population, they may have a vested interest in maintaining a particular version of the past. If they do, the powers of their office could allow them to impose constraints on both historian and informants. Conversely, a friendly interest by local officials could lead to the researcher being regarded by the populace as an agent of the government rather than a disinterested scholar. The people's experiences with other government representatives—for instance colonial anthropologists who may have tampered with their succession system or suppressed ceremonies—could easily have a stifling effect on their willingness to assist the historian in his work.

Traditional political or religious authorities should also be considered, though it is likely that most historians entering the field are more aware of their obligations here. Such authorities may no longer have the power to force researchers to discontinue their work but they may retain the capacity to effect an even worse result: persuade the people not to co-operate, to impart only the most inconsequential information, or even to lie to a researcher who has not gained their good graces. If this happens the researcher has not only wasted his time but comes away believing he has not wasted it.

Whenever possible (and that will be most of the time) the historian should scrupulously work through traditional authorities in such matters as asking advice about interpreters, acquainting authorities with the scope and tenor of his research plans, or providing amenities suitable to their office. He should not allow them to speak for others he wishes to interview but he should realise that they may be among the most useful informants he is likely to encounter. By and large, though, he probably needs their formal approval to consult with local people more than he needs their views about the past.

Being the 'wise stranger'

Dealing with local government and traditional authorities should suggest to the historian that his role in the community is not going to be entirely that of gleaner and processer of data, but that he is likely to become involved in local affairs of greater or lesser moment. For instance, as he collects more and more information he exposes himself to the risk of becoming regarded as an expert on the community's history, with all that this implies. While he assiduously aims to acquire this stature among his peers, he may find that achieving it even before he leaves the field can lead to situations he would prefer to avoid. Local societies, whether oral or literate, are subject to ceaseless political and social infighting, even if it is not always obvious. Both as an outsider and as the recipient of various confidences and points of view, the historian may be called on to serve as arbiter in these disputes.

One of the parties may approach the historian, feeling that the historian will be sympathetic to their interests, or the entire community may want him to listen to their arguments, add his own presumed expertise, and make judgement on the assumption that he has been able to maintain neutrality. If such a request is made the historian will find himself on the spot for several reasons. On a practical level he should realise that if he allows himself to become involved he will surely alienate one group or another, or even all groups if he proves to be unskilled in the fine art of compromise. On an intellectual level he should accept the fact that, because his conception of historical 'truth' may differ from that of the community, he cannot undertake in good conscience to impose his views on theirs. At the same time he will—or should—be aware that the evidence on which to arrive at a firm judgement is not adequate and perhaps never can be to the extent he thinks necessary. Yet any statement to this effect is liable to damage his research prospects because it will disappoint all groups as well as encourage them to doubt his investigative ability. After all, they may think, he has been asking questions for months: why doesn't he know the answers?

All things considered, there is probably no really good course to follow if this situation arises. The best (that is, least bad) expedient may be for the historian to disclaim sufficient knowledge of the past, or better still, of all the particulars in dispute. Of course this will seldom be false humility and, if he is properly diplomatic in his protestations, it should safeguard his research status among his informants, who may be disappointed, but less by promises unfulfilled than by the historian's diffidence. They may even feel that they have not been forthcoming enough in providing him with information.

Forewarned being forearmed, the historian should take care to assure those asking his help, or those he thinks might ask, that at no time during his field research will he be competent to serve as referee. Later, when he begins publishing, he should see to it that copies of his work are made available locally. This will provide useful help, this time the considered reflections of the researcher rather than his undeveloped thoughts. It is also less likely to jeopardise his privileged position in the community although, to be honest, disappointing or alienating informants is one risk the historian must continue to live with [335].

Putting equipment to work

Whether interviews are short or long, with men or women, old people or young people, individuals or groups, most oral historians rely heavily on their recording equipment. The time and effort in learning about using this equipment will be wasted to whatever extent the historian is unable to use it in the field. He must not only hope that he is accepted as a fellow human being but that his equipment is accepted along with him. If the people among whom he is working have had little experience with such technology, they may find the tape recorder and all its accessories slightly daunting and the historian may find it hard to convince the people of its benefits.

Obviously it is both courteous and expedient to ask each informant if he objects to having the interview taped, if he would prefer instead that written notes be taken, or would find just a quiet conversation more appealing. In some ways a tape recorder tucked into a dark corner is less obtrusive than pen scratching across paper placed directly between informant and historian, but the problems could relate more to attitude than visibility. In all cases the informant's feelings must govern, though we might reasonably expect the historian to put forward his best arguments each time the matter rises. We might with even greater reason expect that he would never try to record secretly.

The reverse of this is a situation in which informants will not only fail to find the recorder intimidating but will be greatly stimulated by its presence. A belief that the tape recorder is just the means to communicate a particular point of view effectively is by no means confined to the researcher. The desire to immortalise their views for posterity may mean that the historian is faced with informants who are too voluble or interested only in talking about matters of concern to them but not to the historian. Although the sensible historian will naturally encourage informants to digress from his chosen bounds, he must also develop effective techniques for silencing people without offending them. No doubt several ways will come to mind: equipment malfunction, running out of tape, reminding the informant that he (the informant) must have better things to do, or claiming a previous appointment could be useful.

Here, as so often before, it has been necessary to consider more than one side of the question without firmly taking a stand. But, also as before, it is less important to offer firm but fragile advice than it is to alert historians to the need to be flexible by providing themselves with the widest range of choices without really *appearing* to consider the matter at all once in the field.

Making it all count

Whenever the historian transcribes oral materials the very act of transcription enhances his grasp of their content. The price paid for this is time—valuable time. In fact it is likely that transcribing taped materials will take from six to eight hours for each hour of tape—an unpleasant prospect even if time did not matter. Yet if the historian tries to save this time by simply skimming through tapes to get some idea of their content, he will be for a long time less than sufficiently familiar with what they have to tell him. Taping materials in the field provides the collector only with an impressionistic understanding of the testimony and this is all the more true if his auditory capability in the language is mediocre, forcing him to rely on interpreters for the finer points of the discussion.

In preparing his anticipated research programme the researcher must be careful not to set aside too much of his time for interviewing and too little for transcribing and studying the interviews while still in the field. Whenever possible, and every effort should be made to render it possible, each interview or small group of interviews should be transcribed almost as soon as (and certainly within a few days) they have been conducted. The variable and dynamic aspects of oral research—the living sources—make this procedure absolutely imperative because it is really the only way the historian can detect new areas of discussion or different points of view, as well as anomalies, contradictions, and textual uncertainties that he will need to follow up.

Of course the historian can pick some of this up during the interviews if the interpreter is well trained, understands and accepts the historian's purposes, and is familiar with earlier interviews. But even the finest interpreter should not be expected to stand surrogate for the historian, on whom always rests the major responsibility for pursuing his interviewing in the most effective way.

In transcribing, the historian or interpreter should make a second tape, which can later be used for an independent translation if knotty points of language or interpretation arise. The tape itself and any transcriptions or translations should include data on the informant, the time and place of the interview, and contextual notes on such matters as the numbers and kinds of bystanders and their influence on the informant. When problems arise the historian should note them on the transcript and try to resolve them as soon as practicable. Related tapes and transcripts, particularly when they comment on each other, should be kept together. As long as tape and transcript remain together, it may be acceptable (but no more) to translate while transcribing. However, since tapes and transcripts are often separated by field exigencies it is best to transcribe in the language of the informant and then translate as soon as possible but in any case soon enough to allow a follow-up interview if necessary.

No doubt these procedures seem, and are, laborious and time-consuming. They may also seem, but are not, wasteful of valuable time. No amount of speculating, agonising, or rationalising several thousand miles away from the field can compensate for losing opportunities to seek clarification from an informant whose testimony is carefully examined by the researcher only after he returns home.

Hedging against disaster

Many historians have heard tales about field notes that were lost or destroyed through water damage, fire, mechanical error, theft, errant mails, etc. Although this may happen less often than the telling of it suggests, it is true that dangers of this kind are greater for materials that have no existence beyond that of the historian himself. The most obvious and necessary precaution is making a second tape and a carbon copy of written notes and to keep these in a different place than the originals. Every few weeks the historian should send one copy to his home base and retain the other for continuing study. Packages of duplicates sent off should be numbered and their contents tallied and the person to whom they are sent should notify the researcher as each package arrives. Then, should any materials fail to arrive, it might be possible to copy and send them again.

Doing all this, like transcribing quickly or re-interviewing key informants, can be troublesome. It takes time, energy, and money—all of which are likely to be in limited supply. And if the researcher manages to return home with all copies of his materials intact, this safeguard may seem to have been in vain. Not so, because the existence of a second set of field notes and tapes provides the chance to arrange the body of field materials in several different ways, allowing the historian more readily to abstract and arrange different data for varying purposes. For example he might want to arrange one set geographically and the other by topic, or one set chronologically and the other by informant. Arranging a set by informant would help him gain access to information he identifies mentally with particular interviews.

Last steps

Surprisingly, perhaps, many historians have found it harder than they imagined to leave the field behind. Faced with the prospect of transcribing and translating, organising, interpreting, and writing up the fruits of their research, they have found it easy to exaggerate their commitment to additional fieldwork, to convince themselves that vital information and untapped informants lie just beyond their reach. This may be true, of course, but the historian must decide at some point that the collecting stage of his research has come to an end; sometimes he is helped by running out of money. The decision made, he must give proper thought to leaving the field just as he prepared for and worked in it.

An important facet of this is to thank his informants, interpreters, neighbours, and other friends. They have given their time for his benefit and probably deserve rather more than he can give them in return. He must also make arrangements with the local archives or research institute to deposit field notes and tapes. Preferably this should all be done before he leaves the field but certainly as soon as possible afterwards. In doing this he creates an emergency archive, should his own materials be lost or destroyed. Perhaps more important, he protects his own good name and paves the way for researchers who will follow him and can benefit from his good example.

Once these matters are completed the historian can turn to his own interests. There is little to be said here except to point out the need to be aware of any local currency regulations that could affect his departure, as well as rules about baggage allowances. Although these have changed (based on size instead of weight, a real advantage when heavy field notes are in question) these changes have not yet been universally applied. In order to continue hedging against disaster the historian should carry on board as much material as he can in order to avoid the well-known pitfalls of bagging handling and forwarding.

Perhaps it is too much to expect that, as he sits at the airport or dock or railway station, the historian begins to turn from what he has accomplished to what lies ahead—from the dominance of the largely mechanical, repetitive, and social to the almost exclusively interpretive, tedious, and ruminative. The return home can be either anticlimax or prologue. Any time the historian spends now pondering the road ahead will only be the first of many periods when, probably with no little apprehension, he wonders how he will be able to transform oral raw materials, mere fragments, into a convincing synthesis. It will not really be a transformation, of course, but a slow, uncertain, and tortuous intellectual journey.

CHAPTER FOUR

AFTER THE FIELD: THE INTERPRETATION OF CONTEXT

> Immediately circumstantial evidence became exchanged for direct, the loungers yawned, gave a final survey, and turned away to a subject which would afford more scope for speculation.
> [Hardy, *Desperate Remedies*]

> With the Dinka who do not write, each man will twist it this way and that way. Even if he reports it honestly, the truth gets lost in the middle, but a person who reads can find it all written down.
> [Dinka informant, 119, p. 54]

Once the historian returns from the field he ceases to create his materials but retains the obligation to interpret whatever he has collected. In this and the next chapter we discuss some ways and means to do this to the best possible effect. In Chapter 5 the emphasis is on content—the subject matter—of the data. Here, though, we are concerned with the historian's retrospective thoughts about the circumstances under which he collected his information. In many ways, of course, this discussion relates to the previous chapter and might have been included there. However, it is primarily concerned with issues that remain *after* the historian has collected his data. No matter how carefully and conscientiously he has done this, he will not have met all problems successfully. These have to be dealt with during the interpretative stage of his work.

The pause that refreshes—and chastens

Using the large quantity of oral and archival data he has brought back with him, the historian must begin the task of preparing a work of scholarship. His work will differ from as well as resemble that of conventional historians in a number of ways but the differences in *interpreting* his data will be fewer and less important than they were in *accumulating* them.

Before he begins the arduous work of arranging, selecting, examining, and writing up his materials the historian should take time to establish tentative but explicit points of view about several problems he will be facing. He must remind himself again of the commanding role of memory of his work. He must also remember that what he is doing is an interpretation, in which he pits his own sense of the past against that of members of the society in which he has worked. He must consider the effects of translation on his data as well as that of performance on their past and present transmission. Then he must examine the problem of what standards to use in selecting and rejecting information. Finally, after he has considered all these matters, the historian will find it necessary to deal with some larger issues that are common to the use of oral historical materials. These include such issues as metaphor, mutability, borrowing, and dating and are taken up in the next chapter.

To some extent all historians are concerned with the human memory because both they and it deal with the past; but to the oral historian the role of memory takes on a predominant role in much of his calculation. He can attempt no reconstruction without facing his honest impressions of the mnemonic capacities and inclinations of his informants. Even when he does not attribute to them any conscious desire to distort, he must realise that even their best will to remember—and to remember accurately—begs the question of their ability to do this in ways that will appeal to the historian's own sense of historical significance. As we see in Chapter 6, recent studies on memory, although largely confined to literate societies, suggest how difficult it is to recall the past with detachment and accuracy [295; 315; 342; 359; 383; 445]. There is sometimes talk of 'prodigious' or 'phenomenal' memory among some members of oral societies but before accepting this argument it must be understood that, however attractive it may be, it is largely untested and untestable.

During this period of introspection, when the historian shifts from asking questions of informants to asking them of data, he should remind himself that he is not reproducing his evidence but interpreting it. That is, he is arraying some of his data in new ways and distinguishing his ideas of the best way to see the past from those of his informants. He is taking fragments and trying to fashion them into a recognisable mosaic. While he does this he may recognise that his way of interpreting and that of his informants will never be quite the same, no matter how steeped in the collective mentality of the group he feels he has become. For example, his ideas of time, causality, and the relative importance of certain events and trends, as well as his very ideological perspective, will all be quite different. Moreover, his views on the scope of the past—what its portrayal should encompass in order to be intelligible—will be immeasurably more complex than the views of his sources. This is not because he is literate but because he is a historian.

In reconstructing the past from innumerable tiny fragments, which might be likened to the dots of paint that characterise the pointillist style of art, the historian will never be sure that he has all the pieces he needs or even whether all the pieces he has belong to a single whole. Any views he is likely to have about the past are firmly rooted in these little pieces—the evidence—just as his informants' perceptions of the past have in turn been based on a largely different set of fragments. If we may for the moment consider the past to be like a large forest, then the informants see the forest in terms of the leaves; the first historian who collects testimony from them puts some of these leaves together and makes branches or limbs; the next historian tries to put these together into respectable-looking trees; later historians make other trees and begin to see the forest but still from only one point among the growing number of trees. Only with the passing of many generations of historians can one see this forest in a general view, as from a low-flying aircraft. The historians of most oral societies are still looking at leaves and limbs and branches.

In organising, evaluating, and interpreting his data the historian will constantly need to decide which of them to use, which to reject partly or provisionally, and which to set up and use in another time and place. Sometimes this winnowing and sifting will be explicit and considered, sometimes indistinct and off-hand. As he engages in it the historian is in danger of adopting at least one expedient that might seem quite reasonable, but which is really only convenient and no more. This is a willingness to accept certain testimonies because they are plausible, coherent, and thus generally persuasive, while rejecting others on the grounds that they seem implausible or shapeless, or speak of the frankly impossible. Often the procedure has been to extract such elements as giants, talking animals, or things falling from the sky and regard the residue as some kind of primordial truth to which these improbable elements have been added over a period of time simply to make a good story a little bit better.

To adopt this technique, to separate historical wheat from unhistorical chaff, is to use a sieve whose mesh is far too large to yield a desirable mixture of ingredients. It fails to account, for instance, for the fact that in all societies those kinds of things that have been experienced or observed are most likely to be what is most readily believed so that, for a tradition to be successful enough to have survived into the present *requires* that it have a large part that is true-to-life. Many times of course it will also be true, but frequently its only purpose is to approximate reality. It would be just as artless for historians of Asante to accept a tradition simply because it assigns a commonplace origin to the Golden Stool as it would be to accept the standard version that if fell from the sky. Or for that matter for Biblical scholars to adopt the version of Genesis regarding mankind's origins by reducing the unlikely span of years alloted to early patriarchs by deciding, as some early moderns did, that in Genesis 'year' meant something else than it did in other parts of the Bible. Demythologising elements of tradition in this way is only to confuse the commonplace with the true and to risk exchanging impossibilities for untrue possibilities.

The Golden Stool exists, though when and how it was fabricated and how many there have been, no one knows. Nor would anyone deny that the Israelites of historical times had antecedents, though exactly who they were or where and how they lived we also do not know. In all cases such as these, the historian has little hope at this late date of separating 'fact' from 'fiction' without the guidance of numerous records detailing the progress of the tradition from its very beginning. Barring these, he must content himself with trying to understand the social role of such stories; in attempting this, plausibility (or lack of it) is by itself of little help. Other traditions for which variants still exist can be mined more fully for the truly historical content by such means as identifying the group interest behind each variant, detecting from other sources any changes in these groups, and noting the existence of loan-words, archaic or unintelligible phrases, or data introduced from literate sources.

Some literary critics believe that translating accurately in all respects is not so much an art as an impossibility because the process of translating from one language to another changes more than words. Languages are, they point out, embodiments of culture, so when language changes then so do ideas and perceptions and the ways these are communicated [e.g. 438]. However deeply the translator (who may not be the historian) has immersed himself in the nuances of the second language, he can never have the life experiences that are indispensable to understanding the real, the deeper, the non-lexical meanings of words in that language.

Oral historians are certainly translating literature—sometimes what seems to be straightforward narrative, sometimes more obviously cryptic genres such as poetry or proverbs—but they are in no position to adopt so nihilist an attitude towards the process of translation. Fortunately, they are seldom looking for the same resonances as literary critics and mode of expression is ordinarily less important to them than content. Even so, they would be unwise to assume that translation consists largely of consulting a dictionary to ascertain the possible meanings of a particular term or phrase and then adopting whichever one seems to fit best with what the historian thinks is being said. Much oral historical research depends on translating from languages for which lexical materials are scant and which possess peculiar characteristics such as tonal systems that are conceptually foreign to most researchers. It would hardly be amiss then to dwell a bit on problems of denotation and connotation, on the differing uses of the same word from one culture to another, and even on different uses by an individual from one occasion to the next.

We can illustrate some of the perplexities conveniently by discussing the words 'disinterested', 'uninterested', and 'interested' as they are used by English-speakers. To language purists 'disinterested' means something like 'free from personal bias', whereas 'uninterested' has a substantially different meaning—'apathetic' or 'indifferent'—and the two are not judged compatible enough to meet without creating untold confusions of meaning. Despite the rules, however, most people are inclined to use the two words almost interchangeably in both popular and scholarly discourse. In particular, 'disinterested' has come to mean 'apathetic' or 'indifferent'. But the situation is more complex than this because this new definition of 'disinterested' seems to be more common in British English than it has (yet) become in American English. And of course since it is a change, it is far more likely to be encountered in recent British English than in British English of more than a few generations ago.

Now someone whose native tongue is not English of either variety, but who is attempting to cope with an English text, may resort to an older dictionary that makes clear the semantic distinction; or he may happen to consult a newer dictionary in which the distinction is less clearly made or is even termed obsolete; or he may be fortunate enough to consult a handbook of usage that addresses both the distinction and the history of its fortunes. But doing this for large numbers of words is an onerous task our hypothetical historian is not likely to undertake. Instead, being just familiar enough with English to understand that both words derive from 'interested' in a negative way, but not familiar enough with semantic logic to realise that opposites of the same word are not for that reason identical, he will choose the easy—and in this case wrong—way of using the two terms indiscriminately.

This cautionary tale can be carried further by discussing the word 'interested' itself. Here is a single term—and there are so many of them—that can have several quite different meanings. One of these is 'not free from personal bias', the converse of 'disinterested', at least in the good old days. Another is 'curious' or 'attentive', the opposite of 'uninterested'. The first of these meanings is not very common nowadays and could almost be termed obsolete, though certainly not incorrect. In older texts it occurs more frequently and, if the distinction between 'disinterested' and 'uninterested' is blurred, it is inevitable that the distinction among the various meanings of 'interested' will become equally muddled. And this muddle will extend to any interpretations of texts that are based on false assumptions.

To carry the argument just one step farther, we might point out that, even if the historian decides which meaning of any of these words he thinks his text intended, he cannot be sure that he is right. It is unlikely, after all, that the author will have taken the trouble to clarify the matter since to him there was never anything that needed to be clarified. In this sense then, despite using old dictionaries, new dictionaries, and handbooks, the historian is still uncertain that he has pinned things down.

There are thousands of words in almost any language that have these properties. These three merely illustrate the problem but in addition have the advantage of pointing out that context alone is not always enough to detect semantic ambiguities. Obviously there will be many instances when *either* 'disinterested' or 'uninterested' (each properly used) will make sense in several different contexts. Or for that matter when 'interested' used either way can make sense. When this happens the historian may be forced—without even realising it—to choose on no very clear grounds between two, or even more, possible meanings, even though his informant intended to convey only one.

For local vernaculars the problems will probably be even more intractable. Usage guides seldom exist; any dictionaries may be obsolete or incomplete or both; dialectal variations may be more common and intensive; the use of interpreters will add an imponderable dimension; the lack of native speakers away from the field may force the historian to depend entirely on his own best guesses. The historian can anticipate some of these problems while still in the field but often he will not recognise them as problems until it is too late. If the only available dictionary provides just one meaning for a particular term, it is the rare historian who would not be willing to accept that there is indeed only a single accepted meaning, if only because failing to do this might seem to be allowing himself to be thwarted by his own sense of caution. Once he begins intensive study and comparison of his oral texts, however, he may realise that the dictionary definition was inadequate.

These general points aside, the rest of this chapter is devoted to several important contextual issues that may tax practitioners of oral historiography. They are by no means all specific to oral sources, nor do they exhaust the range of possible issues involved in understanding oral records. However, the points raised here seem to be the most important that are likely to confront historians dealing with the pasts of oral societies beyond the personal recollections of the oldest living members.

Integrating oral and written data

Unless he has been sadly unenterprising, the historian will have gathered some written documentation on topics he has explored in the field. This being so, he will constantly need to decide how he is to integrate the two kinds of sources [23; 58; 65; 338]. This exercise of the historian's skills is not very

different from dealing with a similar variety of written sources, but the degree
of commonness between oral and written materials is likely to be lower, so the
job of making the best of both will be harder. That is, it will be a question of
juxtaposing different materials rather than overlapping largely similar ones
since perspectives can differ so widely as hardly to be recognisable. Broadly
speaking, there are four ways orally-derived and written sources relate to each
other. They can be nearly identical in content; they can complement each
other; they can contradict each other; or they can be so different as to have
almost no common features even though they seem to be describing the same
set of circumstances.

It is rare to find any really substantial similarity between an oral
testimony and a written account since the two sources generally evoke
different time-scales and points of view. Should the historian encounter high
consistency, he should carefully consider the possibility that one of the sources
has directly influenced the other. It may be that his informant was also a
source for the written account—not unlikely in these days of high intensity
fieldwork. Alternatively, the informant may have been repeating what he
heard or read. These touch on the matter of feedback that is discussed in the
next chapter.

It is frequently the case that an oral source confirms or enhances
information from written materials [e.g. 376]. In fact this ability to
complement the written record is the principal purpose of oral historiography.
Perhaps one occasion will suffice to illustrate this. The contemporary written
accounts of the death of Captain James Cook in Hawaii in 1779 contain
abundant details—there were many eyewitnesses—but, despite much
guessing, none of them adequately explained why he was murdered [117; cf.
406]. Testimony collected from Hawaiians a generation later, however,
indicated that the Hawaiians had killed Cook because of certain religious
beliefs—that he died because he happened to be in the wrong place at the
wrong time and little else [138, pp. 115–23]. The full explanation could never
have occurred to Cook's shipmates because they were unacquainted with the
beliefs in question and so were obliged to seek explanations based on their own
experience. In this case the testimony of the European eyewitnesses was
enhanced by adding the answer to the important question: why. Had the
recollections of the islanders not been recorded later, some aspects of Cook's
death would have remained unresolved.

The Hawaiian sources on Cook's death did not contradict the European
accounts by claiming, for instance, that it had been accidental or that he had
been murdered by his own crew. But it does often happen that oral and written
accounts disagree with each other. The eastward expansion of the Cape
Colony and the numerous conflicts with the Xhosa—the so-called Kaffir
Wars—that resulted, provide many examples of the need to weigh one kind of
record against the other. Intent on justifying their insatiable appetite for land,
Cape Colony officials and other observers magnified the most trivial incidents
into occasions for war, attributed such incidents to whatever Xhosa groups
whose land they wanted at the moment, and even invented examples of Xhosa
hostility to justify their aggression. Convincing the authorities that war was
merely a form of self-defence was easily done, as the relentless growth of the
Colony's boundaries testifies.

Historians who have recently tried to see this expansion in a transcultural context and to understand the effects of it on the Xhosa and their neighbours have found that Xhosa versions of these incidents differ in many respects from the accounts enshrined in colonial historiography. It has generally been these last that have been accepted, first by British officials who condoned one annexation after another, and then by historians who saw the expansion as largely a series of defensive reactions to unwarranted Xhosa aggression.

Armed confrontation on the frontier between different cultures is a natural source for the growth of contradictory accounts so it is hardly surprising that Americans have often defended the westward expansion of the United States largely in terms of the preservation of law, life, and order. From the early seventeenth century through to the end of the nineteenth century, self-defence has been the most common political justification for each phase of expansion. This attitude both fostered and was in turn fostered by the appearance of scores of 'captivity tales' that, whether by design or not, fanned resentment towards the Indians and helped provide popular support to public policies of expansion and consequent removal of many Indian groups [429]. Recent studies of the remaining recollections of the Indian groups involved, together with a more careful study of the written sources, show how disingenuous these justifications often were [99; 215].

Nevertheless, it would obviously be unfair to argue that when oral sources contradict written records, they are always correcting them, since just as often the opposite is likely to happen. Suppose that a group of traditions claim that a settlement at the mouth of a particular river was established more than ten generations ago and has existed continuously ever since. However, if there are numerous travellers' accounts from a century or more ago that all flatly state that the area was then uninhabited, it is they and not the oral traditions that are to be believed if we can be certain that the written accounts are independent and represent eyewitness testimony. The task of the historian is then to ask why the traditions make the opposite claim.

Or suppose oral testimony states that a particular chief died in an accident whereas the colonial records state that he was executed for murder. In this case it is probably safe to accept the facts of his death as recorded in the colonial records though not necessarily the reasons they give for the execution. But if the colonial records speak of suicide and oral testimony of murder, or if one group of sources say that his death was accidental and the other that he was murdered, the historian's choice is no longer so clear-cut since self-interest could easily have played a role in developing each version. Here the contradictions encourage the historian to investigate the issue more fully.

Ironically, perhaps, contradiction offers more opportunities than does agreement. When contradiction occurs, the historian must do more than add designated portions of source A to selected parts of source B to arrive at sum AB. Instead, he will probably find it necessary to accept less well-defined parts of each source while rejecting or modifying others. In doing this he has the chance to learn something about the origins, intent, and recent fortunes of each group of sources. Of course this probing should not be left entirely to the time after the historian leaves the field, but aspects of it—the second and third stages of comparison and analysis—will occur at this later date, when the historian has all his sources in hand.

The last group of sources we have defined—those that seem to speak to events not mentioned in another body of materials—will clearly test the historian's ingenuity. He may wonder why none of the oral data he collected so carefully in the field mention something that attracted substantial written comment. Or he may be puzzled by the fact that, whereas his oral sources have a lot to say about a certain revitalisation movement or succession dispute, neither missionaries, colonial officials, or travellers through the area mentioned them at all. In the first case it may be a problem of nomenclature. Europeans on the Gold Coast, American westerners, and other intrusive groups often saw fit to give local people descriptive or baptismal names [e.g. Hawkeye, Captain Dick, Dom João] that had no meaning to, and were never used by, the people themselves [35; 39]. By considering the possibility that oral accounts use different names but still refer to some of the same people and events as the written accounts, the historian may be able partly to reconcile them.

More often than not, though, the problems will not be resolved quite so easily. If the historian is certain that the religious movement or succession dispute mentioned by his informants actually did occur at a time when contemporary documentation is available, he must question the value of his written sources—certainly he must reject any opportunities to argue from their silence. Yet he will seldom have the luxury of certitude. In this never-ending operation of weighing and balancing, sifting and sifting again, all depends on the judgement and discretion of the historian. He alone must decide whether event A or person B were important enough to merit the attention of any sources that dealt in detail and candour with the relevant times and places. If he decides that they were significant for the society he is studying but not necessarily in ways that would be noticed by outsiders, he may decide not to consider the silence of his written sources to be self-condemning. But if he finds recurrent written references to people and events not mentioned by any of his informants he may wonder about the possibility of a conspiracy of silence or the use of allusive language that he never came to understand.

It is important that some of the historian's decisions about the relative value of his sources (written v. oral, anthropological v. missionary, one lineage v. another, etc.) become an integral and explicit part of his published record. If he feels he has triumphantly solved the problems that vexed him most, he will want to bring this to the attention of his readers in order to establish his credentials. If he can claim only a tentative or partial solution, he must warn his readers and in effect solicit their help. It is not enough to relegate blithe generalisations regarding the value of certain important sources to a ritual methodological chapter. The presentation of each major issue should be accompanied, if at all practical, by an explanation sufficient to permit readers to follow the historian's line of reasoning from beginning to end.

The problem of missing links
At least temporarily, both printed materials and oral testimony are the last links in a chain of varying complexity and completeness and often of indeterminate length [104; 286; 368; 487]. Sometimes they are the only link since they have no traceable antecedents. Historians who have been interested in determining the authenticity of their sources have always considered

exploring the 'genealogy' of the most important of them as a necessary part of their work [71; 98; 110]. Like biological genealogies these chains of transmission help to establish the legitimacy of a particular argument by tracing it back through a series of ancestors of unassailable repute. Like biological genealogies then, it is crucial that such chains appear to be unimpaired.

Historians who rely principally on printed sources are often able to trace a statement back through several predecessors to the point of its presumed first appearance. Sometimes this is done by means of footnotes or statements in the text by which a later author credits one or more predecessors for facts or judgements. Sometimes such credit is not given but the reader can deduce dependence through a close similarity or identity of wording. Or sometimes he can infer a specific line of transmission from the repeated use of a particular set of figures, a variant spelling, or a name or names that occur nowhere else.

By doing this historians can often trace an argument all the way back to an indisputably primary point because the original author, like Thucydides or Caesar or Bernal Díaz del Castillo, participated in some of the events he described. Other times it may be possible to follow a line or reasoning or argument back only to an author whose own sources have since disappeared; perhaps they were inscriptions or manuscripts whose whereabouts are no longer known.

In societies using writing it is possible to engage in such detective work or to be certain that, even without it, the scholarly genealogies which the sources provide are accurate. For most oral societies the issue of chains of transmission is only marginally relevant since the historian can seldom do more than trace whatever information he receives one or two transmissions back. He may feel certain that some of the content has been handed down over many generations but he will never know who were involved in this or exactly what was original and what was introduced along the way.

Perhaps the inability to trace the origins of a particular tradition through a recognisable chain of transmitters is not as important as it might seem because it is unlikely that the testimony the historian collects in the field will faithfully reproduce the original testimony. Even with regard to the so-called fixed texts, the occasions for embellishment and suppression are too numerous to allow the historian much peace of mind. At most he can expect relative stability from one informant or a particular group, the result of unconscious memorisation through repetition.

Most of us are familiar with, or have participated in, experiments in which one person passes along a message orally to a second person and asks him to pass it along in turn exactly as he heard it. When the number of participants in such an exercise exceeds four or five and the text is more than a few words, the message given to the last person is almost invariably different from that given to the second. When this is done over long periods of time with the realisation that no internal controls are possible, we can only surmise how much the final transmission, from informant to historian, differs from the very first.

To put the question of transmission over time into a context, we can discuss two historical examples where the chain of transmission from a continuing present back to a receding fixed point was considered important. Both happen to be from societies that possessed writing but that in one case depended on word of mouth and in the other on belated reconstruction.

During the first few centuries of Islam the norms of the new religion were shaped in part by establishing 'tradition' by means of *hadiths*, which were stories about Muhammad's sayings and doings [218; 393; 394; 395; 396]. Eventually six major collections of hadiths were assembled and in these every hadith was prefaced by a list of transmitters. Called *isnads*, these lists were designed to authenticate both the message of the hadith and its attribution to one of Muhammad's companions. Since each compiler wished his own collection to be regarded as the orthodox version, each devised elaborate rules by which to judge the relative merits of each isnad and hence of the hadiths themselves. Needless to say, each isnad had to be uninterrupted and each compiler tried to ensure that its constituent links were regarded in all quarters as impeccable scholars and worthy transmitters.

Several recent studies have shown that hadiths often developed only a century or more after Muhammad's death to be used as weapons in the sectarian wars within Islam [42; 73; 412; 413]. Only then were isnads created to take the hadiths back to Muhammad's time, so that the rules allegedly designed to test isnads were more often used to invent them in the first place. In short, because they had political ends, most isnads were spurious in whole or part [73; 106; 412]. As means adopted to justify the views locked in battle several generations later, they could hardly be genuine, since in many cases there were no doings and sayings of Muhammad to report—could not have been since the issues in question had never been a part of Islam as originally formulated.

The custom of providing scholarly genealogies for points of legal and doctrinal interest has continued in West Africa. There lists of the names of successive teachers are an intrinsic part of Muslim teaching. In some cases they claim to reach back more than a thousand years, far longer than any of the isnads in early Islam, and no more likely to be accurate. The character of their inaccuracies can be of value, though, in showing some patterns of outside influence not otherwise discernible [492].

In the early Christian church the conception of the office of bishop was a matter of dispute, as the church attempted to establish a hierarchy. One view, based on the principle called apostolic succession, held that the importance of the office derived from the fact that only bishops were the direct successors of the apostles or recognised disciples. This argument naturally required that in each diocese there be direct lines of succession from apostolic times. Establishing this was not easy since, once again, the principle to be proved came too late for any proof to survive. Church historians, however, proved adequate to the task and in one diocese after another in the Middle Ages they developed lists of bishops that connected their present with the apostolic past [125; 126; 133; 184]. Sometimes they even provided dates designed to show that the succession had indeed been uninterrupted.

As it happens, in the last century or so scholars have shown that every single one of these lists (and there were hundreds) was, in some part or other, produced by chroniclers and historians who, in order to satisfy local pride, created thousands of fictitious bishops (many sainted of course) [126; 197]. For western Europe there are no reliable lists of bishops extending beyond, at the very earliest, the middle of the second century except possibly that of Rome, and some have questioned the existence of a few early Popes as well [274; 282; 306].

These examples help illustrate the problems in dealing with chains of transmission, real or imagined, in cases when the need for these arose too late to permit their reconstruction accurately. This is nearly always the case, of course, since any suggestion that such an expedient might be needed scarcely arises until wisdom long after the event requires it. If then the proverb that chains are no stronger than their weakest link is true, there are very few examples of unbroken and unchallenged chains. This is the case even in literate societies, where opportunities to maintain, or if necessary invent, chains are much greater and the chances for detecting false links far better than in oral societies, where presumption rather than demonstration must be the rule.

In many oral societies large numbers of variant traditions co-exist [e.g. 472]. In these cases the historian will compare and contrast these in his quest for common features: names, sequences, motifs. When he finds these he can provisionally assume that they are clichés or surviving elements of an earlier—perhaps even an original—version. But this must always be by inference, the result of the historian's applied judgement, and cannot be demonstrated by a series of links from the time of the event recorded until the present.

Informants as artists and advocates

The historian treats the ethnographic interview largely as an intellectual experience—the opportunity to consult informants about the past. However, this idea of the interview will be fully shared by the informant only rarely. As members of a society in which the spoken word plays a prominent social role, informants are likely to regard orality as a performing art [45; 68; 112; 245; 255; 414; 456]. In cultures that communicate largely by the written word, oral performances usually consist of assorted interpretations of an established text, with the audience playing a role confined to expressing approval or disapproval of the quality and immediacy of the interpretation. If the performers depart from the text, all know it and seldom approve because the text is regarded as inviolate.

In predominantly oral societies, on the other hand, the respective role of performers, audience, and text are quite different, for the essence of oral art is the complementary relationship between the artist and his listeners and there is rarely any desire to allow a text to constrain this relationship [33; 414]. Whether the audience is only one person—say, the historian—or whether it happens to consist of many members of the informant's group, the informant will always feel a need to treat what he is doing, among other things, as a living art. It is important, indeed essential, that the historian understands the role of his informants as performing artists and considers the effects of this when dealing with their testimony. He would be quite wrong to isolate the telling from its social setting. While still in the field he can try to take measures to reduce the impact of informants' performing sense—here is another advantage of the private interview. After the field he needs to review his success or lack of it as he judges the value of his material.

Oral performances of traditional historians and storytellers have been central throughout the ages. One can trace the function of oral performance from ancient Egypt through the Greek poets and playrights and the Welsh and Irish bards to the traditional historians of India, central Asia, and scores of other locales right down to the informants of today, wherever they may be [84; 341; 347]. When examining the nature and role of these figures we see that two important and interrelated characteristics stand out. One is that they are intimately associated with, even guided by, their audiences. As a result, there exists a sense of competition—with themselves to surpass previous performances, with other performers for the attention and approval of their listeners, and with the expectations of their audiences as they sense them during the performance. Inevitably then, performers' most valuable assets have been a sensitivity to their listeners' wants and an ability to improvise, embellish, excel, and, ultimately, please. Without these traits there would be no role for them to play.

As a member of the same society as his audience, the oral artist is usually aware of the broader cultural expectations of his listeners, who are likely to demand that each performance improve in some way on earlier ones. Any parent who has tried to coax a child to sleep by telling stories realises the futility of trying to satisfy the child time after time with mere repetition. Once the child learns to anticipate plot development he will demand some elaboration or twist and, failing this, remain adamantly awake, eventually to fall asleep through boredom or exhaustion, neither entirely flattering to the parent's efforts. Losing their listeners' interest is not the aim of most oral performers, who will learn quickly enough that fidelity to a particular text for the sake of consistency and accuracy is likely only to bore, frustrate, and antagonise an audience intent on new experiences. Embellishing a core of stock phrases, set formulas, and standard plots is forever necessary if the performer is to continue to capture and retain his audience's friendly attention.

Enhancing the narrative can take many forms: introducing gestures; altering tone, pitch, or rhythm of speech; adding imaginative twists to existing elements of a story; inventing new characters and situations that can be embellished in their turn. In introducing these modifications the performer may be motivated by a desire to surpass the artistry of other storytellers, who exist because few cultures are able or willing to confer the role of spokesman for the past on a single person. As a result, the many aspirants to the title of most respected traditional historian will constantly be improving their skills at the expense of each other and (if only incidentally) of historical accuracy.

Among those less interested in performing style will probably be the historian, who may naively believe that, whatever the creative aspects of oral performance may be in the society he is studying, in an interview context (as he defines it) interviewees will be able to ignore their role as performers in favour of being no more than informants. Unfortunately, this is likely to be very much a vain hope since it is hard to imagine just why or how such a change might take place. The performer still has an audience, albeit a diminished and slightly unfamiliar one, and the habit of embellishing and pleasing is likely to remain, even though it may assume different forms than if the informant were performing for his friends and neighbours. But even if an informant were somehow able to shed his natural and acquired instincts, how would he be able to peel away the changes of a lifetime—indeed, of many lifetimes—like the layers of an onion and expose, for the edification of the historian only, the small core of unvarnished truth that somehow managed to survive in recognisable form?

The argument that most members of oral societies are, in formal speech situations, performers by inclination and informants only by sufferance, is one likely to make the historian blanch. How, he will wonder, can he reach beyond the artistic instincts of his sources and the consequent additions of generations in order to find material in whose historical value he can have confidence? A realisation that the public recollection of the past is partly a matter of performance, while it introduces the problem, can also suggest ways to meet it, if not always to surmount it. With the aid of the careful contextual notes he has made as a part of each interview, the historian is in a position at least to establish which interviews took place in atmospheres especially likely to have fostered any instinct to perform. All group situations would clearly fall into this category. So too might those occasions when the historian sought to bring information to the surface by telling an informant about data he received from others for this is clearly a challenge to the informant's instinct for one-upsmanship. Often enough, the presence of the historian alone will be sufficient to light the spark.

If in many situations informants are also performers, in other instances they will be acting, often unashamedly, as advocates. In these cases the literary and dramatic dimensions of retelling (and perhaps reliving) the past give way to convincing through argument, exhortation, or the weight of custom. Social, economic, and political relationships in oral societies are necessarily in flux since there is no opportunity to categorise them by referring to an accessible and fixed body of law. Instead, social equilibrium is pursued by means of constant mediation among interest groups. Sometimes differences cannot be resolved by these means and they break out into open dispute. We do not know how often these have occurred in the past of course, but it does seem—to judge from the past 75 years—that much of the historical data in oral societies derives from testimony offered at one kind of dispute or another. These usually concern quarrels over rights to office, differences over grazing or fishing rights, or controversies over matters of supremacy and it does not seem unfair to speculate that these kinds of conditions also stimulated the production of historical knowledge in earlier times.

These differences are usually more than personal disagreements about the past and can often involve large numbers of people, sometimes entire communities. This suggests that, from the historian's point of view, the chances to abuse historical recollections in the interests of litigation are distressingly frequent. In these circumstances the informant who can discuss the past confidently and plausibly will come to be regarded as a valuable member of the community since by his eloquence alone he can contribute a great deal to its well-being. Just how much this is true is evident in the records of the numerous enquiries conducted by colonial authorities. From these we can see how highly regarded (and therefore rewarded) was the appearance of expertise.

Through his reading of the printed sources and particularly of the local archival materials the historian should become familiar, before he begins to interview extensively, with the occasions of disputes and the resulting patterns of the recall of the past that accompanied these. Now that he has reached the point of assessing the answers to his questions he must remind himself that the value of partisan statements—or at least of those made in partisan circumstances—often is less in explaining the past than illuminating the present. In the next chapter we discuss some of the more important ways in which the past is used to help define, delimit, and adjudicate disputes, if only for the moment. Here we only remind the historian of the need to recognise the function of informants as advocates.

After considering the points raised in this chapter the historian may feel that, if he accepts them, it would be pointless to continue—that reconstructing even a tiny bit of the past is impossible. This would be an unnecessarily self-defeating point of view since there is much to be gained if his sights are kept realistically aimed at targets he can reach. We now turn to several aspects of the content of oral tradition that most historians will find themselves dealing with. It will be difficult to separate the good from the bad with these as well, but in dealing with content rather than context it will at least be possible to profit from work already done on similar materials from oral societies elsewhere.

CHAPTER FIVE

AFTER THE FIELD: THE INTERPRETATION OF CONTENT

Discrediting a genealogy through sound knowledge and clear perception is wholly creditable if it be one's business; otherwise it is prying into a matter of no concern, and which will cause disquiet, bother, and anxiety.
[ᶜAbd al-Wadud, 1, p. 135]

Some men's eyes are still so tender as not to be able to beare the strong impressions of Light; especially in what relates to the Antiquities of their own Countrey.
[Edward Stillingfleet, 440, pp. 1–2]

After he has scrutinised his field tapes and notes with regard to contextual problems, the historian can turn at last to consider the content of whatever he has collected. Of course the concepts of content and context are often closely related, as each influences the other. Both present and past contexts have contributed to the distortions and embellishments that are discussed here. Just as the invention of *hadiths* were occasioned by religious wars in Islam, so competing collections of hadiths, once developed, stimulated further conflict and sectarian schisms. For those concerned with the very recent past the next chapter will be more relevant. The discussion that follows here is concerned with the deeper past, from the most faint recollections of a society's beginnings until about the turn of this century. Judgements about contextual issues are necessarily more idiosyncratic because one fieldworker's experiences are never quite those of another. Fortunately, for matters of content there is guidance for the historian willing to see himself as but one representative of a large-scale and wide-ranging enterprise.

Historical data have been collected, as we have seen, from among oral societies since time immemorial and during the past century very widely indeed. From the sum of this work we can learn many things about recollective patterns with various degrees of probability, sometimes nearing virtual certainty. But in reading what follows it must be understood that, while certainty may be approached on a general level, it can never really be attained simply by drawing conclusions from comparative materials, no matter how massive they may be. Scores—even hundreds—of examples can never tell the oral historian what the truth is for his own case. But of course arguing from analogy is a great improvement on mere guessing or, worse still, a feeling that worthwhile aims have to be matched by worthwhile evidence. For convenience the discussion is organised around several major themes; as a result some lesser points are necessarily neglected. Given the constraints imposed by the present work, it seemed best to take the position that if major problems are not solved, the minor ones do not really matter.

Feedback

One way that oral historiography reflects the pursuit of history in general is the way that different kinds of sources influence one another. Like their colleagues, oral historians need to know whether a particular datum is independent or whether it derives from another one, if they are to judge its worth accurately. At the same time they sometimes feel that it is easy to make this distinction, to know what is truly oral and indigenous and what may have been introduced from outside. Occasionally they are even content to assume that any information that has been passed along to them by word of mouth while in the field has been handed down in the same way in the past from one generation to the next. That is, whether or not they believe the information is true, they accept that it has always been oral.

Unhappily, this is often not true at all. A great deal of testimony obtained from informants is really feedback; that is, it originated as information that entered the society and was absorbed into traditions because it proved useful or entertaining. In many cases informants themselves fail to realise this because it happened long enough ago and in subtle enough ways that it quickly became indistinguishable from true oral tradition. People assimilate new information because of a need to find ways to accommodate new knowledge into an existing epistemology that they judge has become inadequate. Whenever societies do this they naturally operate in ways already familiar and they tend to do it in purposeful and not random ways. The reactions of Europe to the discovery of the New World shows this very clearly.

Until 1493 almost everyone in Europe who thought about it at all was content to accept the Biblical account of the creation of mankind and its distribution around the inhabited world as the compilers of the Bible knew it. Of course this version did not take into account all the unexpected plants, animals, and people that were discovered in the new-found Americas. From the resulting intellectual and theological ferment emerged a whole series of hypotheses to explain these awkward new discoveries: the Amerindians were really animals so there was no need for the Bible to mention them (and they could be enslaved); they were descended from pre-Adamites who were not explicitly mentioned in the Bible (a view regarded by many as heretical); they were mentioned in the Bible but under names no longer recognisable; they were descended from the lost tribes of Israel [114; 179; 187; 238; 246; 374; 484]. This speculation went on for centuries and infected the thought of hundreds of scholars. It illustrates particularly well the dilemma that faces any society when it is suddenly confronted with a galaxy of new and unanticipated 'truths' that it must either reject completely or try to accommodate in whole or part.

For most oral societies the written word represented a new orthodoxy that could not easily be rejected because it was accompanied by stark evidence of its efficacy, usually in the form of soldiers, missionaries, and administrators. Inevitably such societies found it necessary to incorporate or co-opt outside data into the local fund of knowledge [e.g. 242]. It was, most felt, the best way to cope with the needs resulting from the introduction of literacy [192]. One of these was the colonisers' attempt to teach many oral societies there own history.

Absorption of new materials could happen at any time and it was by no means confined to the written word, but most feedback the modern historian encounters is likely to have been introduced during the past century. Sometimes it will not be assimilated very well and it will not be hard to recognise it for what it is. Historians can detect most feedback, however, only by being aware of the circumstances that encourage it and the forms it is likely to assume and then by scrutinising both the background of informants and their testimony accordingly.

Few societies have managed to escape the attention of Christian or Muslim missionaries, so it is not surprising that the Bible and (to a lesser degree) the Qur'an are by far the most common and influential sources of outside information. Most often oral societies have borrowed materials directly, if sometimes obscurely, from the scriptures themselves or from missionary teachings based on them, but in many places data derived from the Bible been filtered through such other scriptures as the Book of Mormon [46; 123; 279].

Other feedback stems from the writings of colonial administrators, the publications of early travellers, schoolbooks, local catechisms, and neighbouring peoples. This contamination of tradition might have occurred several centuries ago in some societies or it might have entered the store of traditional lore as a result of a fieldworker's visit only a few years earlier, just as the historian is himself likely to be the source for future feedback. In what follows I draw attention to only a few examples of this phenomenon for illustration only. Then I discuss ways to identify feedback in particular instances.

Historians and anthropologists have closely studied Oceania recently and have detected and analysed numerous instances of feedback [310; 323; 489]. Missionary activity in Hawaii, among the Maori of New Zealand, and elsewhere began early in the nineteenth century, but even before this there had been much visiting between islands by travellers and traders, as well as the Pacific Islanders themselves, often on board European ships [105; 208]. Many observers commented at the time on the alacrity with which many groups accepted scriptural teaching or, for that matter, almost anything else in print. Widespread access to these materials was no problem at all; for example, as early as 1840 missionaries estimated that there was one Bible in New Zealand for every two Maoris [244; 256; 353; 356].

This enthusiasm for the printed word manifested itself quickly in the traditions of the area. Figures representing Adam, Noah, and other Biblical personages soon found their way into genealogies collected later in the century [e.g. 27]. So too did the idea of a creator god [261]. Needless to say, the ubiquitous flood story made many appearances in Oceanic traditions, as did original sin and Garden of Eden-like morality tales. The large numbers of travellers from one island to another only accelerated this propagation and assimilation of Biblical motifs [105; 155; 370; 465].

In the Americas the impact of Biblical lore generally occurred earlier and was probably at least as important, though now somewhat less discernible Some early indigenous historical productions, such as the *Popol Vuh*, which related the history of the Maya of Guatemala, contained allusions to a flood and to other things reminiscent of the Bible [80; 357; 475]. Some early writings of the Incas spoke of their belief in a creator god, again a concept borrowed or adapted from the teachings of the first missionaries [131; 132; 364; 402].

Predictably, though regrettably, many commentators who have noticed these similarities have credited diffusion rather than acculturation. For example many early Spanish chroniclers saw Aztec references to a culture hero named Quetzalcóatl as evidence of a visit by St. Thomas [18; 64; 121; 271; 287; 478]. Later advocates of diffusion, some of them writing nowadays, have used such references to argue that Carthaginians, Irish, Phoenicians, or Africans had long ago discovered the New World. Actually, once we trace the origins of these stories, it is clear enough that they usually resulted from the processes by which the Spanish or hispanised Indians gathered information about the native American past. For the moment we know most about how this worked in Mexico, where Spanish cleric-chroniclers collected data by using catechists and converts who were proficient in Náhuatl and Spanish and who brought together informants and questioned them in ways little different from those of today. Then they helped such chroniclers as Bernardino de Sahagún and Toribio de Motolinía organise the data into forms acceptable to Spanish historical concepts [30; 79; 81; 100; 120; 134; 350; 397].

Fired with the zeal of the newly-converted, these interpreters—for that was essentially their role—often took care either to conceal pre-conquest practices they thought would be repugnant to the Spanish or explained them away in terms of Spanish expectations. As part of this they sometimes felt obliged to explain their own past on the basis of the theological models the missionaries offered [60; 131]. Inevitably these would highlight Biblical motifs and paradigms. Seen in this light, similarities between Mesoamerican and Inca traditional history and mythology on the one hand and the Bible on the other resulted largely from the collecting and acculturative processes that occurred within the first few generations of the conquest [281]. Even Indian historians like Guaman Poma de Ayala, who wrote from an indigenised and largely anti-Spanish perspective, were heavily influenced by Christian world views. Poma de Ayala was careful to orient Inca chronology to the Christian calendar, thought that the Andean Indians descended from Noah, and believed in an early conversion by one of the apostles [5; 17; 354].

We see a set of similar circumstances in North America. The legend of Dekanawidah, the mythical founder of the Iroquois, has numerous parallels with Biblical teachings. Evidence suggests that some of these motifs, though not the character of Dekanawidah himself, sprang from the teaching of French missionaries who worked among the Iroquois in the seventeenth century [54; 127; 150; 151; 337]. In western Canada we find even more explicit motifs in Indian traditions that are based on oral teaching of the early nineteenth century [381].

For Africa the problem is much the same. That is, Biblical and other scriptural themes appear and re-appear in many oral traditions that have been collected throughout the continent. Considering the intensity of missionary activity there, the incidence is probably far greater than we get know. Nor was this activity only a latter-day phenomenon. As early as the middle of the sixteenth century many missionaries worked in lower Zaire, the Zambezi valley, Guiné-Bissau, and elsewhere. The passage of four centuries makes it hard to identify assimilated materials but examples of Christian beliefs, albeit much distorted, have been noticed in the creation theories of groups like the Bakongo [308; 309].

Traditions that have been influenced by Qur'anic teachings and other Islamic literature are also common in north-eastern and north-western Africa. As early as the 1870s the ruler of Buganda told European travellers that his ancestors included a certain Ham (a Biblical figure prominent in Muslim folklore) and perhaps other Islamised names as well [224]. The well-known Dogon beliefs about Sirius have perplexed observers for several decades, inducing at least one to extend the search into outer space [446]. If these beliefs are really indigenous, they are indeed unaccountable, but before accepting a local origin scholars must look elsewhere. Davis has pointed out similarities between Dogon notions and some aspects of Islamic astronomical lore [115]. The study of the skies has always been important to Muslims and the Dogon area has long been subject to Islamic influences. It is not likely that we shall ever know the origins of Dogon concepts of Sirius but it is reasonable to think that modified images of Muslim astronomical beliefs worked their way to the Dogon, who incorporated some of them into their own theories. It is also quite possible—again, we may never know—that French missionaries in the area mentioned the newly-discovered properties of Sirius' companion in the 1920s and that these reinforced the ideas already picked up from the Muslims [61]. Speculation along any of these lines must remain tentative but a hypothesis based on the view that the Dogon absorbed, perhaps more than once, outside (but decidedly terrestrial) notions about Sirius is much more plausible than any that suggests that the Dogon somehow acquired knowledge of this star's peculiar qualities on their own.

As the Dogon example suggests, many other sources than the Bible have been tapped for information that subsequently worked its way into oral tradition. Prominent among these were the writings (and presumably the verbal arguments) of colonial officials, many of whom were intensely interested in the theories of diffusion and cultural evolution that purported to explain racial and cultural characteristics. In Nigeria for instance, H. R. Palmer and others assiduously propagated the idea that the political systems of certain 'advanced' people originated in the Near East. Several of these ideas (probably more than we know) have since taken root in the origin traditions of the area [233].

The Fante of southern Ghana were among the earliest and most eager acculturators in Africa and Fante historians customarily manifested this by using such European points of reference as the building of local trading forts or local European trade wars to anchor their own traditions [229]. The records of the enquiries into the almost incessant disputes over succession, territory, and supremacy during the colonial period permit us to trace fairly systematically the origins and often meandering paths of these traditions. Whatever the particular circumstances, the Fante habitually scoured newly-available printed sources hoping to find information that would preserve or enhance their positions in the complicated and delicate stool hierarchy that the British authorities devised and tried to administer [219; 229; 231].

The sheer number of Fante stools and the many inquests into their history makes their example an extreme one, though instructive. The tendency to absorb secular materials into local oral literature is evident, however, in many other places as well. We have already mentioned Inca Garcilaso de la Vega's efforts to hispanise his version of Inca history and there are numerous examples from Polynesia. With respect to these, it is enough to point out that the wildly grandiose and utterly wrong speculation of Abraham Fornander, Percy Smith, and a host of others about Polynesian origins and migrations still surface from time to time as parts of supposedly pristine local tradition [243; 424].

The educational experiences of members of oral societies, particularly those who serve as informants, also influence feedback. Among the Shona and the Kongo we find references to events and figures that could not possibly have come to the notice of either group except from some outside source, in this case colonial schoolbooks that emphasise European history to the near exclusion of local events. Of course recourse to outside materials has not been confined to the realm of history. In Tonga, to cite just one example, local variations of the Cinderella tale and the story of Dick Whittington's cat have been collected—folklores culturally specific enough to make it certain that they are not coincidental repetitions of life experiences that often characterise the folktale idiom [183; 466].

It would seem that one need only look for evidence of feedback in order to find it. Though perhaps uncongenial, this prospect should scarcely be unexpected. Uncontaminated oral tradition simply does not exist any more, except possibly in the most remote areas of Amazonia, the Philippines, or New Guinea. The historian must be willing to give very high research priority to examining his data with an eye to learning which have been affected by outside sources. Fortunately, there are several ways he can go about this. As mentioned, while still in the field he should collect as much information as he can about his informants' education, travels, occupational contacts, partisan roles in past disputes, and the like [e.g. 498]. In this way he can begin to differentiate, if sometimes only roughly, those informants who may have acquired extraneous knowledge from those less likely to have done so.

The historian may be in danger of believing that he alone has been able to unlock the past of the group he is investigating. To prevent this notion and to detect outside influences, he should trace back as far as he can any previous incarnations of particular traditions—a procedure we would expect any historian to subject his data to. His most useful sources for this are likely to be local government and missionary archives, though the observations of earlier travellers and residents can sometimes be useful.

Broadly speaking, there can be three possible outcomes to such an investigation. The historian can find no earlier record of the tradition, which is bound to perplex him a bit unless he prefers to believe that it lay dormant until he came along and awakened it. Or he may find that all accounts from the very first to be recorded mention a particular set of circumstances, so that he may provisionally feel confident that the tradition is largely, maybe even entirely indigenous. Finally, he may discover that at some time an old tradition changed or a new one appeared that was propagated and accepted locally. Of course this last possibility will interest the historian most because it exemplifies the problem of dealing with the dynamics of tradition. We can briefly discuss two examples of this phenomenon to indicate its purposes and effects.

During the nineteenth century Fiji was heavily visited and proselytised. Many visitors and missionaries asked about the origins of the Fijians, in line with the quest of Melanesian and Polynesian origins already mentioned and about a dozen published accounts reported that the Fijians had no traditions about their origins at all. Then in 1892 there appeared a sketchy account—later to be much elaborated—of a migration from the west at a specified time back in genealogical time. Basil Thomson, the author of the work in which this new tradition appeared, was a magistrate in Fiji as well as an advocate of the schemes of Fornander and Smith and, from all accounts he took no pains to conceal his views from the Fijians. In a short time both Europeans and Fijians began to embellish and then to codify this migration story. Times were ripe for this new version of Fijian origins and the story of Kaunitoni's settlement fits in well with the more outlandish ethnography of the time, which tried on philological grounds to argue that the Fijians derived utlimately from ancient Egypt. After about 1900 the Kaunitoni legend became the orthodox version. It appeared in general histories of the island, in schoolboy writing contests, in the press and on the radio, and in anthropological accounts of Fijian culture [165; 178; 454]. It is now virtually impossible to collect accounts of Fijian origins that do *not* attribute the settlement of the island to Kaunitoni [e.g. 182].

The central figure in current traditions about the early history of Elmina paramount stool in southern Ghana is one Kwamina Ansa. These traditions claim that Kwamina Ansa was ruling when the Portuguese arrived in 1482. But Kwamina Ansa never appeared in the many traditional accounts of Elmina history collected before 1915, even though he has never failed to appear since. This may at first seem puzzling, but the conditions accompanying his appearance provide a ready explanation. Shortly before 1915 several published accounts of the Portuguese expedition of 1482 appeared in the Gold Coast. Basing themselves on Portuguese chronicles these mentioned a certain 'Caramansa' who had met the Portuguese and from whom they rented land to build a fort. These sources imply that Caramansa was not the ruler of Elmina itself (then a tiny village) but the fact that the Portuguese encountered him there was enough for some European historians—quickly emulated by Elmina traditionists—to claim for him, under the name of Kwamina Ansa, a place in the local past. In the years that followed, which were characterised by several animated stool disputes, Kwamina Ansa was repeatedly put to such effective use that today his position in traditional (though scarcely oral) historiography is sacrosanct. He has become indispensable [227].

Although Kaunitoni and Kwamina Ansa, and of course many others, have been unmasked as imposters, many like them still repose undetected in the traditions of oral societies. If these figures have an outstanding common characteristic, it is their usefulness and this undoubtedly handicaps efforts to eliminate them. But, whatever the other difficulties, special care must be taken in exorcising them because so often this depends on risky arguments from silence that can never be conclusive and that can easily be misused if all the relevant literature is not ransacked thoroughly enough. The absence of certain figures and events in the accounts of early passers-by is by no means sufficient cause to consider their appearance later to be fraudulent. Even the most well-grounded arguments from silence exist precariously, since only a single substantiated early reference can undermine the best-prepared case. If, for example, an authentic reference to Kwamina Ansa should turn up in an Elmina tradition recorded by the Dutch sometime in the nineteenth century, then any arguments that he was invented as a result of his appearance in European books fall to the ground. But if the historian is thorough in canvassing the available sources and even in turning up a few new ones, and if he believes that some of these sources would certainly have mentioned certain things in the *natural* course of their writing, then he is obliged to question any later traditions on the grounds that they were introduced from the outside and adapted locally because they were seen as potentially useful. It is noteworthy in this regard that both Kaunitoni and Kwamina Ansa have been adopted by their respective communities completely and not simply by partisan elements within them.

Clearly it will not always be easy to identify feedback and it will be even harder to know to what uses to put such discoveries. Although the quest for historical accuracy ('what really happened') is still important for any historian, we have already seen and will see again that inaccurate recollections of the past can be more interesting than simple facts in that they help to penetrate the collective mentality of a society. This is nowhere more true than in the matter of feedback. In this sense seeking, finding, and segregating borrowed elements of tradition is very much legitimate work for historians.

Culture heroes and other minor metaphors

Every society, whether oral or literate, has a stock of set expressions that serve to interpret circumstances that are frequently encountered. These expressions are sometimes rooted in the past [53; 198]. By virtue of repeated use they become increasingly streamlined until they lose all literal meaning, serving instead as a kind of shorthand to describe in as few words as possible what once may have taken thousands. As a result of this compression, even members of the society that use them no longer understand exactly what they mean and naturally they have no meaning—except a literal one—to outsiders. As a result informants may not be aware of the essentially metaphorical nature of clichés, which may be embedded in testimonies in forms that are quite indistinguishable from material that can be taken as historically factual. Clearly the historian needs to be careful in trying to make distinctions that even his informants cannot make. Fortunately, most clichés concern the purely personal level—routine daily chores, and the like—and so are of more interest to folklorists and sociologists than to historians. Expressions of wider importance are usually culturally specific and can be decoded only through close study of local epistomology.

Two examples of clichés that relate to the past can show how even the most common expressions can allude to events that might interest the historian. We have all heard the expression 'all roads lead to Rome'—a bit ambiguous these days when roads seem to lead everywhere and Rome is just another large European city. But of course Rome was for a long time more than that, first as an imperial capital and then as the seat of the Papacy. In the

Middle Ages, especially, all important ecclesiastical disputes in any part of western Europe were subject to the judgement of the Papal Curia and the Popes were often strong enough to enforce their decisions on reluctant secular rulers and local church dignitaries. Ultimately, then, for a time all roads *did* lead to Rome.

Another familiar expression is 'leaving no stone unturned'—good advice in fact for historians and their sources. Although it now has no applicable literal meaning, the expression refers to an actual event in the Greek-Persian wars. Herodotus tells us that a Persian treasure was unearthed because the Delphic oracle told the Greeks to leave no stone unturned in their search for it and, so the story goes, it was found under the unearthed stones [164]. These clichés and others are used constantly with no thought to their derivation, which of course is now usually impossible to ascertain since the sayings have been popularised for so long.

A few motifs are so widespread that they are likely to be encountered by most oral historians. Aside from the matter of origins discussed below, perhaps the most important of these is that of the Culture Hero, a term used to describe an individual who may or may not have existed but whose role tradition has so magnified that he personifies great cultural processes and long periods of time. Recollections of a 'great personage' who was thought to be responsible for introducing new political, social, or economic skills to a previously ignorant people is a popular figure in oral literature [289]. It is probably safe to argue, for example, that if the United States and Great Britain had been completely oral societies, such figures as George Washington, Henry VIII, or Queen Victoria would be remembered even more deeply in the popular mind because people would credit them with the accomplishments of their more obscure predecessors and successors as well as their own, since doing this would seem entirely appropriate and would help in remembering these events through association.

The recollected history of nearly every oral society seems to include at least one Culture Hero and sometimes more: the 'five good emperors' of archaic China; Jimmu Tenno in Japan; Manco Capac and Pachacuti among the Inca; Dekanawidah and Hiawatha among the Iroquois; King Arthur in early medieval Britain; Romulus and Remus in Rome; Krishna and Rama in Vedic India; Kisra and Sunjata in West Africa; Kintu and Kimera in East Africa; Alexander the Great throughout much of the medieval and Islamic world [12; 55; 56; 89]. The litany is endless. Drawn from a variety of cultures scattered throughout the world, these are examples of the ways in which traditions form around an archetypal figure who is used to explain an early cultural stage or, perhaps more often, to serve as slightly larger-than-life precedents for the state of things as they now exist. There is little evidence other than the traditions themselves that most Culture Heroes ever existed, either in the periods attributed to them or at any other time. They occupy mental but not historical space and, if the historian wishes to put them to work at all, it can only be as obscure images of a long-forgotten reality that may suggest to him some sequences of actual events or cultural influences but that are more closely related to the collective mentality of the people who invented or transformed them.

Used with caution and sensitivity then, Culture Heroes can play a role in oral historiography. If a tradition says that Culture Hero X came from direction Y and introduced iron working, religion, or advanced fishing techniques, then the historian could feel justified in seeking connections of some kind in direction Y since it is possible that the Culture Hero embodies a series of events, some of which were actually connected somehow with direction Y. This search will often show that the Culture Hero's origins were concocted later when there were reasons to associate him with a group in direction Y. Or the historian may discover that certain directions (including up and down) have symbolic attributes and are yet another kind of cliché—one that attributes all things deemed to be good to that direction thought to be auspicious, and vice-versa.

Other kinds of metaphors are likely to interest the historian. One candidate that has received some attention of late, though not as metaphor, is the matter of famine and drought. Ideas of cause and effect in any society are very different. They will range from the precise, though not necessarily correct, knowledge of a small group of acknowledged experts all the way to the beliefs of those who see a supernatural or extraterrestrial explanation for every circumstance whose causes are not immediate or obvious. It is possible that some ideas about ultimate causes will get such a grip on a society that its members automatically attribute all good things to one set of circumstances and all bad things to another. The Israelites believed that their Egyptian captivity, the crossing of the Red Sea, their enforced wanderings in the desert, miscellaneous falling city walls, the frequent invasions of their enemies, and the several destructions of Jerusalem were due either to God's wrath or his goodness and seldom looked for other causes. In effect these events became metaphors expressing Israel's travails and triumphs.

As familiar as they were with the heavens, Chinese and Babylonian astronomers tended to see the movements and other activities of heavenly bodies as prophesies of political changes or natural cataclysms. And the Chinese historians developed a model metaphor to explain dynastic change: the rise, apogee, decline, and fall of each dynasty was viewed as a remorseless cycle that depended on the personal ethical behaviour of various emperors. To the outsider this explanation confuses cause and effect but to the Chinese the matter was comfortably unambiguous.

It is not unlikely (but it probably can seldom be proved) that many societies that depend for their well-being entirely on the timing and intensity of the rains have come to use metaphors of famine or drought—first as occasional reasons, then as explanations for recurring events, and finally as interpretations not only of hunger but also of political discord, wars, enforced population movements, and other misfortunes. Whenever this is true, recalling a famine is simply an integral part of recalling any calamity. In other words, if one or more unhappy event is recalled, then a famine to account for them and hunger as a part of them are also remembered, not necessarily because these also occurred but because they have come to be regarded as the second side of the coin, the shadow to the substance.

Drought, famine, hunger, and misfortune become inseparable, no longer with some being occasional causes and others occasional effects, but as inherent parts of a standard set of circumstances. Authenticated cases of famine can be important for historians. They help in the understanding of the economic system of a group and in appreciating its adaptive capability. They may also help to date a few events in the past if they can be correlated with outside records. Their potential value means that the temptation will be strong to put what may only be metaphor to work as historical fact and to attribute remembered famines to particular times in the past. Often, of course, famines as metaphor will be indistinguishable from famines as historical occurrences since they are so much a fact of life in many oral societies [103]. In dealing with this dilemma the historian must first explore as far as he can any possible associative thought patterns and test, if he is able, the memory of recent famines against the historical record regarding them. Without at least some evidence from contemporary sources, accepting famine traditions is likely to be of no value.

Groups who regard themselves as distinct may still recognise in their neighbours so many familiar customs and characteristics—language, art forms, kinship systems, diet, titles—that they inevitably wonder how they came to be distinct from one another. Such speculation often leads to stories designed to explain both the differences and the similarites by means of some specific incident. Often there is a quarrel involved—between father and son, uncle and nephew, or siblings. What is interesting is that the reasons traditions usually cite for these quarrels are so implausibly trivial. Such things as arguments over slight social blunders, the ownership of an item not worth owning, or the sharing of goods not worth sharing are advanced to explain the most far-reaching events. Perhaps the Biblical stories of the banishment of Ham and his son Canaan and the quarrel between Jacob and Esau are the most familiar examples of this kind of story, but the theme of the petty quarrel to explain the presumed separation of peoples ranges worldwide. When the historian encounters it in his own work he should not see it as necessarily reinforcing the evidence of linguistics, or physical anthropology, or the same tale told by a neighbouring group. Instead he should regard it as a possible example of a society seeking to recover and explain its past in terms of everyday familiarity.

The major metaphors

No question has so vexed historians over the centuries as that of origins [43; 118]. The debate has ranged from the issue of the beginnings of the human race through those of individual peoples and states down to those of ruling groups and individuals. There have been times in fact when learned speculation about beginnings has dominated historical thought to the point of monopolising it. We have all measured ourselves, it seems, by our supposed origins, no matter how remote. The search has never been confined to the writing of history but has spilled over into philosophy and theology as well [13; 316]. There is no need to try to take account here of the arguments of philosophers, theologians, and scientists over origins, although it is not always easy to disentangle them for the approaches of historians. It should be pointed out, though, that understanding why a study of oral historioigraphy needs to dwell so long on the matter requires that we carry the discussion beyond the narrow confines of historical thought.

Attempts to locate origins in time and space through the medium of oral tradition have been central to the work of both informants and historians. One trait nearly universal in tradition has been its interest—maybe fixation—with the earliest times. This interest has often been paralleled, if not surpassed, by historians who have thought it possible and desirable to pinpoint the beginnings of states, cultural complexes, and linguistic families, no matter if trying to do so is both undesirably mechanistic and hopelessly unrealistic. We must study these facets of tradition and of its historians within a larger context.

Two features stand out sharply in nearly all theories of origins (and there have been thousands of them) that have been put forward at every opportunity. These theories have a genealogical character and they incorporate some kind of migration. All peoples originated but few seem to have originated where they actually were when speculation on their origins took place [e.g. 43]. The examples used here are intended to indicate the nature of the problem rather than provide specific answers to particular sets of circumstances. For two reasons these will not be drawn entirely from oral societies. In the first place written sources often provide the tools for their own analysis. Moreover, there seem to be few important differences between the styles of origin theories among oral, marginally oral, and wholly literate societies, except that there is a move towards increasing complexity in the direction of literate societies.

In detailing theories of origins we encounter the Bible once again, for its version of creation is the most widespread and influential and an important model for others. Besides its account of the creation of man and matter, Genesis devotes considerable attention to the peopling of the world as its compilers knew it. This peopling is presented in a genealogical framework, beginning with Noah and his sons, who spawned the undifferentiated 'races'. Beyond this the compilers provided eponymous ancestors for each of the ethnic groups that fell within their range, as well as the 12 tribes of Israel and similar smaller groups.

Later on, Greek and Roman mythology was to prove a fertile source for explaining the origins of various peoples [43]. In addition to having an elaborate pantheon to explain existence before man, the Greeks found a mythical or heroic ancestor for each of their own sub-groups and cities, and of course for all the non-Greeks they happened to encounter. Relying on Greek precedent, the Romans developed a system of their own. Rome itself was held to have been founded by a descendant of the most prominent survivor of the Trojan war. Moreover, most of the tribal groups with which the Romans came increasingly into contact were allocated ancestors appropriate to their relationship with the empire: important ancestors for important allies; wicked ancestors for important enemies; and obscure ancestors for unimportant allies [43; 59]. And of course these affiliations changed as friends became enemies, unimportant groups suddenly became important, and so forth. In effect genealogy was wielded as an instrument of foreign policy.

With the triumph of Christianity the Biblical version of global demography came back into fashion, though it had become inextricably entwined with the various Greco-Roman models. But the standard operating procedure remained the same: leave no distinct group of people without a specific ancestor. Various sons and descendants of Noah (not all mentioned in the Bible, but no matter) were brought into service as more and more peoples were added to Europe's growing consciousness of the wider world. The hard-pressed descendants of Noah were supplemented by previously unknown offspring of Troy, Phoenicia, Egypt, and Greece to meet the demands of this exercise of providing names for the nameless [101; 135; 189; 217; 266; 403]. So successfully was this accomplished that eventually there were more ancestors than peoples who needed them. Rather than waste these, rival theories began to grow up, providing much sport for imaginative medieval and early modern chroniclers.

Away from western Europe the game was played much the same. Genealogies traced many of the important families of Caucasia to legendary Persian rulers, David of Israel, even Chinese emperors [206; 235; 458]. The Khazars of western Russia were held to be descended from the handy lost tribes of Israel, as were several other groups whose religious practices were thought to have debased Mosaic overtones [284]. In the Islamic world Noah's sons were well known, for the Muslim version of origins had an overlapping set of players with that of Europe [423]. In India the Puranas and other supposedly historical works divided the area's ruling lines into two groups, the solar race and the lunar race, and then traced them back to the fourth millennium, a point of view still widely accepted in India [20; 86; 288]. In Malaysia, Persia, Armenia, and several other places Alexander the Great was regarded as the progenitor of numerous ruling houses [55; 56; 89; 385].

We have already seen how this genealogical structure came tumbling down in Europe with the discovery of the New World. Within a single lifetime new peoples were discovered in numbers and in places that finally stretched the previously elastic bounds of genealogical imagination too far. More than anything else this destroyed European ideas that origins could be discovered and explained solely by means of genealogies and with the rise of modern evolutionary theory this genealogical mania was relegated to little more than an embarrassing memory and dread example. For the rest of the world, though, this realisation was slower to come. Here the Bible alone did not serve as an inexhaustible source of ancestors, but ancient Egypt and the Near East, notable Indian dynasties, and figures from pre-Islamic Arabian legend were effective substitutes.

Until recently many Africanists argued that the more advanced African states were somehow related, perhaps genetically, to ancient Near Eastern states. If the more extravagant schemes sometimes cited are now largely disowned, pale imitations survive and sometimes flourish. Historians have seen the Bacwezi of eastern Africa as kind of latter-day Trojans, producing the ancestors or founders of several ruling lines in the area. The Almoravids and other early north African groups are also sometimes credited with producing later lines of rulers in northern and western Africa. In Ghana many stools trace their origins to Bono, an important state in the seventeenth and eighteenth centuries and of residual prestige ever since. Early rulers of Ife and Benin, whose existence many historians do not accept, are nevertheless widely considered to have been ancestors of numerous royal families in western Nigeria.

In India most of the more than 200 princely states under British rule traced their ancestry of one or another prominent medieval dynasty, particularly to the Rajputs [20; 448]. In Polynesia the ruling lines on several islands traced their beginnings back to Tonga or even farther to a place called

Hawaiki, while in early medieval Ireland enough sons of the legendary Míl, who was thought to have come from Spain, were invented to account for all the groups in Ireland then regarded as separate [76; 273; 352]. Several groups of racial isolates living in mountainous areas of the eastern United States now claim descent from Carthaginians, Roanoke colonists, or West African groups. In most cases historians and anthropologists implanted these ideas in the nineteenth century but they have since gained local belief in the telling and retelling [221].

The fact that historians have ordinarily traced peoples to a fairly limited pool of ancestors has meant that migrations have been an indispensable feature of most interpretations of the uncharted past. How else could descendants of Noah, firmly located in the Near East by those who accepted his existence, have turned up all around the world, even as far as China [373; 468]? For other reasons, too, migrations have always been a popular explanation for the state of things at any particular time. The ancient Jews wrote of a great migration from Egypt, short in distance maybe, but accompanied by suitably miraculous events [303]. The Greeks claimed that their ancestors had arrived at particular times and in well-defined groups, many of them under the descendants of Hercules [34; 85; 200; 449]. Ancient historians, and some modern ones, believed that the Etruscans migrated from Asia Minor to Italy and the Carthaginians from Phoenicia to North Africa, in both cases in a body [82].

Until recently European historians saw the settlement of the Visigoths, Ostrogoths, Vandals, and other groups as an abrupt culmination of only a few centuries of spectacular mass migrations, a view reinforced by the occasional incursions of the Huns, Alans, and others, who seemed to come suddenly from deep in central Asia, only to recede as quickly as they came, presumably to trek still elsewhere [72]. This view, so influential in the historiography of western Europe, encouraged desperate chroniclers to conjure up their own local versions of the peopling of their countries. Migrations from Italy (Geoffrey of Monmouth) or Spain (the Irish annalists) or Asia Minor (the Hapsburg historians) were the historiographical order of the day [124; 135; 480]. To read their stories is to be told that there had never been any original inhabitants in western Europe at all.

In the Americas the Aztecs seemed to remember—or so they told the Spanish chroniclers—a long migration from an area they called Aztlan, which some thought was in the south-western United States [113; 319]. Likewise the first Incas were thought to have come from the area around Lake Titicaca. But, for the New World, honours must go to the testimony of the pictorial history of the Delaware Indians called the *Walam Olum*, which claimed to trace a migration reaching all the way from Siberia to the eastern coast of the United States [481]. According to this record, the trek lasted for over 90 reigns, yet the migrants arrived virtually intact and retained their collective memory until the very end.

Most of the Hinduised states of peninsular and insular south-east Asia boasted that the ancestors of their ruling lines originated in India, migrating to establish states where, this argument ran, none had existed before [e.g. 97]. In India itself conventional wisdom regards the peopling of northern India as occurring when large groups of 'Aryans' migrated from central Asia in the third and second millennia B.C., fought great battles with the indigenous peoples, and drove them to the south of the peninsula—a view that seemed to reinforce the testimony of the Puranas and similar works [69]. In Africa most historians of the earliest periods covered by traditions accepted the idea that the Bantu-speaking areas of the continent were largely populated during a series of large-scale migrations. In placing arrows on their maps, they often built on the evidence of oral tradition, supplemented in many cases by linguistic and archeological interpretations.

Even so, probably the most impressive example of extreme migration theory is to be found in the works of early historians of the Pacific. The fact that most of the islands share many elements of a common culture and language necessarily implies that population movements by sea did occur, perhaps even frequently. Beginning in the 1860s some of those interested in Pacific history began to develop quite elaborate schemes that required—or simply took for granted—frequent migrations, both long and short [243]. Generally they assumed that these were purposeful colonising missions. The most influential proponent of this view, Percy Smith of New Zealand, believed that he could trace the movements of the first Polynesians all the way back to India and even to Mesopotamia. While few of his contemporaries were willing to follow Smith quite so far, all seemed willing to believe, and to attempt to demonstrate, that innumerable colonising expeditions had characterised the last millennium. At the time, these views seemed to be firmly supported by the information in numerous traditional accounts and extended genealogies that the Europeans were then collecting with the greatest enthusiasm [232; 353; 424; 425; 430].

The explanatory power of migrations accorded well—almost too well, it might seem to sceptical minds—with the diffusionist and evolutionary speculation of the times. Most scholars did not consider independent local development of cultural traits to be as likely as the introduction of traits from a few selected spots. The belief that most of the world was populated by 'primitive' groups precluded any approach that seemed to grant these people any capacity beyond the wit to accept good ideas already developed by more civilised races.

In recent years, however, migration theories have been in retreat, if not actual flight [63]. In most cases it has been realised that posing historical questions in terms of mass population movements was part of an intellectual tradition that sought to explain cause and effect by discrete, discernible events, denying the complex interplay among processes that are quite impossible any longer to give shape to. At one level the movement of people (that is, mobility rather than migration) is so common that it could be used to explain anything, and thereby nothing. In any case, historians find migrations by themselves to be less important, even when they can be shown to have occurred, than their antecedents and aftermath.

Beyond this, more serious study of the sources and presuppositions underlying old views, second thoughts on the effects of transculturation, and work being done on an increasing body of archeological and linguistic data have demonstrated that population movements are usually so subtle as to be detectable only by hindsight [e.g. 6; 10]. The classic model—wave after wave of barbarian hordes pounding down the gates of Rome—has been superseded by a view of several centuries of largely peaceful infiltration, of constant flux and reflux occasionally highlighted by pitched battles and momentarily discernible movements of people, but overall an inexorably slow and steady process [72].

More thoughtful and less engaged use of archaeological and literary evidence for the Israelite 'conquest' of Palestine has also begun to show that the long-accepted version of the Book of Exodus is an unsatisfactory explanation of a longer and more complex series of events. Excavation at sites that figure prominently in the account in Exodus, most notably Jericho, show that they did not even exist when the conquest was alleged to have taken place [166; 327]. Moreover, study of the term 'Hebrew' in the records of the time suggests that it was applied much more indeterminately than later and that those who eventually became the Israelites were only one group among many who lived in the area practising transhumance, becoming more sedentary, and eventually settling in the area where they are historically noted [78; 194; 254; 258; 322]. Later the Israelites developed an account of their beginnings that seemed to them to link up more closely with their belief that they alone were God's chosen people, and this account included appropriate migration and conquest themes.

Students of Delaware culture and history now believe that the *Walam Olum* was a by-product of a revival movement among the Delawares, who were trying to retain their self-identity in nearly impossible circumstances [248; 344; 482 488]. Years of missionary activity are not only likely to have acquainted the Delawares with the prevailing view that the Indians had reached the New World via the Bering Strait, but certainly must also have impressed on them the heroic dimensions of migration, especially one across a body of water as shown by the Israelites' flight from Egypt.

In Oceanic studies a debate has raged for more than 20 years over the capacity of traditional shipbuilding and navigational techniques to overcome the great distances and treacherous currents of the Pacific by plotting courses from one group of islands to another [155; 422]. This debate remains unresolved, but numerous studies have thoroughly discredited the actual historical details offered by the proponents of inter-island colonisation. In fact their arguments were never more than loosely based on the various traditions collected throughout the area, and particularly in New Zealand [424]. Once in hand, these were subjected to shameless editing and manipulation by those who wanted to use their evidence to reinforce the claims of the comparative philologists of the time. To do this they set about tidying up by adding, substracting, or transferring genealogical details with blithe disregard for scholarly standards. In addition to recent findings of textual criticism of these sources, extensive archaeological work demonstrates that supposed dates and directions of these movements are often hopelessly impossible [e.g. 102].

For Africa of course, relatively little archaeological evidence is yet available. Although archaeologists have made a good start, they have not yet been able to compensate for the immensity of the continent and the ravages of climate. Such evidence as there is begins to tell a story similar to recent innovations for Europe, Palestine, and Oceania. In place of the long-distance and large-scale *Völkerwanderungen*, a different picture emerges. The 'Bantu migrations' are in process of becoming 'Bantu expansion', even in gross outline a complicated series of slow movements by small groups, who took many different paths, often retraced their steps, and nowhere left much evidence that what they were doing was in the nature of a conquest [160; 161; 470]. Linguistic evidence from the Bantu-speaking areas largely supports these archaeological conclusions when both can be applied to a particular situation. At present the weight of such evidence (always subject to change as new data come to hand) is that many events to which traditions give a relatively recent date and a short time span actually may have occurred longer ago and taken centuries to happen [415; 416]. In other words, the African experience in this respect seems not to have been very different from that of areas for which we have more abundant data.

While it may be difficult to explain satisfactorily, it is clear enough that the notion of coming from somewhere else, whether it is somewhere best suited to the preconceptions of outsiders or to members of the society, is one that is uncannily attractive [e.g. 447]. It seems that there is little glamour in autochthony, perhaps because it often seems desirable to distinguish the ruling classes from the rest of the population. After all, how many Americans would prefer to believe that they are descended from Indians rather than from passengers on the *Mayflower*? And how many Britons have tried to show that their ancestors crossed the Channel with William in 1066?

Or maybe it is just that being in one place for as long as the collective memory reaches back seems too unenterprising because it fails to provide elements for a good story with a dramatic beginning. In any case, longstanding autochthony and undistinguishable infiltration is the clear verdict of the presently available literary, archaeological, and linguistic evidence from most areas. Moreover, the more such evidence accumulates, the more certain this verdict seems to be.

Dating

No history without chronology, runs one dictum of historians. No one is likely to dispute that dates are the historian's staple fare, but the historian who deals with oral societies must learn to accept that he will probably be on a strict lifelong diet. More than any other aspect of the past, measuring it is very much a by-product of being able to write things down. It is rare in any society that anyone but historians are much interested in knowing such things as: exactly how long ago a war, earthquake, or other event occurred and how long it lasted; how much time intervened between two particular events; which of two or more events preceded the other(s); or how old somebody was when he did something. A degree of precision is obviously useful to anyone who wants to establish cause and effect relationships but of doubtful value to others. In societies that possess some form of writing, it is no trouble to jot down dates of various events, even if there seems to be no compelling reason for them at the time. In contrast, in an oral society a great deal of people's time and intellectual skills must be devoted—over and over again—to maintaining a record of this kind.

Although no one has ever advanced good reasons why any society should want to keep chronological records, a surprising amount of recent work on the earlier past of oral societies takes it for granted that they can and do manage this very thing, even if only in terms of generations. Historians seem to have been little astonished to find that informants can offer them, with a little coaching perhaps, raw data relating to reign lengths or generation placement that the historian can later use to arrive at his own dating system. In extreme cases this yearning for chronological preciseness has actually led some to assign nearly exact dates of more than one thousand years ago to events that themselves are unlikely ever to have happened. These instances should be regarded, of course, as acts of faith not binding on other historians.

The approach offered here is quite different. The desire to give time to the timeless by calculating dates for events that are undatable has always been a favourite activity of historians, beginning with the compilers of the Sumerian King List at the end of the third millennium B.C. Much of this activity—all too much of it—has tended to be undone as the weight of evidence told against these efforts to make too much of too little. By now the data drawn from hundreds of studies, combined with the realisation that it is unlikely that members of oral societies would care to remember incidental details about reign lengths and exact genealogical placement accurately for perhaps hundreds of years, tells us unequivocally that exact dates have often been will o' the wisps [222]. Here we discuss the three major sources of chronological detail in non-calendar keeping societies: genealogies, datable astronomical phenomena, and archaeological dating.

Genealogies
The uses to which countless genealogies have been put, in efforts to give dates to names, is the most eloquent testimony of the mania for chronology among students of oral societies. No form of historical document has suffered more from the ravages of self-interest than the genealogy. This has been true whether they have been long or short, royal or private, or from literate or oral societies. And yet no historian can fail to use them if they are among the sources available to him. In these times, when ancestor-hunting enjoys a popularity greater than ever before, it is probably easier to appreciate the considerations that go into the making of pedigrees and to realise how often they serve, not so much as tools for plumbing the past, but as weapons for preserving or subverting the present. More than any other form of credential, genealogies can provide instant legitimacy, self-esteem, and enhanced status [e.g. 51; 128; 332]. It is not very surprising then that they are an extremely ancient and persistent form of explanation. The earliest known genealogies traced ancestry back to gods and many pedigrees collected in the field nowadays still reach back to equally unlikely figures.

Genealogies can be lists of rulers or no more than a line of direct ancestors going back to some desired point of origin, and historians can use either variety in attempting to infer dates for individuals named in them. When a new field of oral historical research opens up, it seems that one of the first activities of historians is collecting pedigrees and then devising figures for an 'average' generation, so that by applying simple mathematics they can assign approximate dates to any point on the list. For example, the Polynesian Society decided in the 1890s that 25 years was a reasonable figure to give to personages in genealogies collected in the Pacific, while in the study of early African history a range of 25 to 30 years has ordinarily been used [36; 267; 275]. Evidence from numerous well-documented genealogies indicates that these figures are generally reasonable, but it is questionable whether any average really ought to be applied to a particular genealogy or list of officeholders, a point that historians often seem to miss [222, pp. 121–44].

Even averages that can actually be shown to be correct for entire dynasties or series of officeholders will not hold true for individual segments of these, which may vary wildly from the overall average. In England, for instance, the average length of reigns between 1066 and 1951 is 22.3 years but only two of the 39 rulers reigned between 22 and 23 years. In France the average length of reign between 987 and 1793 is 24.4, yet no king ruled for a period between 22 and 29 years. And of course these are merely two examples of many. This means that using averages could determine the *beginning* of each period but only by sheer luck will any point along the way be approximated.

Historians who collect genealogies in oral societies will usually find that there are many more versions that they might have preferred. The question then arises how to reconcile these variants by deciding which parts to accept and which to reject as untrustworthy. In this the first step will be to consider the circumstances in which each genealogy was collected, just as it would be for any other datum [49; 252]. If it happened to have been collected during a dispute, experience shows that it is almost certain to be wrong, probably in many different ways. If, on the other hand, it was collected in circumstances which seem unrelated to matters of local or personal prestige, then questions of informant reliability and internal consistency must be considered, as well as the likely tendency of the informant to recall such information accurately. Even then the historian can seldom know if it has been affected by earlier disputes about which he knows nothing. In short, no matter how many tests he is able to subject it to, the historian may find it impossible to know just how a genealogy is wrong or to be certain that it is correct. Many of the steps in determining this will be related to specific local circumstances, but several general observations can be made.

Well-remembered founder figures will often appear in several genealogies, but at different points back. One bad expedient to attempt to resolve this kind of contradiction has been to take the average number of generations in the relevant genealogies and adopt that as a working figure. Of course, using averages in this way makes even less sense than using them to establish the length of a typical generation. Any range in a particular individual's genealogical placement will be better accounted for by assuming that the shorter genealogies have been telescoped or the longer ones embellished, or perhaps even a bit of both. In fact, since all distortions to genealogies result in one way or another from sins of omission or commission, we can best frame our discussion in terms of ways to detect and cope with these.

The evidence as we have it might suggest that genealogical embellishment is more common that genealogical forgetfulness. However, this is really an illusion. After all, the need for embellishment is created by forgetting ancestors in the first place. Then too, it is much easier to detect additions since this involves finding what the historian is looking for rather than trying to find what is not there. Additions to genealogies may take several forms: duplicating names; combining variants; inserting etiological names; including eponyms; making collaterals into direct ancestors; making gods into men; and sheer invention [222, pp. 27–64].

Duplicating names in order to lengthen genealogies has naturally been a popular expedient because it requires so little imagination. It has occurred in East Africa, in the genealogies recorded on the surviving inscriptions of ancient and medieval India, among some of the chronicles of ancient Peru, and in the work of such medieval fabulists as Saxo Grammaticus. The appearance in a genealogy of many persons of the same name should alert the historian to the possibility of this kind of alteration, but by itself this can only be suggestive since there are many known examples of families which use a few royal names over and over again. Sometimes, though, a genealogy will contain many instances of duplicated names in a society where the naming patterns or the contents of recent genealogies do not reflect any duplicative tendencies at all. When this happens the historian is right to suspect that he has been given false information.

Another easy way to transform an undesirably short genealogy into an attractively long one is to combine variant pedigrees. For example, there might be three distinct traditions about a sequence of five rulers: ABCDE, ABEDG, and BCFGH. When faced with this historians of the past and present have sometimes decided that the memory of eight different names means that eight different people ruled and at once five rulers become eight: ABCDEFGH. This would be a natural thing to do and it could even be right. On the other hand the eight different names could simply be variations of the actual names of only five individuals—or maybe even fewer if such expansion has already occurred. And, once this procedure is adopted, the eight rulers may become twelve in due course, then seventeen, and so on, as the additive process is repeated. The oral historian who wishes to do this with his data must be very certain that he can provide proper historical credentials to any extra names he adds.

It is also common to make kings and ancestors out of animals, places, and other things. This is usually less wilfully distortive than the duplication of names because members of a society might easily feel that a place name, title, or lineage should be traced to an ancestor or prominent hero after whom they are named. There are, after all, hundreds of places in the United States named after George Washington, Thomas Jefferson, Abraham Lincoln, and Robert E. Lee. But, as usual, great caution is required before assuming that this form of eponymy is universal. For instance, there are few places in Great Britain named after the heroes of its history and the historical use of eponymy does not lend confidence to those who would accept it.

In the records of early Mesopotamia there are several instances of lists of 'rulers' which, on closer inspection and comparison, have turned out to be lists of tribal groupings and place names. The same is true of several Biblical genealogies, the pedigrees of pre-Islamic Arabia, early Ireland, and others. Often enough, however, eponymous 'ancestors' are created from a desire to embroider the past for reasons of the present. Geoffrey of Monmouth was only the most blatant of the many medieval chroniclers who created scores of non-existent rulers by taking the names of towns, rivers, mountains, and the like and making kings' names from them. The chroniclers then claimed that the kings they invented founded the towns or named the rivers, which in turn were used to prove that the kings had really existed! [e.g. 50]. Several centuries later, this carefree approach can be rather amusing, until we remember that it was long regarded as acceptable history because it was what people wanted to believe.

Collaterals, whether they ruled or not, seem to be genealogists' forgotten people, unimportant in reaching back from the present to the furthest reaches of the past. Sometimes they are forgotten entirely by virtue of being (or becoming) collaterals and sometimes they are remembered, but as direct descendants who occupy their own generational space rather than sharing it with others. In such cases the genealogists use names of persons who actually belong in the genealogy but rearrange them to make the genealogy seem to occupy a longer period of time. It will not be easy to discover when this has happened, particularly many generations after the individuals lived. Sometimes there may be hints in stories that indicate that specific persons were contemporaries, whereas the genealogies place them several generations apart. It will be easier to suspect possible examples of collaterals applied directly to the main line when the historian is dealing with lists of officeholders because it is very rare (only about .02% incidence) that succession to an office follows directly from father to son (or uncle to nephew) more than eight consecutive times [224, pp. 71–94]. When this happens in oral genealogies, the historian can assume that his data are incorrect.

Making gods into men, or euhemerism, was a characteristic feature of early Greek genealogies, but has occurred in China, India, Oceania, and Africa as well, largely as a result of the introduction of Christian teaching [e.g. 7; 66]. When this occurs the historian learns something about chronology and other things as well. For the former he realises that these figures do not occupy historical, but mythical, time. But the presence of gods disguised as humans in genealogies should also tell him something about cultural developments. The transformation may have been a real one, prompted by a desire to dispense with old religious practices in favour of new ones by downgrading old gods into new humans [230]. Or it may be a case of genealogies being used to encourage authorities to believe that there were no old gods.

About invention little can be said. It happens, and it happens more often than we can ever know. The Catholic church, for example, has only recently begun to rid its liturgical calendar of the hundreds of saints who were created to justify local cults or to fill up the Christian year with feast days, or who were simply doublets or triplets of other saints or pagan gods (an example, it will be seen, of euhemerism as well).

Sometimes inventing needed names is done crudely and haphazardly. No historian should fail to notice that a genealogy contains undisguised Biblical names, the names of current political figures, or names that are really numbers. But a historian can seldom be expected to detect the modest juxtaposing or shuffling of names already in the genealogy and in common use in the society. Successful genealogical invention is a bit like the perfect murder: simplicity pays.

The process of telescoping—shortening or omitting entire portions of a society's past—is a classic characteristic of the collective memory. Most often, the part of the past that is forgotten is the period between the time of origins and the recent past. That genealogical forgetfulness should assume this form stems from the demands of myth on the one hand and the increased ability to remember the past few generations on the other. Telescoping occurs in genealogies and other forms of historical recollection when events associated with a society's earliest remembered times—'beginnings', if you will—are simply attached to whatever recollections remain of fairly recent times [222, pp. 27–38]. By itself telescoping is often haphazard and artificial and therefore not hard to detect if the historian happens to be looking for it. Sometimes, though, it results from cultural norms that may not easily be discerned by the outsider.

For instance, the Mbundu of Angola have transformed the earliest period of the history of the major lineages that constitute Mbundu society into historical figures that are not unlike the typical Culture Hero. Like the Culture Hero these 'people' represent corporate groups that must have taken a long time to form and as a result many centuries have mistakenly been attributed to only a few lifetimes [329; 330]. Seeing the duration of the Mbundu past in this way helps fit it better into the cultural complex of which the Mbundu are part, but recognising this form of telescoping at all required not just a desire to find instances of telescoping but an awareness of Mbundu notions of kinship organisation.

Finding that the telescoping has occurred, or feeling certain that it must have, is one thing; trying to measure its extent is quite another. Sometimes radiocarbon dating can help, at least in broad terms, if an archeological site is plausibly associated with a certain figure whose existence the historian is prepared to accept [207; 415]. When doing this, it is useful to bear in mind that major sites are frequently connected with important figures in tradition because this seems reasonable and proper to the society and not at all because the site and figure (who may not be historical) were actually associated.

Calculating the contemporaneity of certain people from the testimony of two or more sets of traditions in order to gauge the duration of the past, and by inference the effects of telescoping, will usually be fruitless. Bringing in names from neighbouring societies is a common form of feedback designed to strengthen and legitimise particular versions of traditional history, so that the historian must avoid using one suspect source to check another. Only rarely will the historian be able to estimate the chronological implications of telescoping with any hope of precision and reliability.

Besides genealogies that claim to show biological relationships among previous rulers or ancestors, the historian will sometimes collect lists of office-holders that are simply sequences of names with no claim to genetical relationship. Trying to attribute dates to incumbents of such lists can be even more risky than using genealogies for this purpose. There are certainly no good reasons for granting more credit to lists of office-holders than to genealogies since they too are often used to justify both the *status quo* and the hope of changing it. But even when the historian feels he can accept such lists, applying dates to tenures in office is virtually impossible. Unlike generations, there are no biological constraints placed on officeholding and hence no consistent or predictable range with which to work. We know that the length of tenure in both hereditary and elective offices has ranged from mere moments to more than 90 years, that is, about three times the range we might normally expect for a generation. It is true that most tenures are in the 15- to 35-year range, but overall patterns of dispersal are much greater than for biological generations and change from one time and place to another. In any case, a range of 20 years, each one with roughly equal probability, has no meaning for chronological reconstruction.

It may be possible to narrow this range for particular societies by using what details we know about the succession system, if there is reason to believe that these can be trusted. In rotating systems with importance placed on maturity (the Papacy, for example) or where eligibility is broad (Gaelic Ireland, and Akan stools) short reigns are to be expected. Where there is ultimogeniture (as in Burundi) or reincarnation (as in the Tibetan Buddhist complex) longer reigns are more likely. The great majority of cases will fall somewhere—but almost anywhere—between these extremes and will depend on such factors as differential mortality, personal inability, and bad luck, which are hardly useful tools for historians interested in measuring the past.

In sum, while there is obviously value in seeking to establish an accurate list of officeholders, the results of this will normally be limited to understanding succession patterns, dispute procedures, the range of vested interests and the way these work together, and the differences between ideal and actual practice. This is a sufficiently interesting group of subjects and should compensate the historian for his inability to measure the duration of the past in oral tradition.

A final word can be said about the value of age sets and named epochs in helping to establish chronologies. Many uncentralised societies have developed institutions by which members move from one status to another as they grow older. There may be many such age grades or only a few but they usually seem to be fairly fixed in length in each society. Generally they are given names to distinguish the relative standing of contemporaries and if these names are remembered they can act in the same way as the names of rulers, with the advantage that the length of each of them is fairly similar to all the others. When it can be shown that they have been remembered accurately, they can be helpful for periods of a century or more. In the same fashion, naming short periods of time, ordinarily a calendar year but sometimes only a season, can occasionally prove accurate [e.g. 181].

There is an irony in the study and practice of generational dating. When outside data show that oral records are accurate, they also render such oral records at least partly superfluous. Though outside data are useful, if often misleading, corroboration of the possibility of fairly precise oral recollection over several generations, they are of no help just where we need it most—in those societies which have fallen beyond the scope of contemporary documentation.

Eclipses and their companions
Investigators have collected a number of traditions that refer to celestial events, most often described as solar eclipses by those analysing them. Historians have naturally been quick to use these because solar eclipses can be dated to the very minute, no matter where or how long ago they took place and even one such exact date in the midst of uncertainty is bound to be treasured by any historian. We find, for instance, that Biblical scholars many times have mobilised the stories of the sun standing still at Jericho or the sky's darkening during the crucifixion to push a particular dating scheme and to authenticate the stories themselves [e.g. 409; 439]. Likewise, African historians have

recently made several efforts to use such apparent eclipse references, but few of these can be called successful [223].

As usual, the problem is one of interpretation and validation. It is seldom wise to accept every reference to some kind of celestial phenomenon at its face value, either as to description or timing. A great deal of evidence shows how seldom observers have recognised eclipses as such if they are neither expecting them nor understand their physical properties. Then too it is obvious that such extraordinary natural events as eclipses, earthquakes, volcanic eruptions, and tidal waves are frequently wrenched from their proper context and connected with local events that seem to make more fitting companions [48; 116; 346; 360; 427; 479].

Under these circumstances we can hardly afford to take any reference to the sun doing strange things to be a potentially datable eclipse. Nor can we, even if we occasionally accept such a reference, take for granted that it has been placed properly in the past. Before we do, it is always necessary to ask ourselves *why* a society should have remembered only one particular eclipse, which they sometimes place far back in time, and have forgotten more recent ones. If we are unable to answer this question satisfactorily, it is best that we refrain from attempting any far-reaching dating exercises at all. There is always value, however, in mentioning an apparent eclipse reference, discussing it, and judging its possible value as a chronological landmark in hopes of stimulating more research and possible verification.

Sometimes eclipses may acquire the status of metaphor that we have mentioned with respect to famines. The lack of more than one or two eclipse references in most oral traditions suggests, though, that this has seldom occurred or has been discouraged because visible eclipses take place far too infrequently to achieve the status of the commonplace.

Oral tradition and archeology
Short of finding a calendar during excavation, it is unlikely that archaeological data can help confirm or contradict any dates inferred by techniques such as generational dating. Such evidence can still be of value in establishing sequence and broad dating ranges as well as providing certain kinds of relative dating. For instance, such yields at a site as coins or datable foreign pottery can tell the historian that the site was occupied after a certain date, though not by whom or for how long before or after. Locally-derived goods can be more loosely dated by means of radiocarbon dating. If done carefully, this widely-used technique can yield accuracy rates of over 99% but only at the expense of a range of possible dates too great to be useful to the historian if he has already reached the point of juggling generations. If he desires narrower dating he must settle for a statistical chance of only two in three. Other dating techniques, for example bristlecone pine calibration and thermoluminescence, are being developed, but the reliability of these remains in dispute and it may be some time before historians can use them with confidence.

As it happens, archaeological dating has helped show historians how dangerous it is to rely too heavily on genealogical dating methods. For example, radiocarbon dates have been secured for most island groups in the Pacific that turn out to be hundreds or even thousands of years earlier than those indicated by the genealogies for the peopling of the area [93; 149; 171;

205; 280]. In eastern and central Africa we find a similar situation [415; 464]. Part of the problem lies in the fact that oral traditions habitually speak of populating previously uninhabited land, a cliché which has found ready belief when dating is sought.

Historians have displayed a similar lack of caution in accepting whatever dates happen to come to their attention for the earliest settlement of an area. Such hypotheses seldom survive for more than a few years until new excavations bring new and earlier datings [e.g. 142]. It should be easy to realise how likely this is to happen, yet the impulse to accept earlier evidence lingers on, whether with regard to the earliest man anywhere or to the dating of a particular local culture.

If archaeology is likely to be of little use in dating oral tradition, traditions have occasionally helped locate important archaeological sites. Igbo-Ukwu in Nigeria, Katuruka in Tanzania, and many sites in western Europe and the south-western United States are among those to which archaeological interest was first drawn by local lore [9; 408]. Such traditions often associate these sites with figures whom they connect with more recent times than those dates which the sites themselves have been given by archaeologists. This indicates the tenacity with which the popular memory can retain elements from the deepest past, even though much distorting them in the telling and retelling.

When considering the relationship between pots and pedigrees, the historian must keep several things in mind. Local people may not actually remember anything about particular sites but may have developed stories to account for their presence. Alleged gravesites, earthworks, and other large ruins inevitably attract first speculation about their origins and then more certain associations between men, events, and ruins [162; 203; 230; 460; 469]. The pueblos of the south-western United States, the Easter Island statues, the large ruins on Sardinia, the Maya temples, the Zimbabwe ruins—to name only a few—have all been attributed, often with great circumstantial detail, to peoples who never existed beyond the minds of later observers. In some cases these peoples were invented because observers were not willing to credit the local people with the imagination to conceive or the technical competence to create such monuments. Bearing this in mind, most historians should be satisfied to have sites pointed out to them so that they or others can attempt to date them on archaeological grounds, without forgetting of course that some of the traditions about the site may be correct.

In order to develop hypotheses capable of being tested, historians and archaeologists are often obliged to make certain assumptions about the identity of the former inhabitants of a site. In this process sites, areas, and types of artifacts become associated with specific groups of people but without any certain evidence, since archaeological remains can tell us nothing about the language of a people if they did not write it. Sometimes the evidence from physical anthropology can be of some help but often this is not clear-cut enough to lead to firm conclusions. The study of the remains of the Indus civilization, Bronze Age Greece, and the Bantu expansion are recent examples of the problems involved in trying to connect specific remains with specific groups of people who might be known from later literary or linguistic evidence. The extensive literature on the Bantu expansion during the last two decades has been characterised by an unusual amount of debate over the timing and direction of the various population movements, where they began and why, and how far the available data can explain things [160; 161; 470]. No matter how divergent the interpretations, it is interesting that each is based in varying degrees on the association of certain sites and pottery types with one or another alleged group of Bantu-speakers.

As more archaeological data become available some of these identifications will become more refined, others strengthened, and yet others abandoned. This situation will continue to characterise the study of the Bantu for a long time to come, perhaps forever, just as it has other historical problems that have relied heavily on linking archaeological, linguistic, and literary evidence [e.g. 311]. All historians who deal with the remote past will need to consult the interim conclusions of historical linguists, archaeologists, ethnomusiocologists, botanists, and others. In doing this, though, they must avoid being bold in their ignorance of these complex fields lest they accept as solid fact those things that are only based on recognisably incomplete data.

We have discussed here the major interpretative issues that are likely to face historians who use oral tradition—data which come to them only after passing through the mouths of many generations of tellers. Again I should point out that each historian will encounter in his own work a host of minor or particular problems as he works with his oral materials. In some cases he may need to know more about subjects like geomorphology or hydrology if he is to complete his work. We cannot hope to discuss these here but we have tried to convey a sense of the complexity of dealing with oral tradition to the reader, who can then consider this in his study of the problems connected with a particular piece of research.

CHAPTER SIX

ORAL HISTORY: TESTIMONY ON THE RECENT PAST

I did not think I could get so much profit from the contents of books as from the utterances of a living and abiding voice.
[Eusebius Pamphilii, 143, Bk 3, p. 39].

Biography is the only true history.
[Carlyle]

So far we have been concerned mainly with the collection and study of oral tradition, which we have defined as the recollection of the more distant past that has been transmitted for several generations and has become more or less the common property of a society. Since no living members experienced these events or saw the people whose names and deeds they remember, informants in these circumstances can be considered as primary sources only in the sense that the historian cannot go beyond them in his quest for information.

Many oral historians are less interested in what happened many generations ago than they are in the more recent past, believing that what happened in the last few generations is more relevant to our times. They also regard it as an advantage that they can interview actual participants in the events in which they are interested. This practice of interviewing people about their own experiences is generally called oral history, or sometimes life history. Several of the problems associated with oral history are of a different nature than those involved with the study of oral tradition and we need to treat them separately.

The first problem is one of nomenclature. Although the terms 'oral history' and 'life history' are often used interchangeably, it is best to make a distinction between them. 'Life history' is a concept that is used in anthropology and psychiatry as well as in history [75; 296; 333]. As its name suggests, life history is essentially a spoken autobiography in which the informant is asked to relate at some length those parts of his life that seem *to him* most interesting and important. In these circumstances the interviewer tends to learn more about the informant than about the larger world he lived in. In some cases this may be just what the historian is after but more often it is likely to be an inefficient way to learn about the recent past.

This knowledge may be more successfully gained by means of oral history. Here the historian guides the informant in the same way as he does with regard to collecting oral tradition. The personal experiences of the informant are still what the historian wants but in the context of the larger problem on which he is working. Because they are *personal* experiences, the attitude of the informant is likely to be different than when he is merely recounting what he has been told or what he regards as common knowlege. It is this special relationship between the informant and his testimony that raises most of the issues discussed in this chapter.

In oral societies personal recollections are usually lost in the ever-moving current of oral tradition. By surviving into the present oral tradition has demonstrated a capacity to appeal to the interests of enough people to ensure its success. In this it differs markedly from personal recollections, which seldom survive the lifetime of the individual or, at best, the lives of any children.

To a greater degree than the study of oral tradition, the practice of oral history has been characterised by a feeling that each collector can be his own historian. This can be seen in some of the advice about transcribing to be found in several of the many oral history manuals that have made their appearance recently [e.g. 32]. While preaching fidelity to the oral text, they allow such editing practices as omitting 'crutch words' used by interviewees and, even worse, comments by the interviewer that are not direct questions. These are, they say, minor corrections but they are significant since they tamper with the primary source, producing paraphrases disguised as verbatim testimony. Eliminating indications of hesitations, or moments of doubt and embarrassment, either to protect the image of the interviewer or that of the interviewee makes it impossible to produce a historical document and not just an amusing or readable vignette. The primary source is destroyed rather than preserved and oral history is reduced to the status of dilettantism.

Historians who find this slightly deplorable are pleased that lately the pursuit of the past has begun increasingly to draw the attention of serious scholarship. This growing interest is in part a reaction to the undeniable fact that most conventional written history and oral tradition is elitist history, being largely the history of society's winners as they choose that it be remembered. This view helps account for oral history's growing vogue within literate societies [140; 202; 210; 452; 453].

This is not to say that oral history has not also been the history of the elite. In fact the modern course of the collection and study of personal recollections is usually held to have begun with the establishment of the Columbia University Oral History project in 1948. Designed to collect the reminiscences of major figures in contemporary American public life, it served as a kind of oral appendix to the published memoirs of many of these people. In this way its work offered a complementary perspective of their activities rather than differing views of a larger historical context [427]. (However, it established one indefensible precedent by failing to retain original tapes and relying on transcripts instead.)

But, although it remains the largest single undertaking of its kind, the Columbia project was (or became) anomalous in its interest in those who made a visibly significant impact on their times. The more orthodox current view, already presaged by the ex-slave narratives discussed below, is that oral history provides an opportunity to explore and record the views of the underprivileged, the dispossessed, and the defeated—those who, by virtue of being historically inarticulate, have been overlooked in most studies of the past. In Britain, France, and the United States oral history has closely reflected this interest, with studies of farmers, miners, and members of the urban working class being featured prominently [390; 441; 453].

The considerable interest at present in oral history is reflected by the fact that, after little more than 30 years of systematic collecting, there already exists more than 150 000 hours of taped interviews and perhaps 1 500 000 pages of transcripts in the United States and Britain alone, as well as a very substantial, but indeterminate amount elsewhere. This outpouring has led to formalising the work of oral historians through such organisations as the Oral History Association in the United States and the Oral History Society in Britain. In addition to *Oral History Review* and *Oral History*, the respective organs of these groups, numerous other journals—for example the *Bulletin of the Society for the Study of Labour History*, *History Workshop*, and *Ethnologie Française*—and innumerable local bulletins publish interviews or studies based on interviews [239; 451]. Finally, *The International Journal of Oral History*, which attempts to treat oral history more comparatively and theoretically, began publication in 1980.

Beyond this prominence in literate societies, oral history is beginning to gain popularity among historians of oral or partly oral cultures. This is demonstrated by such publications as *Oral History* and *Yagl-Ambu*, published in Papua New Guinea, and several others devoted to Oceania and the Third World generally. In part this rising interest reflects the intellectual and ideological outlook of many historians of these areas and in part the more practical fact that studying the past few generations in oral societies permits a more fruitful integration of oral and written materials.

In Africa several studies have appeared that, through the medium of either oral history and life history, have investigated the past [e.g. 26; 96; 108]. Moreover, the use of oral history to throw new light on the period of colonial rule has been particularly common in Africa, and more lately in Oceania [170; 326; 358; 442; 491]. The study of labour unionism, cash cropping, labour migration, and military recruitment has relied more and more heavily on the testimony of those who participated and less on official documentation.

But recent studies of such topics as early resistance to colonial rule have necessarily tended to rely on second-hand oral and written accounts (some of which include early interviews) since few who took part are still alive. For our purposes we can treat such studies as oral history if we argue that hearing about the experiences of one's parents is in itself an experience and can be retold as such even if in some circumstances it might be considered as little more than hearsay. These instances are probably a relatively minor aspect of oral history and the discussion here assumes that oral historians are primarily interested in events personally experienced and attitudes personally acquired.

Just as for other recent approaches to the study of history—psychohistory and quantitative history, for instance—many proponents of oral history have consciously set out to justify their approaches, methods, and goals to show, as one of the most prominent among them has put it, that oral history can be 'a means for transforming both the content and purpose of history' [453, p. 2]. This is a large order and has seldom been met, but the attempts to justify oral history by defending the integrity and uniqueness of personal recollections as historical sources has led to a richer debate among practitioners of oral history than among historians whose principal concern has been oral tradition. Most of the latter have been satisfied to work within a larger scholarly framework without creating a more distinct sense of self-identity. These differences require that several points discussed earlier only in passing are considered here in relation to the growing use of oral history.

How trivial is too trivial?
One of the more frequent and telling criticisms of oral history is that, by attempting to democratise the past, it has rendered it trivial [349; 461]. According to this line of reasoning the principal task of the historian is to identify and reconstruct the *significant* and *relevant* aspects of the past—those that have left traces almost in spite of themselves because they had widespread or long-term effects that require continual study. In their attempt to enshrine the ordinary and the obscure, this argument continues, those who practise oral history are really turning the role of historian on its head. They are modern-day antiquarians, unable to distinguish the fascinating but unimportant aspects of the past from those that really mattered.

It is true that much of the work of oral history has been to listen to those who happened to be the objects of authority rather than its wielders, the done-untos rather than the doers, those whose impact never extended beyond the circle of family and friends and who might not otherwise have left any permanent trace of their activities. When historians regard the study of the lives and views of these people *as an end in itself*—as an effort to rewrite the past by reclaiming from its debris only this single facet—and when they shape their methods of enquiry, transcription, and preservation accordingly, then the arguments of the critics must be considered a strong one.

Many historians of course realise that oral history is only one feature of any attempt to extend the study of events recent enough to permit personal recollections to play a role. In this regard the work of oral historians is seen to be more valuable in oral rather than literate societies. For example, studies of trade unionism, military service, and wage-earning in oral societies have seldom been made in anecdotal terms but have been juxtaposed and integrated with other sources, both official and unofficial, so that a fruitful discussion can emerge. There has sometimes, however, been too great a personal and ideological commitment in these studies and personal recollections are not criticised when compared or contrasted with other evidence. In part this results from the sympathy which an interviewer has for an informant who is relaying, often with great feeling, his own experiences, in contrast to written accounts or oral tradition, which transmit more corporate and impersonal versions of the past.

If the historian is to cope with oral history's tendency for the unique, then he must avoid allowing his informants merely to reminisce, in the belief that this gives a flavour to their testimony more important than substance. Personal reminiscences are at once the most unstructured and most tailored form of oral testimony. By allowing an interviewee to control the direction of the interview as well as the kinds of data he provides by means of apparently aimless reminiscing, the historian concedes that rambling is a virtue.

If, say, the historian is interested in early manifestations of economic change during the colonial period, it is important that he define, for his informant and himself, the nature of this interest. Otherwise he will not be able to avoid undue emphasis on events and attitudes that are so intensely personal to each informant that they can never be combined in a coherent overall argument. It may be hard to persuade informants, intent on reliving moments of their own pasts, to concentrate on the more collective aspects of the events that interest the historian. He must balance the need to leave new paths of enquiry open while remaining ready and able to close them if they promise to lead nowhere. A series of introspective life histories—no matter how many—can only lead to a cellular rendition of the past, with each cell hermetically sealed, rather than combining to form a fuller and more integrated picture.

Unless interviews are tightly structured and informants are chosen with the aim of providing complementary data, it will be another instance where the sums of all the parts may be of little more value than any one of them. The historian who might be interested in exploring the history, role, and effects of colonial education in a particular area should study the schools available to the traditional elite as well as any that served the rest of society. He should interview teachers (and if possible, parents) as well as students, gardeners as well as headmasters, colonial officials as well as those who preferred traditional systems of learning. While he is doing this he will naturally not be completely uninterested in such seeming diversions as anecdotes or even jokes because they are often telltale embodiments of larger issues he might not otherwise notice. But to rely on these almost entirely, no matter how interesting or revealing they might be, is to sacrifice structure and larger significance in favour of the memorable but humdrum.

Dealing with this aspect of oral history is almost the opposite of the historian's problems in interpreting oral tradition, where he is trying to filter out the components of a collective version in the hopes of understanding how and why it was put together as it was. But in oral history, the historian will find that one of his major challenges is to persuade his informants to go beyond the personal and idiosyncratic by making connections, discussing issues, and providing wider perspectives. Again, this calls for care in choosing informants. To do this well is especially hard for oral history, where each story is the property of only one person, because death will already have done its own selection, particularly for events that occurred 40, 50, or more years ago.

Memory and perspective
Oral history, like the interpretation of oral tradition, inevitably faces the issue of the role of memory in its work [21; 22; 186; 295; 315; 342; 473]. Whether we like it or not, memory eventually makes cheats of us all, so that it may not be so absurd to suggest that sometimes an individual is not best qualified to remember his own experiences accurately. Oddly, perhaps, this problem stems in part from the fact that we spend too much time thinking about—remembering—the past: the more important or pleasant or unpleasant certain experiences seem to us to be, the more likely we are to dwell on and imperceptibly modify them. The effects of this will vary according to the type of experiences. Facts and events may be remembered but the attitudes we had toward them at the time may have been forgotten and replaced by new viewpoints. And events that were of little interest to us are likely to be remembered more accurately, if less fully, than those in which we were heavily, perhaps emotionally involved.

In a sense the repeated recalling of individual experiences can be compared to the chain of transmission. That is, the most recent time we recall an experience will be different—who knows how much?—from the first time. No matter how careful we may try to be, remembering is just too casual and too unconscious to be adequately controlled. Each time we recall something to mind (or only pass it briefly through our unconscious), modifications occur [22; 172; 185; 237; 295]. These may result from omitting or suppressing unpleasant aspects of an experience, blaming them on others, or minimising their role and effects. The advantage of hindsight may allow an informant to claim greater or more certain knowledge of particular events. Or the extraordinary (as the informant defines it) may crowd out the ordinary. This constant blending and reblending is commonplace, the more so when doing it permits the informant to credit himself, or those he thinks highly of, with a more prominent role. It may also allow the informant to be wise before as well as after the event, or able to shift blame unto others instead of sharing it.

When an informant claims credit for initiating an activity or for taking a greater part in it than any other sources indicate, the historian is faced with his perennial task of comparing and evaluating various strands of evidence. This returns us to the earlier discussion, although we can point out again that the historian can test the truth of such informants by encouraging them to comment on matters for which abundant data exist. It is often the case, though, that the events in question never reached the public record and there are few or no other individuals left either to dispute or verify a particular informant's version. When the historian is at the mercy of a single informant he needs to realise more than ever that self-aggrandisement is by no means only the result of deliberate fabrication. On the contrary, it can easily be the predictable result of many years of conscious and unconscious refashioning of the past little by little, including assimilating the roles of other actors who have since died.

Should seeing be believing?
It is often taken for granted that eyewitness testimony is by nature reliable, or at least more reliable than other forms of recollection because seeing something happen impresses a kind of indelible image on the memory. This is far from true, however, even during the immediate aftermath of an event and before any of the modifications we have mentioned occur [21; 298]. The problem here is often one of out-and-out bias. Since no two people have had the same blend of training and experience, no two people will ever see a complex event—and all events are ultimately complex—in quite the same way. For example, two spectators at a soccer match will later remember different parts of the play—depending on their own interest in particular teams or players, their level of understanding of the games' intricacies, or simply their point of observing. One person may remember a goal saved rather than a goal scored, or regard an offside call or a foul as determining the outcome. And so on.

Reasons for these differing recollections are almost too numerous to identify. It may be that one spectator had once been a goalkeeper, another a striker, so that each identifies with, and thereby remembers more clearly, events that recall his own experiences. Or two spectators may admire two particular players and each sees the entire game as an extension of the deeds of those players. Or it may simply be that one spectator was absent or inattentive at one stage and another was equally so at another moment. As time passes these individuals may forget these peculiarities in their recollections (if they ever recognised them at all) but each recollection based on them will remain in its own way incomplete and personal. Because of this, the historian who would like to learn about what happened in the game will seldom be successful without the aid of other contemporary sources, which of course may carry their own biases.

To gain prestige, an informant may sometimes falsely claim eyewitness status. Even so generally responsible an observer as Bartolomé de las Casas claimed to see things that could not have been, in order to support his extravagant charges of Indian mortality in the early years of Spanish rule [228]. And future historians will have to deal with those who claim to have seen or taken part in such events as D-Day, the eruption of Mt. St. Helens, or the assassination of a prominent public figure. If such claims are made often enough, contradictions among them may alert the historian. But even when he is convinced that an informant did 'see' at least part of what happened on a particular occasion, he cannot place too much faith in such a testimony. A glance at the extensive experimental literature on the vagaries of eyewitness testimony, almost enough to caricature the term, should be reason enough to breed mistrust.

Is older really better?
We have already mentioned the question of aged informants but more needs to be said in this regard with respect to personal recollections. For what it may be worth, the empirical record of psychology suggests that most people's ability to remember declines as they grow older [22; 52; 146; 417; 445]. The ways in which this happens vary from one person to another but it is fair to say that the long-term memories (that is, from a few days to infinity) of the elderly are likely to be less retentive, less accurate, and less able to be mobilised quickly than those of their juniors. If there is one common thread tying together the disparate activities of oral historians, it is that their sources have usually been older people who, they presume, can recall times far enough back to interest them. This alone is enough to justify some mention of the apparent relationship between memory and age.

Two points about the observed patterns are of interest. In the first place, any decline may take the form of memory loss. Here the capacity to remember things accurately simply diminishes so that some things once remembered will be forgotten completely or be recalled with an increasing degree of inexactitude. In some cases, though, it is the ability for *quick* recall that is eroded. When this happens some older adults will retain most of their recollective abilities but will need more and more time to put them into motion. In these cases an informant, embarrassed by being unable to remember as easily as he once could, may replace recall with glib improvisation. When an unusual amount of hemming and hawing accompanies answers, when there is simply an uncomfortably long silence, or when the historian notes a disparity between an informant's testimony and that of others, he should consider the possibility that this improvisation is taking place.

If the informant happens to be recalling events about which few other informants can speak with first-hand knowledge, the historian might find it easy to convince himself that any hesitancies are owing to something other than an inability to remember promptly. And of course it sometimes will be. But, particularly when dealing with older informants, the historian may be able to anticipate this problem by assuring them that he wishes them to consider carefully before answering (in order to give them time to recall), by pointing out that other informants were seldom able to answer quickly (in order to stifle any competitive urges), or by devising other ways that help to put the informant at ease by giving him time to gather his thoughts. He could also encourage informants to do a little unstructured reminiscing in order to fix their attention on the past and then begin to focus on the chosen topic. As long as the historian does not abuse this tactic it can help 'loosen up' informants so they will speak with greater care and accuracy. Finally, as a kind of last resort, the historian who suspects that he has a case of 'slow' memory could leave a set of questions and return later to discuss them. He runs the risk here, though, of the informant discussing the questions with others or consulting written sources for help.

Confidentiality

No single issue has perplexed oral historians recently as much as the role of privacy and confidentiality in their work [130; 144; 159; 236]. In addition to the implications of confidentiality for publishing discussed below, several other dilemmas face the historian. Those who deal with personal recollections certainly face this issue more often and more squarely than those who use oral tradition or written documents. For instance, historians interested in the colonial period have found that very often neither they nor their informants are able to be dispassionate without considerable effort. As a result many interpretations of that era represent one extreme view or the other and, not surprisingly, provocative and sensitive testimony is common.

Of course the problem of privacy is not confined to the practice of oral history. Even those archives with liberal terms usually make exceptions with regard to personal data and other materials that may reflect directly on living persons or their families. But, for better or worse, the historian who deals with oral sources is practically free from such impediments. With this, however, comes a set of accompanying duties which can be broadly classified as legal and ethical, with the two not being entirely separable in most cases.

Questions of ownership and copyright naturally arise for materials recorded or transcribed in the field [398; 399]. Since these vary from one jurisdiction to another and since statutory provisions respecting copyright have in any case barely begun to take note of the special issues raised by oral historiography, it is impossible to know what conditions might be in force in particular areas at particular times. But oral historians should lobby to take part in any process by which these laws are drafted and implemented so that the laws provide realistic guidelines to safeguard the interests of both historians and informants when these are incompatible. For the moment, a few observations can be made about field procedures that will anticipate problems once the historian leaves the field.

Tapes of interviews and any transcripts that result are the joint creation of historian and informant and in most cases ownership privileges are vested in both parties. It could easily prove awkward then for the historian if he were obliged to consult with his informants each time he wanted to put data from interviews into the public record [335]. It is clearly advisable that he obtains some kind of permission by which his informants concede to him 'fair use' of the results of his interviews. The need to do this is a new departure for historians, and researchers in oral societies—our main concern here—have rarely done so.

Securing these waivers will require certain negotiating skills. Above all else, the historian must take care to explain clearly and fully why he needs such permission, how he intends to use it, and how having it protects both his ability to use informants' testimony and their rights to impose reasonable or necessary constraints. Moreover, he must learn to be honest in presenting the issues of this arrangement, so that informants are not discouraged from being open and candid.

All this will not be easy and it can prove to be an unpleasant feature of research, stressing the businesslike and instrumental sides of a relationship that all researchers would like to think of as primarily intellectual and social. Yet the trends in copyright law seem to warrant this measure as a sensible precaution against objections that informants or their heirs could raise about data the historian has already put to use.

Although the term 'fair use' seems simple enough on the face of it, it probably is not. Legalities aside, from time to time the historian is certain to confront difficult ethical dilemmas in deciding whether and how to use some of his materials even if he has safely in hand all the waivers he needs. Sometimes he will find that he must decide to what extent he is willing to embarrass, or even endanger, certain informants by using data they have provided and documenting that use by naming names. At the same time he will realise that if he uses information without identifying its source he runs the risk of having it doubted on the grounds that it is inverifiable. This dilemma could be aggravated by the fact that, the more interesting and valuable the information is, the more likely that it will raise the question of confidentiality. In these circumstances, merely having a waiver does not absolve the historian from thinking long and hard about using certain kinds of data.

The problem, and the consequent soul-searching, become the greater when dealing with the recent past, when the reputation, integrity, and even safety of living people—perhaps important people—may be brought into question. It is not hard to imagine any number of situations where this could happen: collaboration with an enemy or colonial power; rigging elections; financial wrongdoing; crimes against humanity. Possessing this kind of information, and it matters little whether it is true or not, the historian holds, however unwillingly, the well-being of some of his informants in his hands. In some cases he can do nothing with information of this nature, not even try to cite it anonymously if there is the possibility that it can be traced to a particular person or even used as a means of random reprisal. At other times he may be in doubt as to the controversial nature of certain data, which may appear less volatile to him than to more knowledgeable members of the society. If he has *any* doubts about the wisdom of using them he must begin by relying on any cultural familiarity and specific knowledge he has gained in the field and, where possible, supplement these by communicating with his informants, asking advice from members of the society that may be nearer at hand, or seeking the aid of other scholars who have worked among the group. If his doubts persist he can refrain from using his information, or perhaps manage to couch it in terms that suggest he has based his conclusions on a variety of details from scattered sources, but this must be done with care.

Suppose the historian learns that some of his informants have had second thoughts about data they have given him—thoughts that may spring from later events, the advice of friends, or a belated realisation of their sensitive nature? If it is not already too late, the historian must respect these afterthoughts. Whether or not he believes them to be well-founded should not be his main concern. Should they be resolutely ignored? Should they be treated in conjunction with the original testimony to demonstrate the fluid nature of such testimony? Should they be held to replace or negate earlier testimony? In most cases the historian should choose the last alternative. Adopting the first course would offend his conscience, while the opportunities offered by the second should be resisted until such methodological manoeuvres can be carried out safely, if ever.

As is so often true, patience can be the historian's most useful virtue. Waiting until the informants in question have died or moved permanently out of the society may make it possible to use controversial materials, provide verifiable sources, and still protect the informants. Naturally, waiting is a calculated risk. Using the information later could still jeopardise the informant's family or friends; the historian may be pre-empted by another, less scrupulous, scholar who has gathered similar data; or he may die before his informants.

Another alternative the historian may find himself considering is using only those parts of a certain testimony he thinks are useful but innocuous. There is another danger here, though, since segregating portions of testimony on these grounds may well destroy its integrity, intelligibility, and value. It would hardly make sense, for example, to talk only about the visible public career of an organisation without pointing out the nature, direction, and success of its activities were largely the result of the corruption of its leaders, since this partial tale would leave readers with a completely false impression. But if mentioning this corruption seems to the historian likely to lay a trail back to particular informants, he may not be able to discuss the organisation's true history at all for the moment.

Finally, there is the real possibility that the use of certain information, even if accurate, may lead to libel suits. This is becoming a more common danger to historians and in many cases the charge has not been that the material was incorrect or the interpretation of it unfair, but only that the historian has used unfavourable information gratuitously, and hence maliciously. Litigation has a habit of feeding on itself and the incidence of such suits may become a truly serious impediment to free scholarship on the present or recent past.

In view of these various considerations, to offer firm advice on confidentiality would not necessarily be to offer sound advice. The dilemma in deciding whether to use controversial material or whether to suppress it at least temporarily, whether to make assertions citing anonymous informants or none at all, or whether to provide full documentation regardless of possible risks, is simply an integral part of the oral historian's work. He must be willing to accept the burdens these impose if he is to be a competent yet considerate scholar. But in coping there are two things he should never do. He must never allow himself to make decisions solely on the self-serving basis of his own plans for future research, and he should never use the cloak of confidentiality to withold from his peers information that is necessary to judge his work.

A case study: the ex-slave narratives
Studying a single example of collecting personal recollections and the scholarly response to it can illustrate some of the issues raised in this chapter. The government-sponsored collection of testimony from former slaves in the American South is a particularly appropriate body of material for this exercise since it is the only example for which the original interviews are available for study and which has attracted enough scrutiny and interest to draw forth useful conclusions. Carried out during the 1930s, this project was large and diverse—over 2 000 interviews were conducted in 17 states [141; 432; 501]. These activities preceded the development of modern oral history methods so that mere distance makes the project especially interesting. More important it has received intensive, if somewhat belated, attention [24; 47; 141; 176; 324; 384; 432; 497; 501].

Although these narratives (not entirely an appropriate term, but the one by which they are known) remain useful for understanding some aspects of American slavery, several important defects diminish their value. Blacks conducted fewer than one-fifth of the interviews, violating the cardinal principle that interviewers should be culturally sympathetic to the outlook of those they interview [324; 501]. The racial etiquette that governed relations between blacks and whites in the American South during the 1930s inhibited, indeed prevented, frank and honest communication between the two groups on any subject as sensitive as that of slavery. So it is not very surprising that most of the information the ex-slaves provided was compliant and routine. When such awkward topics as miscegenation, corporal punishment, and passive resistance were raised, informants usually prudently disclaimed any knowledge whatever. This entirely natural reticence was only reinforced by the assumptions, methods, and attitudes of many of the interviewers, who routinely used derogatory terms for blacks during their questioning. It would be easy to dismiss this condescension as unconscious, but even if both parties accepted it as normal, it clearly intruded into the data-gathering process.

While the sample of 2 200 interviews is a large one by any standard, this figure represented only about 2% of the surviving ex-slaves. Even so, there was no attempt to choose interviewees at random, either by background or geography. Beyond some general guidelines, each interviewer was left to his or her own devices and inevitably there were great variations in every aspect of the exercise. A high proportion of those interviewed had been house servants who could not speak directly about the harsher conditions under which the great majority of slaves laboured as field hands. The bias in terms of geographical distribution was even greater: almost half the interviews took place in Texas and Arkansas, neither important slaveholding states, while there were few interviews in Virginia, the Carolinas, and Mississippi, where plantation slavery flourished [47; 324].

Another problem, though not one over which interviewers had any control, concerned the ages of the former slaves. On the one hand, about half of them had been under ten years of age when slavery was abolished and their recollections of it were naturally fragmentary and untypical. On the other, those who had experienced some years of adulthood in slavery were in their nineties or older, not necessarily an age too advanced to allow them to provide useful information, but certainly reaching, and sometimes exceeding, the point at which fragility, fading memories, and the desire to please played a large role.

At its establishment, project leaders devised a list of questions to guide the interviewers in their unaccustomed work [501]. They phrased many of these questions in terms that encouraged or demanded certain answers, for this was before the study of survey research techniques had raised issues about the forms questions should take. In principle this was bad enough. In practice it was even worse, because informants were often asked simply to agree or disagree that slavery had actually been more benign than most had suspected (was your master a kind man? were you fed well?) [432]. Given the nature of the existing relations between blacks and whites, many slaves grasped at the chance to answer these questions in a way (yes; yes) that produced a picture of conditions under slavery that was at best idyllic and at worst hopelessly tendentious.

There were those informants, however, who refused to be intimidated by the conditions and discussed candidly the hardships they had experienced or been told about. In some cases interviewers deleted these comments from the versions eventually placed on public deposit [47; 432]. Other kinds of editing also took place, despite the claims of the programme organisers that there be no editing for content, style, or language. The language of informants was sometimes changed to 'improve' intelligibility, while on other occasions the opposite principle operated and transcriptions were made that caricatured black idiom to suit the preconceptions of the interviewers. This kind of tampering was made easy by the lack of original tapes but in some cases more than one transcript survives and permits modern scholars to detect the changes. In other cases interviewers unabashedly noted in their comments the changes they had made.

Analysing the body of ex-slave narratives as a whole also shows that both interviewers and informants tended to concentrate on aspects of slavery that suited their own preferences. Some interviewers saw no harm in pursuing their own theories freely, whereas ex-slaves would generally be more candid with black interviewers. As a result if often seems as if different informants were actually recalling two different systems of slavery—one benign, the other harsh.

All things considered, the combination of weaknesses that characterises the ex-slave narratives restricts their reliable data to such matters as childhood under slavery, some aspects of family life, some details on slave genealogies, and some unintended insights into the nature of memory and of interview psychology. Despite this, since their rediscovery a decade or so ago, these materials have been put to some rather ambitious uses—sometimes to support arguments that southern plantation slavery was a mixture of benign efficiency and rational economics, sometimes to claim that it was both inhumane and unprofitable and resented by almost all slaves. Certainly it is possible, indeed easy, to gain support for nearly any point of view in these narratives and to take too seriously their evidence without carefully exploring the situation in which they were created. Now that this is being done, close scrutiny and comparison are demonstrating the limitations of the narratives as accurate sources for conditions under slavery as seen from the bottom up, although their testimony provides a few insights on attitudes that are nowhere else available. For what it tried to do, the project was largely an opportunity lost because its organisers failed to exercise enough care in structuring the interviews and in selecting interviewers and informants. Its greatest merit may be in showing the value of extensive textual analysis on a body of orally-derived data, given the willingness of a group of historians to undertake it. In this way it serves as both an example and an incentive for further studies of oral materials, so many of which have been collected and so few analysed and evaluated.

CHAPTER SEVEN

SHARING PRIMARY SOURCES

Historians need not be curious to preserve old Manuscripts and Records, after they have form'd their Histories by them: for else no Historian could ever be secure, if the not being able to show their Warrands [Proofs] after many ages, might discredit their History [George Mackenzie, 312, p. 8].

I remember noting their statement and finding myself unable to accept it. They cited no evidence and gave no particulars. A mere *ipse dixit* has no evidential value
[R. Austin Freeman, *The Stoneware Monkey*]

I

Some may be surprised to find an entire chapter devoted to the issue of providing access to sources. Yet this question, largely peculiar to oral research, has generally been ignored. This is somewhat strange and not a little disconcerting since scholars have long recognised that their arguments and conclusions need to be tested by their peers before they are widely adopted. Enduring such unending surveillance arose partly in reaction to the attitude before about the sixteenth century, when referring to unspecified and inaccessible 'authority' was all that was required to support any argument. The example of Copernicus and the heliocentric theory of the solar system illustrates this. For many centuries before Copernicus, everyone accepted that the earth was the physical centre of all creation, a 'fact' presumed to have been demonstrated by the appearance of Christ there. Both Christian and Muslim astronomers long held that all known heavenly bodies revolved in assorted ways around a stationary earth. But gradually centuries of observation and notation, and the development of instruments and techniques that made it possible to discover new heavenly bodies and calculate more accurately the movements and distances of the familiar ones, all combined to suggest that an earth-centered model of the universe was no longer tenable. Even so, it took many decades before most people were willing to admit that earlier notions of celestial mechanics had been wrong.

Testing and verification of ideas takes different forms from one branch of knowledge to another. In the sciences, the developing of hypotheses is preceded by a set of suppositions and followed by extensive and repeated tests that may in turn lead to new hypotheses. Since the scientist is usually dealing with observable and measurable phenomena, he can repeat any experiment, with or without variations, as many times as needed in order to establish a point beyond doubt. While doing this, he is careful to maintain precise records of each phase of the experiment and it is on the basis of these that he advances a hypothesis to explain what he has seen. Stimulated and guided by these records, other scientists are able to repeat the original experiment to test the accuracy and reliability of the conclusions of the first scientist, sometimes by introducing new variables or by adopting new measuring techniques or mathematical approaches, all designed to test and, if possible, refute the conclusions already reached. As a result of this well-established and widely-accepted system, hypotheses that are accepted in the sciences represent the best interpretation of knowledge then available. Even so, many of them are eventually modified or overthrown entirely by other hypotheses.

The problem of verification or confirmation becomes much less clear-cut once we leave the physical sciences. No longer is it possible to confirm, modify, or refute established wisdom or attempts to revise it by duplicating the work of others. In most of the social sciences and humanities the ability of an argument to gain and maintain support depends largely on the ways in which the problem is framed and the evidence gathered and handled. In this regard the preliminary collection of evidence must always be as wide-ranging as possible. Sometimes a scholar demonstrates that he has been properly industrious by showing those sources he has consulted but not used directly, while at the same time justifying his choice of whatever materials he actually uses.

A noteworthy example of work whose authors had the courtesy to include what turned out to be the seeds of their own destruction is the published work of Robert W. Fogel and Stanley Engerman on slavery in the American South [163]. In their *Time on the Cross* these authors proposed a view of slavery quite different from any then accepted. Relying heavily on numerical evidence and statistical extrapolation, Fogel and Engerman argued that plantation slavery was generally both benign and efficient. In short—and to oversimplify a great deal—happy slaves made productive slaves. Because the authors laid out their statistical arguments and the evidence on which they were based fully, critics were able, after a brief period of unguarded enthusiasm, to cite crippling deficiencies in the authors' choice of sources, in their statistical techniques, and in their assumptions of randomness. As a result, little of the interpretation of *Time on the Cross* has survived its critics but its authors have at least demonstrated the value of permitting access to their sources and method. Had they not arrayed their evidence and techniques so thoroughly, it is just possible that much of their argument would remain unchallenged.

No doubt few of us want our work to suffer the same fate as *Time on the Cross* and its example may discourage much of the argument that follows here. Nonetheless, it is undeniable that scholars in all disciplines have agreed that the best way to safeguard advances in knowledge is to array their evidence and procedures for interested parties, without going so far as to encourage actively sustained scrutiny of it.

II

At the same time that we argue the importance of providing opportunities for verifying scholarly work, we must admit that oral historical materials present unusually difficult problems. The rest of this chapter is devoted to the nature of these problems and even more to the argument that they not only can be, but must be, overcome if oral historiography is to earn respect. This involves some repetition of points made in passing in earlier chapters but any such emphasis will not really be amiss. If we made these points earlier in an effort to instruct, we make them here in an effort to persuade.

As we have already seen, using oral sources to throw light on otherwise obscure corners of the past is by no means a recent phenomenon. Since its use has increased markedly in recent years, the discussion presumes that the issue of verifiability is closely connected with the use, abuse, and preservation of field-recorded tapes and their transcriptions and translations.

Historians usually divide their sources into several categories: primary, secondary, tertiary, and so on. As the term suggests, primary sources are those materials dealing with a subject on which any work on that subject *must* be based if it is to have lasting value. Conventionally, primary sources have included such things as inscriptions, charters, coins, and original holograph correspondence. But even though a particular group of sources is considered primary, it should not be forgotten that these sources were once based on other sources, now presumed lost. For example, a particular inscription may summarise several earlier ones, or even change earlier records to fit new circumstances. A letter from one party to another will be based in part on information and opinions the writer has read or heard from others and that he in turn reports to the person to whom he is writing. But since the earlier inscriptions or the information that provided the basis for our hypothetical letter no longer exist, historians have no choice but to regard the available sources as 'primary' since they are near to truly original sources as the historian can *now* secure. These kinds of sources might be relegated to secondary status as new data are uncovered. For instance, a summary census of Nigeria published during the colonial period would no longer be regarded as primary if the actual tallies on which it was based come to light.

By this argument, the primary sources for most oral historians are their informants. However, this will become less true as time passes for, just as records are destroyed or lost, so informants die. Whenever it is possible then, informants should be consulted about their own testimony, whether by the original collector or someone else interested in it [335]. Failing informants themselves, it is inescapable that the tapes will be considered the historian's primary sources. After all, no other materials intervene between them and the informant's testimony and they alone can provide certain information needed to establish the value of the data they contain. For instance, only tapes provide such useful signals as pauses or other hesitations, variations in inflection, or interruptions and indications of dissent from bystanders. Even then, the quizzical look or impatient gesture will be lost.

The editors of the best editions of collected works of important figures have been careful to indicate crossed-out words, mis-spellings, and marginal notes in the original manuscripts, since they realise that these apparently unimportant trifles can be useful indications of a person's views or frame of mind when the document was prepared. But it is quite impossible to indicate oral anomalies in words in any systematically intelligible fashion. Only by listening carefully to the tapes can we detect and attempt to understand these.

In these circumstances, even though the conscientious fieldworker has been careful to transcribe his tapes in the language of the interview at the earliest possible moment, his transcripts can never be considered as tapes in another form and therefore of equal value as evidence. Regardless of the best efforts, many adjustments are made in transcribing, however unwillingly or unwittingly. In some cases they are simple slips of the pen, due perhaps to the investigator's unfamiliarity with the language, background noises, too much haste, or simply fatigue after a long day's work. In other cases, being insufficiently trained in the local language, the historian feels more comfortable leaving the work of transcription to his interpreter. The intervention of another party between source and historian is not typical of most historical work and inevitably it helps to create serious and sometimes unresolvable problems.

Besides making simple literal errors, a researcher might underestimate the importance of such linguistic aspects as tone, or he may be aware of these but become careless in noting them fully and accurately. If the interview was held in the midst of an audience the investigator may have failed to appreciate and to note in his transcription the effect this audience might have had on the informant. Even an apparently passive group of onlookers can affect the testimony and commentary an informant provides. Silence is often eloquent, but it can hardly be transcribed effectively.

In short, like all secondary sources, the transcripts of taped interviews are inferior and less desirable because they can reproduce adequately some information in the primary sources but they are unable to provide help in appraising whatever they reproduce. Although transcripts are valuable in so far as they afford safeguards against the destruction of tapes, as *sources* they must always remain inferior to the tapes.

III

Historians who have collected oral tradition have been notably reluctant to make the full range of their materials available for consultation. After all, they have actually helped to create many of the materials with which they work, and own them in ways that historians working with written sources never can, since their sources are normally in the public domain and available to other qualified scholars who wish to use them. Many oral historians probably share the feelings of one collector who expressed concern over 'making available all of my fieldwork to others who perhaps have more opportunity to write it up than I do'. This may help explain why the fate of the very large body of material on which oral historians have relied is largely unknown. In discussing the nature and magnitude of this problem I will (perhaps unfairly) concentrate on the experience of African historians since this is large and important as well as typical of work done with oral sources everywhere.

The number of tapes collected by African historians and the amount of data they represent can only be described as presumably very large. Despite some 20 years of extensive historical investigation there, we still know surprisingly little about the oral data behind this work. It is true, of course, that numerous publications have appeared that speak expansively of assiduous interviewing. However, this only indicates the industriousness of fieldworkers and does not answer a number of more important questions. For example, the whereabouts of the tapes (as well as of transcripts and translations) are seldom revealed.

This reticence naturally raises concerns about the preservation of tapes. Are they languishing on dusty shelves or in musty closets, or have they already perished in hot attics and humid cellars? Have they simply died of old age and neglect or have they been thrown out as the collector turns his attention to new enthusiasms and discards the unwanted remains of the old? If we accept that tapes are the oral historian's most important source, the answers to these questions are likely to discourage us, for we must certainly assume that a large, if indeterminable, proportion of the tapes collected by African historians has suffered one or another of these unnecessary and untimely fates. We may be equally certain that much of what remains is likely to receive similar treatment.

These elusive tapes have of course inspired many books and articles, but without the evidence on which this legacy has been built, of what value can it be? Can conclusions and arguments be irretrievably separated from the evidence on which they are based and still be regarded as contributions to knowledge? How is this procedure different from that of Geoffrey of Monmouth, who claimed to create his pastiche of the British past on the authority of 'a very old book' that no one else ever saw and which almost everyone now regards as a pious fiction? These are rather uncomfortable questions and ones that seem to suggest a lamentable lack of concern in the work of friends and colleagues. However, much of the recent work of oral historians has been designed to correct and supplement the work of their predecessors of not too long ago. We have already seen that this recent work has undermined many of yesterday's theories, while many other concepts, still accepted, are sure to follow. This continuing redefinition of the past has also begun to occur with work based on interpreting oral tradition. Here too, what historians once accepted as well founded has in many cases been questioned or rejected by later testimony or by reinterpreting earlier conclusions.

The magnitude of this reinterpretative enterprise is reflected in the fact that most of what we think we know of the pre-nineteenth century history of tropical Africa, Oceania, and elsewhere is based on traditions collected during the past 75 years, and largely within the last 25. And we have seen that a flourishing historiography of the colonial period rooted in oral rather than archival sources has also developed. All in all, it is probably no exaggeration to estimate that as much as one-half of recent work in these areas depends heavily or even solely on oral sources. Yet, when we begin to survey this published work, we find that not much of it is supported by accessible evidence and is little more than simple assertion when judged by the traditional demands of historical enquiry—the tying together of evidence, argument, and conclusion.

A survey of a dozen recent works that deal with the East African interior and rely extensively on oral tradition shows that only three authors appear to have deposited any taped materials [226]. Furthermore, even in these cases only part of the tape collections were deposited and two of the three depositors have restricted access even to these! Asante is as thoroughly and ably studied as any area in tropical Africa. Scores of studies of the Asante past have appeared during the past two decades, but, once again, despite the fact that copies of previously widely-scattered archival materials have been collected together, no similar effort has been made to secure tapes or other kinds of field materials. More than 200 histories of Asante stools have been compiled. In their available form these show signs of heavy editing, but the extent and character of this editing must remain uncertain because no tapes or even verbatim transcripts are available to help judge the reliability of the histories. In the same way, an attempt to provide life histories of important Asante historical figures has been in progress for several years, but the value of these is diminished by the inaccessibility of the oral sources on which important parts of this work are based.

Many similar examples could be introduced from all parts of Africa to the point where the entire fabric of early African history becomes suspect. It seems surprising that the extent of this problem has not begun to trouble most Africanists very much or very noticeably. Instead, there has been a marked absence of critical comment in the review literature. As a species of historical enquiry, African history is in its infancy and perhaps it is too early to expect that this aspect of its work should engage the interest of historical scholarship at large to any great degree. But the claims of Africanists and other oral historians to equal merit in terms of sources and argument are certain eventually to draw the attention, and perhaps the scorn, of historians who find themselves utterly unable to test them.

Whatever losses have already occurred to taped sources cannot be restored, nor can they even be calculated, since they have left traces behind only in the form of scattered footnotes, imprecise methodological chapters, and lists of informants, many of whom are no longer alive. Since it is fruitless to lament the past, we must be satisfied to learn from it in order to salvage the future.

IV

Solving the dilemma of verifying oral sources requires a two-fold but complementary programme. Scholars who collect oral data must accept the responsibility of making them available at the earliest possible moment, subject to the qualifications mentioned below. Copies of tapes should be made as soon as the researcher returns from the field, if not sooner, so that tape deterioration can be checked. At this point the researcher may expect—and is entitled to—sole use of these materials and would be justified in temporarily restricting access to any copies. But restrictions should be lifted at the very latest before the publication of any materials (including dissertations where, as in the United States, they are freely available) that are based on such sources. Here the researcher will need to consider confidentiality, which was discussed in the last chapter, and decide which of the suggested courses (or another) he should adopt. The principle must remain, however, that no scholar has the right to seek both the approval of his peers and immunity from any criticism based on their familiarity with his sources.

There are several ways to gain access to tapes but neither individually nor collectively are they sufficient in themselves. At present a few universities with strong area studies programmes stipulate that a substantial amount of supporting text be submitted along with the dissertation. This requirement shows that some have begun to realise that oral sources present unusual problems of evidence, but is far from a solution. Since translated texts are secondary or tertiary sources, accepting them in place of the tapes only permits the latter to remain tantalisingly inviolate. Then too, the chance to be selective encourages the historian to deal only with the most straightforward materials, rather than always with the most valuable, in order to finish his research promptly.

To date most research in the Third World has been funded by private or governmental granting agencies. Holding the purse-strings bestows on these agencies the kind of effective power that only money can exert. So far, though, these agencies have seldom done more than instruct grantees to leave some traces of their work in the host country. This has seldom been particularly effective because it has never been either systematically defined or widely enforced. What must be done is that some portion of the grant be paid only when all such tapes and/or transcripts have been deposited in at least one place that will in turn permit their dissemination after a waiting period of up to five years.

Host countries should also be able to exercise some pressure in this regard. However, ill-will owing to the failure of researchers to leave copies of their materials behind demonstrates that efforts made over the past 20 years have not been very successful. The unhappy results are doubled in this case. Not only is it impossible for local scholars to verify work based on tapes, but scholars who travel in the wake of the defaulters find themselves being punished for the sins of their predecessors.

How then are we to encourage and sustain a sense of obligation among scholars? Beyond what we have already suggested, answers to this question are by no means easy to find. One way would be for methodology courses in Third World history to stress this aspect of oral research in addition to the usual attention to the mechanical and interpretative sides of collecting and using oral data. A slightly different way would be to insist that oral history students be exposed more fully to the ways other historians treat their sources. A good example would be medieval historians, who, for many scholarly generations have diligently unearthed charters, inscriptions, and the like, and prepared scholarly editions of them for common use. As a result there are numerous extensive series of such works, many running to hundreds of volumes. In contrast, for Africa there are only the *Fontes Historiae Africanae*, devoted largely to Arabic-language materials; an undeveloped series on early Portuguese travellers' accounts; the publications of the Van Riebeeck Society on sources for southern Africa; and scattered volumes in the Hakluyt series. The collections of oral materials are distinguished only by their scantiness [119; 499]. Still another way to motivate historians would be to use manuscript assessment procedures and book reviews to emphasise the vulnerability of any interpretation that is virtually undocumented in the accepted sense of that term.

V

If oral historians are to go public with their sources, they need to find despositories prepared to seek out and identify oral materials actively; process and index them effectively and sensitively; and disseminate them, and information about them, promptly and economically. For the moment there are no despositories that fulfil all these functions satisfactorily with regard to Third World materials. It is true that some institutions—for example, the Archives of Traditional Music at Indiana University—have been established to meet this need. It is no less true that they have failed to stimulate interest (except among musicologists) either in depositing materials or in permitting free access to them. Nor have they been able to index, retrieve, and distribute copies readily.

It is necessary then to develop such depositories almost literally from the ground up. Even the largest research libraries have demonstrated time and again that they are unable or unwilling to absorb non-print materials in practical ways. All information retrieval systems have 'cracks' in them into which odds and ends fall, sometimes never to be seen again. For whatever reasons, the cracks in libraries seem to attract microforms, cassettes, filmstrips, and tapes almost magnetically. Even when such materials are processed quickly and realistically, the problems of storage and retrieval obtrude. Libraries have always been primarily intended to hold books and journals and their construction reflects this. This usually means that non-print materials are held in temporary or controlled storage areas and may be available only at certain times, to certain classes of patrons, or for restricted periods. Nor are libraries usually equipped to provide copies of such materials; in any case the threat of copyright law, so ambiguous in intent and so haphazard in application, would probably hinder carrying out this service effectively.

Specially-designed and equipped depositories, however, could be affiliated with existing research libraries with strong interests in the study of oral cultures, encouraging a partnership between trained information scientists and practitioners of oral historiography. Only a relatively few depositories would be needed if recruitment and distribution are to be effective—no more than two or three in each major area of the Third World and a like number in Europe and in the United States. Keeping the number of despositories low would enable larger numbers of depositors and curators to work together and would permit economies of construction, storage, and distribution. An important function of these depositories would be to provide tape indexes and union lists similar to *The National Register of Microform Masters* and *The National Union Catalog of Manuscript Collections*, issued by the Library of Congress.

All tape collections should be accompanied by typescript indexes of appropriate size and detail. Obviously the collector himself is best qualified to prepare these; in fact this can readily be done at the transcription stage. The most effective format would include major sub-topics that could be identified by their foot location on each numbered tape, together with an index of all proper names keyed to the topical index. In addition all informants should be listed, located, and identified, with details on their age, status in life, and qualifications, as well as data on the circumstances of the interview. Finally, information on the conception and execution of the project should be included.

Depositories that exemplify these aims are not entirely lacking. Several of the major oral history projects—for instance, those conducted by Columbia University, several American presidential libraries, and Leeds University—have developed impressive technological capabilities that enable them to prepare fairly detailed accounts of their holdings. However, the aim of most oral history collections has been to gather raw data for future use and they do not consider the reproduction and distribution of their holdings to be an immediate priority. There is no little irony in the fact that for most of the oral history projects in the United States and Great Britain, the materials are deposited before use, whereas among historians of oral cultures the tapes have been widely used without ever being deposited in public institutions at all.

VI

At best it will be many years before it will be possible to provide a core of orally-derived primary sources that will support the published work relying on them. This means that much recent oral historiography can be accepted only provisionally. Meanwhile the almost complete absence of adequate supporting documentation will allow sceptics to thrive, secure in the knowledge that their doubts cannot properly be answered—that they can ask 'where's the evidence' and know it will not be produced. As the first enthusiasm for oral historiography begins to wear off, it is likely that both the number of these sceptics and the vigour of their criticism will increase. This disconcerting possibility should force oral historians to take the necessary pains to provide access to their sources and to teach their successors to do the same. If this happens, this period of infancy will eventually be regarded only as an episode—a harbinger of greater maturity and self-assurance.

CODA

[Rundi oral traditions] are not at all weighty, yet they are indispensable.
It is truly a challenge.

    [Jan Vansina, 472, p. 219]

We must hurry. The present generation no longer knows anything of its
ancestors.

    [E. de Bovis, 53, p. 368]

I

We might best close by returning to the beginning and reviewing our opening
arguments in the light of the intervening discussion. In doing this, it is
particularly important to emphasise that, although oral history has, as we
have seen, its own peculiar problems, among the best ways to resolve these is to
keep in mind that the study of the oral past must be conducted on the same
lines as the study of any other past. We began by asking the basic question:
what is history? If we agree that history is not so much a record of the facts of
the past as it is a series of accepted judgements based on carefully considered
probabilities, then we must concede that historians themselves play a major
role in determining how the past will look to the present.

  Oral historians who would doubt the truth in this, and thus their own
dominant share in shaping the past they reconstruct, might do well to emulate
the practice of Torben Monberg, an anthropologist who worked in Oceania.
Several years after publishing a set of stories and tales he had collected during
fieldwork, Monberg returned to his field locale specifically to learn what effects
his book had had on the people among whom he had worked [335]. To his
chagrin, and with a wonderful sense of understatement, Monberg reports that
reaction to his published work was 'not entirely favourable'. This criticism
took several forms, some of them unexpected. Not surprisingly, some people
objected that there were 'bad stories about ancestors of people who are still
alive'. Others complained that *their* traditional stories [were] not in the book'
and would therefore soon be forgotten in favour of those that were. Yet other
informants were distressed because their own testimony had not been included
whereas that of others had been. One informant had an answer for
Monberg—a solution that would not appeal to many historians: he should
'make a new book containing all the different versions of stories' since this
would be a work that 'nobody would fight about'. In short, Monberg learned
that only a very few of his informants were satisfied completely with the way he
went about using the data he had collected from them, even though the
resulting product was much less heavily edited and abstracted than the work
of historians would have been.

  Monberg's exercise in submitting his work to the judgement of his
informants was an admirably bold one, but one that has failed to attract many
imitators. Fortunately, in his own work Monberg was not especially interested
in extracting factual historical data, so his work was less diminished by the
criticism it received. But his example does remind us that, in attempting to

reconstruct any experience, especially collective experience, any scholar pursues an elusive quarry. This is especially true when dealing with word of mouth rather than words captured in writing.

II

Maintaining a delicate balance between introspection and action, hearing and believing, thinking and writing, is indisputably the most crucial need for any historian going about his work. It does not require a particularly close look at the broader historical canvas to realise that there is scarcely a cause or an effect, an event or process anywhere about which there is universal agreement among historians. Instead, historians are constantly challenging the interpretations of a century ago or a year ago; and it will always be so. All historians agree that Napoleon lost the battle of Waterloo, but they have argued for more than 150 years about every aspect of the battle, its prologue, and its aftermath.

The past has happened and cannot change, but the interpretation and understanding of it continues to happen and will never stop changing. This perpetual but salutary kinesis ensures that the work of some historians will survive—either because it is better or because it proves more useful in fitting later views more closely or in providing a good summary record—whereas the work of others will fall into disuse or disrepute, not always for good reasons. Future generations are bound to appraise some of our own work as harshly as we have judged that of some of our predecessors. While we look to the past, then, we must also anticipate the future.

Looked at in this way, de Bovis' words quoted at the beginning of this chapter take on new meaning in today's world of oral historiography. In the century since then, oral historians have not failed to echo his concern and sense of urgency. By both word and action they have shown that they realise that the recollection of things past in oral societies is shrinking and changing under the impact of the modern world. The extent of oral historical research undertaken just in the past 30 years certainly suggests at least a sense of feverish haste at times, and this can only be a mixed blessing. Much work impetuously done will fall fair victim to scholarly norms of organised criticism because it has not been based on rigorous historical method with regard to sources and analysis.

It may, then, be time for a brief and partial respite, a chance for introspection and retrenchment. One outcome of such an interlude will probably be a realisation that recent work is not always the culmination of all that preceded it, or a necessary point of departure on which all future work must be based. Seen in perspective, a more modest appraisal may emerge. Part of this will be a sense that it is wise always to work as though our most energetic critics (after ourselves) are watching from the wings. If this helps us to formulate problems carefully, collect and evaluate data intelligently and thoroughly, and arrange to make them available fully and spontaneously, we should be able to rest satisfied that the contribution of oral historiography to the store of historical knowledge will be both important and lasting.

BIBLIOGRAPHY

The following bibliography is confined to works cited in the text and is intended to serve two purposes. The first, of course, is to provide documentation to support the arguments and quotations in the text. The other is to suggest the riches available to the oral historian. What follows is no more than a sampling; for further relevant materials published since 1970 see the annual bibliographies that have appeared in *History in Africa* since 1974 and that now add up to more than 3 000 items. Readers interested in keeping abreast of relevant published books and articles should also consult the following periodic bibliographies: *Anthropological Index of Current Periodicals*, published by the Royal Anthropological Institute; *Anthropological Literature*: *Bibliografia Missionaria*; *International African Bibliography*, published by the International African Institute; *International Bibliography of Historical Sciences*; *International Bibliography of Social and Cultural Anthropology*; *Recently Published Articles*, published by the American Historical Association and, except for Oceania, very comprehensive and up-to-date; and *Répertoire bibliographique de la philosophie*. In addition, *Anthropos* and *Current Anthropology* list the contents of selected journals and anthologies, while *Biography* and *International Journal of Oral History* include recent materials on the subject matter of Chapter 6.

ABBREVIATIONS

AHR	*American Historical Review*
APS	*The African Past Speaks*, Miller, Joseph C. (ed.), Folkestone, 1980
AQ	*Anthropological Quarterly*
ARA	*Annual Review of Anthropology*
BJRUL	*Bulletin of the John Rylands University Library*
FOAS	*Fonti Orali. Antropologia e Storia*, Bernardi, Bernardo, *et al.* (eds.), Milan, 1978
HA	*History in Africa*
HTR	*Harvard Theological Review*
IJAHS	*International Journal of African Historical Studies*
JAF	*Journal of American Folklore*
JAH	*Journal of African History*
JAOS	*Journal of the American Oriental Society*
JFI	*Journal of the Folklore Institute* [Indiana University]
JPH	*Journal of Pacific History*
JPS	*Journal of the Polynesian Society*
JSA	*Journal de la Société des Américanistes*
MS	*Mediaeval Scandinavia*
NZJH	*New Zealand Journal of History*
OHR	*Oral History Review*
PEQ	*Palestine Exploration Quarterly*
RMSS	*The Recall Method in Social Surveys*, Moss, Louis, and Goldstein, Harvey (eds.), London, 1979

1   ᶜAbd al-Wadud b. Ahmad Mawlud al-Shamsadi, 'The Ancient History of the Mauritanian Adrar and the Sons of Shams al-din', in Norris, Harry T., *Saharan Myth and Saga*, Oxford, 1972, pp. 126–59.
2   Abel, E. L., 'The Psychology of Memory and Rumor Transmission and Their Bearing on Theories of Oral Transmission in Early Christianity', *Journal of Religion*, 51, 1971, pp. 270–81.
3   Acton, John Dalberg, Baron, *Lectures on Modern History*, London, 1907.
4   Adam of Bremen, *History of the Archbishops of Hamburg-Bremen*, ed. Tschan, Francis J., New York, 1959.
5   Adorno, Rolena, 'Felipe Guaman Poma de Ayala: An Andean View of the Peruvian Viceroyalty, 1565–1615', *Journal de la Société des Américanistes*, 65, 1978, pp. 121–43.
6   Afigbo, A. E., 'Ibibio Origins and Migrations: a Critique of Methodology', *Nigeria Magazine*, Dec. 1970–Aug. 1971, pp. 62–69.
7   Africa, T. W., 'The One-Eyed Man Against Rome: an Exercise in Euhemerism', *Historia*, 19, 1970, pp. 528–38.
8   Aikin, J. P., 'Pseudo-Ancestors in the Genealogical Projects of Emperor Maximilian I', *Renaissance and Reformation*, 13, 1977, 8–15.
9   Alagoa, E. J., 'Oral Tradition and Archaeology: the Case of Onyoma', *Òdùmá*, i, 1, Oct. 1973. pp. 10–12.
10   Allaire, L., 'On the Historicity of Carib Migrations in the Lesser Antilles', *American Antiquity*, 45, 1980, pp. 238–45.
11   Allan, S., 'The Identities of Taigong Wang in Zhou and Han Literature', *Monumenta Serica*, 30, 1972/73, pp. 57–99.
12   Alster, B. 'The Paradigmatic Character of Mesopotamian Heroes', *Revue d'Assyrologie et d'archéologie orientale*, 68, 1974, pp. 49–60.
13   Amsler, M. E., 'Literary Onomastics and the Descent of Nations: the Example of Isidore and Vico'. *Names*, 27, 1979, pp. 106–16.
14   Andersson, Theodore M., *The Problem of Icelandic Saga Origins*, New Haven, 1964.
15   *Antiquités russes d'après les monuments historiques des Islandais et des anciens scandinaves*, Rafn, Carl C. (ed.), 2 vols, Copenhagen, 1850–52.
16   Archambault, Paul, *Seven French Chroniclers: Witnesses to History*, Syracuse, 1974.
17   Arguedas, J., 'The Encounter of Two Worlds in Garcilaso de la Vega's "Royal Commentaries of the Incas"', *Sussex Essays in Anthropology*, 1, 1976, pp. 13–22.
18   Arjona Santos, A., 'Quetzalcóatl: la historia y el mito', *Cuadernos Hispanoamericanos*, 310, April 1976, pp. 94–123.
19   Armayor, O. K., 'Sesostris and Herodotus' Autopsy of Thrace, Colchis, Inland Asia Minor, and the Levant', *Harvard Studies in Classical Philology*, 84, 1980, pp. 51–74.
20   Asopa, Jai N., *Origin of the Rajputs*, Delhi, 1976.
21   Baddeley, Alan D., 'The Limitations of Human Memory: Implications for the Design of Retrospective Surveys' in *RMSS*, pp. 13–30.
22   Baddeley, Alan D., *The Psychology of Memory*, New York, 1976.
23   Bailey, C., 'The Negev in the Nineteenth Century: Reconstructing History From Bedouin Oral Traditions', *Asian and African Studies*, 14, 1980, pp. 35–80.
24   Bailey, D. T., 'A Divided Prism: Two Sources of Black Testimony on Slavery', *Journal of Southern History*, 46, 1980, pp. 381–404.
25   al-Baladhuri, Abu-l-Abbas b. Jabir, *The Origins of the Islamic State*, Hitti, Philip K. (ed.), Beirut, 1966.
26   Barnett, Donald L. and Njama, Karari, *Mau Mau From Within*, New York, 1966.
27   Barrère, D. B., 'Revisions and Adulterations in Polynesian Creation Myths', *Polynesian Culture History*, Highland, Genevieve (ed.), Honolulu, 1967, pp. 105–17.
28   Barzun, Jacques and Graff, Henry F., *The Modern Researcher*, New York, 1970.
29   *Basic International Bibliography of Archive Administration*, comp. Duchein, Michel, *Archivum*, xxv, Munich, 1978.
30   Baudot, Georges, *Utopie et histoire au Mexique: les premiers chroniqueurs de la civilisation mexicaine (1520–1569)*, Paris, 1977.
31   Bauer, Wilhelm, *Einführung in das Studium der Geschichte*, Tübingen, 1928.
32   Baum, Willa, *Transcribing and Editing Oral History*, Nashville, 1977.
33   Bauman, Richard, *Verbal Art as Performance*, Rowley, Mass., 1977.
34   Baumbach, L., 'A Doric Fifth Column?' *Acta Classica* [Cape Town], 23, 1980, pp. 1–12.

35   Beach, D. N., 'The Mutapa Dynasty: A Comparison of Documentary and Traditional
        Evidence', *HA*, 3, 1976, pp. 1–18.
36   Beach, D. N., 'The Shona Generation', *Central African Journal of Medicine*, 25, 1979,
        pp. 45–51.
37   Benediktsson, J., 'Some Problems in the History of the Settlement of Iceland', in *The
        Vikings*, Uppsala, 1978, pp. 161–65.
38   Bernheim, Ernst, *Lehrbuch der historischen Methode und der Geschichtsphilosophie*, Leipzig,
        1903.
39   Berntsen, J. L., 'The Enemy is Us: Eponymy in the Historiography of the Maasai', *HA*,
        7, 1980, pp. 1–21.
40   Best, Elsdon, *The Maori School of Learning: Its Objectives, Methods, and Ceremonial*,
        Wellington, 1923.
41   Best, Ernest, 'Scripture, Tradition and the Canon of the New Testament', *Bulletin of the
        John Rylands University Library*, 61, 1978/79, pp. 258–89.
42   Bianquis, T., 'La transmission du hadith en Syrie à l'époque fatimide', *Bulletin d'études
        orientales*, 25, 1972, pp. 85–95.
43   Bickerman, E. J., '*Origines gentium*', *Classical Philology*, 47, 1952, pp. 65–81.
44   Billington, Ray A. (ed.), *The Historian's Contribution to Anglo-American Misunderstanding*,
        London, 1966.
45   Blackburn, S. H., 'Oral Performances: Narrative and Ritual in a Tamil Tradition', *JAF*,
        94, 1981, pp. 207–27.
46   Blanke, G. H., 'Early Theories About the Nature and Origin of the Indians and the
        Advent of Mormonism', *Amerikastudien/American Studies*, 25, 1980, pp. 243–68.
47   Blassingame, J. W., 'Using the Testimony of Ex-Slaves: Approaches and Problems',
        Journal of Southern History, 41, 1975, pp. 473–92.
48   Blong, R. J., 'The Krakatoa Myth and the New Guinea Highlands', *JPS*, 84, 1975,
        pp. 213–17.
49   Blount, Ben G., 'Agreeing to Agree on Genealogy: A Luo Sociology of Knowledge',
        Sociocultural Dimensions of Language Use, Sanches, M. and Blount, B. G., (eds.), New
        York, 1975, pp. 117–36.
50   Borchardt, Frank L., *German Antiquity in Renaissance Myth*, Baltimore, 1971.
51   Bosworth, C. E., 'The Heritage of Rulership in Early Islamic Iran and the Search for
        Dynastic Connections with the Past', *Iran*, 11, 1973, pp. 51–62.
52   Botwinick, Jack and Martha Storandt, *Memory, Related Functions, and Age*, Springfield, Ill.,
        1974.
53   Bovis, E. de, 'Etat de la société tahitienne à l'arrivée des Européens', *Revue Coloniale*, ii,
        14, 1855, 368–408, 510–39.
54   Boyce, D. B., 'A Glimpse of Iroquois Culture History Through the Eyes of Joseph Brant
        and John Norton', *Proceedings of the American Philosophical Society*, 117, 1973,
        pp. 286–94.
55   Boyle, J. A., 'The Alexander Myth in Central Asia', *Folklore*, 85, 1974, pp. 217–28.
56   Boyle, J. A., 'The Alexander Romance in the East and West', *BJRUL*, 60, 1977,
        pp. 13–27.
57   Boyle, J. A., 'Rashid al-din, the First World Historian', *Islamic Culture*, 44, 1970, pp. 9–17.
58   Braukämper, U., 'The Correlation of Oral Traditions and Historical Records in
        Southern Ethiopia: A Case Study of the Hadiya-Sidamo Past', *Journal of Ethiopian
        Studies*, 11, 1973, pp. 29–50.
59   Braund, D. C. 'The Aedui, Troy, and the Apocolocyntosis', *Classical Quarterly*, n.s. 30,
        1980, pp. 420–25.
60   Bravo, G., 'Revitalización del mito de origén en la étapa final de la historia incaica', *Actes
        du XLIIe Congrès International des Américanistes*, Paris, 1976, 5 vols. Paris, 1978,
        iv, pp. 327–33.
61   Brecher, K., 'Sirius Enigmas', *Astronomy of the Ancients*, Brecher, Kenneth, and Feirtag,
        Michael (eds), Cambridge, Mass., 1979, pp. 91–115.
62   Brewer, D., 'The Gospels and the Laws of Folktale', *Folklore*, 90, 1979, pp. 37–52.
63   Bronson, B., 'Against Migration: A Negative Perspective on Population Movements in
        Prehistoric Southeast Asia', *Kabar Seberang/Sulating Maphilindo*, 1, Jan. 1977,
        pp. 29–43.
64   Brotherston, G., 'Huitzilopochtli and What was Made of Him', in *Mesoamerican
        Archaeology: New Approaches*, Hammond, Norman (ed.), London, 1974, pp. 155–66.

65   Brown, M., 'The Use of Oral and Documentary Evidence in Historical Archaeology: Ethnohistory at Mott Farm', *Ethnohistory*, 20, 1973, pp. 347–60.
66   Brown, T. S., 'Euhemerus and the Historians', *HTR*, 39, 1946, pp. 259–74.
67   Brown, T. S., 'The Greek Sense of Time in History as Suggested by Their Accounts of Egypt', *Historia*, 11, 1962, pp. 257–70.
68   Bruford, A., 'Recitation or Re-creation? Examples From South Uist Storytelling', *Scottish Studies*, 22, 1978, pp. 27–44.
69   Brunswig, R. S., 'Radiocarbon Dating and the Indus Civilization: Calibration and Chronology', *East and West*, n.s. 25, 1975, pp. 111–45.
70   Buck, P., 'The Value of Tradition in Polynesian Research', *JPS*, 35, 1926, pp. 181–203.
71   Búrca, S. de., 'Aspects of Transmission', *Eigse*, 15, 1973, pp. 51–65.
72   Burns, T. S., 'Theories and Facts: the Early Gothic Migrations', *HA*, 9, 1982, pp. 1–20.
73   Burton, John, *The Collection of the Qur'an*, Cambridge, 1977.
74   Burton, John H., *Life and Correspondence of David Hume*, 2 vols., Edinburgh, 1846.
75   Butler, R. N., 'The Life Review: An Interpretation of Reminiscence in the Aged', *Psychiatry*, 26, 1963, pp. 65–75.
76   Byrne, F. J., '*Senchas*: the Nature of Gaelic Historical Tradition', *Historical Studies*, 9, 1974, pp. 137–59.
77   Campbell, A., 'Saxo Grammaticus and Scandinavian Historical Tradition', *Saga-Book of the Viking Society*, 13, 1946/53, pp. 1–22.
78   Campbell, E. F., and Miller, J. M., 'William Foxwell Albright and Historical Reconstruction', *Biblical Archaeologist*, 42, 1979, pp. 37–47.
79   Canedo, L. O., 'Toribio Motolinía and His Historical Writings', *The Americas*, 29, 1972/73, pp. 277–307.
80   Carmack, Robert, *Quichean Civilization*, Berkeley, 1973.
81   Carrera Stampa, M., 'Historiadores indígenas y mestizos novohispanos, siglos XVI–XVII', *Revista Española de Antropología Americana*, 6, 1971, pp. 205–43.
82   Carrington, P., 'The Heroic Age of Phrygia in Ancient Literature and Art', *Anatolian Studies*, 27, 1977, pp. 117–26.
83   Cason, M., 'A Survey of African Materials in the Libraries and Archives of Protestant Missionary Societies in England', *HA*, 9, 1981, pp. 277–307.
84   Chadwick, Hector M. and Nora K., *The Growth of Literature*, 3 vols., Cambridge, 1932–40.
85   Chadwick, J., 'Who Were the Dorians?', *La Parola del Passato*, 166, 1976, pp. 103–17.
86   Chattopadhyaya, B. D., 'Origin of the Rajputs: The Political, Economic, and Social Processes in Early Medieval Rajasthan', *Indian Historical Review*, 3, 1976, pp. 59–82.
87   Ciklamini, M., 'Old Norse Epic and Historical Tradition', *JFI*, 8, 1971, pp. 93–100.
88   Ciklamini, M., 'Ynglinga saga: Its Function and Its Appeal', *Mediaeval Scandinavia*, 8, 1975, pp. 86–99.
89   Cizek, A. N., 'Alexander the Great as God's Champion in the South-East European Folkbooks', *Orientalia Lovaniensia Periodica*, 9, 1978, pp. 189–211.
90   Clanchy, M. T., *From Memory to the Written Record: England, 1066–1307*, London, 1979.
91   Clanchy, M. T. 'Remembering the Past and the Good Old Law', *History*, 55, 1970, pp. 165–76.
92   Clark, G. Kitson, *The Critical Historian*, New York, 1967.
93   Clark, J. T., and Terrell, J., 'Archaeology in Oceania', *ARA*, 7, 1978, pp. 293–320.
94   Cline, H. F., 'Reflections on Ethnohistory', in *Handbook of Middle American Indians*, 16 vols, Austin, 1964–76, xii, 1, pp. 3–15.
95   Cochrane, E., 'The Transition From Renaissance to Baroque: The Case of Italian Historiography', *History and Theory*, 19, 1980, pp. 21–38.
96   Codère, Helen, *The Biography of an African Society: Rwanda, 1900–1960, Based on Forty-Eight Rwandan Autobiographies*, Tervuren, 1973.
97   Coèdes, Georges, *The Indianized States of Southeast Asia*, Honolulu, 1968.
98   Cogan, M., and Tadmor, H., 'Gyges and Ashurbanipal: A Study in Literary Transmission', *Orientalia*, n.s. 46, 1977, pp. 65–85.
99   Cohen, B. J., 'Nativism and Western Myth: The Influence of Nativism on the American Self-Image', *Journal of American Studies*, 8, 1974, pp. 23–40.
100 Colston, S. A., 'The "Historia Mexicana" and Durán's *Historia*', *JSA*, 62, 1973, pp. 35–42.
101 Connell, C. W., 'Western Views of the Origin of the 'Tartars': An Example of the

Influence of Myth in the Second Half of the Thirteenth Century', *Journal of Medieval and Renaissance Studies*, 3, 1973, pp. 115–39.

102   Cordy, R. H., 'The Tahitian Migration to Hawaii, ca. A.D. 1100–1300: An Argument Against Its Occurrence', *New Zealand Archaeological Association Newsletter*, 17, 1974, pp. 65–73.

103   Cove, J. J., 'Survival or Extinction? Reflections on the Problem of Famine in Tsimshian and Kaguru Mythology', in *Extinction and Survival in Human Populations*, Laughlin, Charles D., and Brady, Ivan A. (eds), New York, 1978, pp. 231–44.

104   Crépeau, P., 'The Invading Guest: Some Aspects of Oral Transmission', *Yearbook of Symbolic Anthropology*, 1, 1978, pp. 11–29.

105   Crocombe, R. G. and M., *The Works of Ta'unga: Records of a Polynesian Traveller in the South Seas, 1833–1896*, Canberra, 1968.

106   Crone, Patricia, *Slaves on Horses: The Evolution of the Islamic Polity*, Cambridge, 1980.

107   Culley, R. C., 'Oral Tradition and Historicity', in *Studies on the Ancient Palestinian World*, Weems, J. W., and Redford, D. B. (eds), Toronto, 1972, pp. 102–16.

108   Curtin, Philip D. (ed.), *Africa Remembered*, Madison, 1967.

109   Curtin, Philip D., 'African History', in *The Past Before Us: Contemporary Historical Writing in the United States*, Kammen, Michael (ed.), Ithaca, N.Y., 1980, pp. 113–30.

110   Curtin, Philip D., *The Atlantic Slave Trade: A Census*, Madison, 1969.

111   Curtin, Philip D., 'Field Techniques for Collecting and Processing Oral Data', *JAH*, 9, 1968, pp. 367–85.

112   Darnell, R., 'Correlates of Cree Narrative Performance', in *Explorations in the Ethnography of Speaking*, Bauman, Richard, and Sherzer, Joel (eds), Cambridge, Mass., 1974, pp. 315–36.

113   Davies, Nigel, *The Aztecs: A History*, London, 1974.

114   Davies, Nigel, *Voyagers to the New World*, New York, 1979.

115   Davis, R. W., 'Review of Robert Temple, The Sirius Mystery', *IJAHS*, 10, 1977, pp. 655–67.

116   Davis, Ronald W., 'Volcanic Dust in the Atmosphere and the Interpretation of African Eclipse Traditions', *HA*, 4, 1977, pp. 31–41.

117   Daws, G., 'Kealakekua Bay Revisted: A Note on the Death of Captain Cook', *JPH*, 3, 1968, pp. 21–23.

118   Delmaire, B., 'Les origines russes d'après les travaux soviètiques récents', *Annales: Economies, Sociétés, Civilisations*, 29, 1974, pp. 151–65.

119   Deng, Francis M., *Dinka Cosmology*, London, 1980.

120   D'Olwer, L. N., and Cline, H. F., 'Sahagún and His Works', in *Handbook of Middle American Indians*, 16 vols, Austin, 1964–76, xiii, 2, pp. 186–239.

121   Dorsinsang-Smets, A., 'La place et le sens de Quetzalcoatl dans la pensée mexicaine', *Bulletin de l'Académie royale des sciences d'Outre-Mer*, 1974, pp. 114–24.

122   Dorson, Richard M., *The British Folklorists: A History*, Chicago, 1968.

123   Douglas, N., 'The Sons of Lehi and the Seed of Cain: Racial Myths in Mormon Scripture and Their Relevance to the Pacific Islands' *Journal of Religious History*, 8, 1974/75, pp. 90–104.

124   Dubois, Claude-Gilbert, *La conception de l'histoire en France au XVIe siècle (1560–1610)*, Paris, 1977.

125   Dubois, J., 'Listes épiscopales', *Catholica*, 7, 1974, pp. 829–37.

126   Dubois, J., 'Les listes épiscopales: témoins de l'organisation ecclésiastique et de la transmission des traditions', *Revue d'Histoire de l'Eglise de France*, 62, 1975, pp. 9–24.

127   Duchet, M., 'Discours ethnologique et discours historique: le texte de Lafitau', *Transactions* of the 4th International Congress on the Enlightenment, New Haven, 1975, 5 vols, New Haven, 1976, ii, pp. 607–23.

128   Dumville, D. N., 'Kingship, Genealogies, and Regnal Lists', in *Early Medieval Kingship*, Sawyer, P. H., and Wood, I. N. (eds), Leeds, 1977, pp. 72–104.

129   Duri, A. A., 'Al-Zuhri: A Study of the Beginnings of History Writing in Islam', *BSOAS*, 19, 1957, pp. 1–12.

130   Du Toit, B. M., 'Ethics, Informed Consent, and Fieldwork', *Journal of Anthropological Research*, 36, 1980, pp. 274–86.

131   Duviols, Pierre, *La lutte contre les religions autochthones dans le Pérou colonial: 'l'extirpation de l'idolatrie' entre 1532 et 1660*, Lima, 1971.

132   Duviols, Pierre, 'Los nombres quechua de Viracocha, supuesto "Dios Creador" de los evangelizadores', *Allpanchis*, 10, 1977, pp. 53–63.

133   Dvornik, Francis, *The Idea of Apostolicity in Byzantium and the Legend of the Apostle Andrew*, Cambridge, Mass., 1958.

134   Edmundson, Munro S. (ed.), *Sixteenth-Century Mexico: The Work of Sahagún*, Albuquerque, 1974.

135   Ehmke, E. G., 'Gauls and Franks in XVIth-Century French Historical Writing', *Proceedings* of the Western Society for French History, San Diego, 1979, pp. 78–87.

136   Einhard, *Vita Karoli Magni/The Life of Charlemagne*, Firchow, Evelyn S. and Zeydel, Edwin H. (trans.), Coral Gables, Fla., 1972.

137   Elert, C. C., 'Andreas Kempe (1622–1689) and the Languages Spoken in Paradise', *Historiographia Linguistica*, 5, 1978, pp. 221–26.

138   Ellis, William, *Narrative of a Tour Through Hawaii or Owhywhee*, 2 vols, London, 1828.

139   Elton, G. R., *The Practice of History*, London, 1969.

140   *Envelopes of Sound: Six Practitioners Discuss the Method, Theory, and Practice of Oral History and Oral Testimony*, Grele, Ronald J. (ed.), Chicago, 1975.

141   Escott, Paul D., *Slavery Remembered: A Record of Twentieth-Century Slave Narratives*, Chapel Hill, 1979.

142   *Ethnoarchaeology: Implications of Ethnography for Archaeology*, Kramer, Carol (ed.), New York, 1979.

143   Eusebius Pamphilii, Bishop of Caesarea, *The Ecclesiastical History*, 2 vols., Cambridge, 1959–64.

144   Eustus, T. W., 'Get it in Writing: Oral History and the Law', *OHR*, 1976, pp. 6–18.

145   Fairchild, W. D., 'Evidence of Improvised Speaking in Thucydides', *Classical Bulletin*, 51, 1975, pp. 4–8.

146   Fallot, R. D., 'The Impact on Mood of Verbal Reminiscing in Later Adulthood', *International Journal of Aging and Human Development*, 10, 1979/80, pp. 385–400.

147   Falnes, Oscar J., *National Romanticism in Norway*, New York, 1933.

148   Farmer, H., 'William of Malmesbury's Life and Works', *Journal of Ecclesiastical History*, 13, 1962, pp. 39–54.

149   Feinberg, R., 'Archaeology, Oral History, and Sequence of Population on Anuta Island', *JPS*, 85, 1976, pp. 99–101.

150   Fenton, W. N., 'The Lore of the Longhouse: Myth, Ritual, and Red Power', *Anthropological Quarterly*, 48, 1975, pp. 131–47.

151   Fenton, W. N., 'Problems in the Authentication of the League of the Iroquois', in *Neighbors and Intruders: An Ethnographical Exploration of the Indians of Hudson's River*, Ottawa, 1978, pp. 261–68.

152   Ferguson, Adam, *An Essay on the History of Civil Society* second ed., London, 1768.

153   Fernandez, J., 'The Mission of Metaphor in Expressive Culture', *Current Anthropology*, 15, 1974, pp. 119–45.

154   *The Fieldworker and the Field*, Srinivas, M. N., Shah, A. M., and Ramaswamy, E. A. (eds), New York, 1979.

155   Finney, Ben R., *et al.*, 'Hawaiian Historians and the First Pacific History Seminar', in *The Changing Pacific: Essays in Honour of H. E. Maude*, Gunson, Niel (ed.), Melbourne, 1978, pp. 308–16.

156   Fischel, Walter J., *Ibn Khaldun in Egypt: His Public Functions and His Historical Research (1382–1406)*, Berkeley, 1967.

157   Fischel, Walter J., 'Ibn Khaldun's Use of Historical Sources', *Studia Islamica*, 14, 1961, pp. 109–19.

158   Fitzgerald, Frances, *Revising America: History Textbooks in the Twentieth Century*, Boston, 1979.

159   Flaherty, D. H., 'Privacy and Confidentiality: The Responsibility of Historians', *Reviews in American History*, 8, 1980, pp. 419–29.

160   Flight, C., 'Malcolm Guthrie and the Reconstruction of Bantu Prehistory', *HA*, 7, 1980, pp. 81–118.

161   Flight, C., 'Trees and Traps: Strategies For the Classification of African Languages and their Historical Significance', *HA*, 8, 1981, pp. 43–74.

162   Fodor, A., 'The Origin of the Arabic Legends of the Pyramids', *Acta Orientalia* [Budapest], 23, 1970, pp. 335–63.

163   Fogel, Robert W. and Engerman, Stanley, L., *Time on the Cross*, 2 vols, Boston, 1974.
164   Fontenrose, Joseph, *The Delphic Oracle*, Berkeley, 1978.
165   France, P., 'The Kaunitoni Migration: Notes on the Genesis of a Fijian Tradition', *JPH*, 1, 1966, pp. 107–13.
166   Franken, H. J., 'The Problem of Identification in Biblical Archaeology', *PEQ*, 108, 1976, pp. 2–11.
167   Gabrieli, Francesco, *Arab Historians of the Crusades*, Berkeley, 1969.
168   Galbraith, V. H., *The Making of the Domesday Book*, Oxford, 1961.
169   Galbraith, V. H., *Studies in the Public Records*, London, 1948.
170   Gammage, B., 'The Rabaul Strike, 1929', *JPH*, 10, 1975, pp. 3–29.
171   Garanger, J., 'Tradition orale et préhistoire en Océanie', *Cahiers d'ORSTOM, sér. sciences humaines*, 13, 1976, pp. 147–61.
172   Gardiner, J. N., *et al.*, 'Memory for Remembered Events', *Journal of Verbal Learning and Verbal Behavior*, 16, 1977, pp. 45–54.
173   Gardiner, K. H. J., 'On Translating Paul the Deacon', *Parergon*, 21, August, 1978, pp. 43–51.
174   Gartrell, B., 'Is Ethnography Possible? A Critique of *African Odyssey*', *Journal of Anthropological Research*, 35, 1979, pp. 426–46.
175   Gates, J., 'Model Emperors of the Golden Age in Chinese Lore', *JAOS*, 56, 1936, pp. 51–76.
176   Genovese, Eugene D., *Roll, Jordan, Roll: The World the Slaves Made*, New York, 1974.
177   George, H. B., *Historical Evidence*, Oxford, 1909.
178   Geraghty, P., 'How a Myth is Born: The Story of the Kaunitoni Story', *Mana Review*, 2, 1977, pp. 25–29.
179   Gerbi, Antonello, *The Dispute of the New World. The History of a Polemic 1750–1900*, Pittsburgh, 1973.
180   Gerhardsson, Birger, *Memory and Manuscript. Oral Tradition and Written Tradition in Rabbinic Judaism and Early Christianity*, Uppsala, 1961.
181   Gibson, G. D., 'Himba Epochs', *HA*, 4, 1977, pp. 67–121.
182   Gifford, Edward W., 'Fijian Mythology, Legends and Archaeology', *University of California Publications in Semitic Philology*, 11, 1951, pp. 167–77.
183   Gifford, Edward W., *Tongan Myths and Tales*, Honolulu, 1924.
184   Gilliard, F. D., 'The Apostolicity of the Gallic Churches', *HTR*, 68, 1975, pp. 17–34.
185   Ginet, Carl, *Knowledge, Perception, and Memory*, Dordrecht, 1975.
186   Gittins, D., 'Oral History, Reliability, and Recollection', *RMSS*, pp. 82–99.
187   Gliozzi, Guiliano, *Adamo e il Nuovo Mondo*, Florence, 1977.
188   Goldkind, V., 'Anthropologists, Informants, and the Achievement of Power in Chan Kom', *Sociologus*, n.s. 20, 1970, pp. 17–41.
189   Göllner, G., 'Legenden von der skythischen und trojanischen und kaukasischen Abstammung der Türken im 15. und 16. Jährhundert', *Revue des Etudes Sud-Est Européennes*, 15, 1977, pp. 49–61.
190   Gomme, George L., *Folklore as an Historical Science*, London, 1908.
191   Goodman, L. E., 'Ibn Khaldun and Thucydides', *JAOS*, 92, 1972, pp. 250–70.
192   Goody, J., and Watt, I., 'The Consequences of Literacy', in *Literacy in Traditional Societies*, Goody, Jack (ed.), Cambridge, 1968, pp. 27–68.
193   Gossiaux, P.-P., 'La guerre des Songye Bena Tshofwe contre les Songye Beekalebwe: comparison des traditions recueillis en 1916 et 1957', *Revue Universitaire du Burundi*, 1, 1972, pp. 122–28.
194   Gottwald, Norman K., *Tribes of Yahweh*, New York, 1979.
195   Gransden, Antonia, *Historical Writing in England, c. 550 to c. 1307*, London, 1974.
196   Grant, Michael, *The Ancient Historians*, London, 1970.
197   Grant, R. M., 'Early Episcopal Succession', *Studia Patristica*, 11, 1972, pp. 179–84.
198   Graulich, M., 'The Metaphor of Day in Ancient Mexican Myth and Ritual', *Current Anthropology*, 22, 1981, pp. 45–60.
199   Gravel, P. B., '"And Sometimes All For Naught": Reflections of an Anthropologist on his Return From the Field', *Western Canadian Journal of Anthropology*, vi, 4, 1976, pp. 103–23.
200   Greenhalgh, P. A. L., 'How are the Mighty Fallen?' *Acta Classica* [Cape Town], 21, 1978, pp. 1–38.

201   Greenway, John L., *The Golden Horns. Mythic Imagination and the Nordic Past*, Athens, Ga., 1977.
202   Grele, R. J., 'A Surmisable Variety: Interdisciplinarity and Oral Testimony', *American Quarterly*, 27, 1975, pp. 275–95.
203   Grinsell, L. V., 'The Legendary History and Folklore of Stonehenge', *Folklore*, 87, 1976, pp. 5–20.
204   Grobman, N. R., 'Eighteenth-Century Scottish Philosophers on Oral Tradition', *JFI*, 10, 1973, pp. 187–95.
205   Groube, L. M., 'Tonga, Lapita Pottery, and Polynesian Origins', *JPS*, 80, 1971, pp. 278–316.
206   Gulbenkian, E. V., 'Significance of the Narrative Describing the Traditional Origins of the Armenians', *Muséon*, 86, 1973, pp. 365–76.
207   Gulløv, H. C., and Kapel, H., 'Legend, History, and Archaeology: A Study of the Art of Eskimo Narratives', *Folk*, 21/22, 1979/80, pp. 347–80.
208   Gunson, W. N., 'Tahiti's Traditional History–Without Adams?' *JPH*, 10, 1975, pp. 112–17.
209   Halkin, Léon E., *Eléments de critique historique*, Liège, 1966.
210   Hand, S. B., 'Some Words on Oral Histories', *Scholarly Publishing*, 9, 1977/78, pp. 171–85.
211   Hanson, R. P. C., *Tradition in the Early Church*, Philadelphia, 1963.
212   Harrington, D. J., 'The Reception of Walter Bauer's *Orthodoxy and Heresy in Earliest Christianity* During the Last Decade', *HTR*, 73, 1980, pp. 289–98.
213   Hartland, E. S., 'On the Evidential Value of the Historical Traditions of the Baganda and Bushongo', *Folk-Lore*, 25, 1914, pp. 428–56.
214   Hartwig, G. W., 'Oral Data and the Historical Function in East Africa', *IJAHS*, 7, 1975, pp. 468–79.
215   Hauptman, L. M., 'Mythologizing Westward Expansion: Schoolbooks and the Image of the Western Frontier Before Turner', *Western Historical Quarterly*, 8, 1977, pp. 269–82.
216   Hay, Denys, *Annalists and Historians*, New York, 1977.
217   Heath, M., 'Renaissance Scholars and the Origins of the Turks', *Bibliothèque d'Humanisme et de Renaissance*, 41, 1979, pp. 453–71.
218   Heffening, W., 'Shahid', *Encyclopaedia of Islam*, second ed., iv, pp. 261–62.
219   Henige, David, 'Akan Stool Succession Under Colonial Rule: Continuity or Change?' *JAH*, 16, 1975, pp. 285–301.
220   Henige, David, '*Bibliotheca Missionum*: A Case of Benign Neglect', *HA*, 5, 1978, pp. 337–44.
221   Henige, David, 'Carthaginians, Lost Colonists, and Other *dea ex machina*: Origin Traditions of American Racial Isolates' (forthcoming).
222   Henige, David *The Chronology of Oral Tradition*, Oxford, 1974.
223   Henige, David, '"Day Was of Sudden Turned Into Night": The Use of Eclipses in Dating Oral History', *Comparative Studies in Society and History*, 18, 1976, pp. 476–501.
224   Henige, David '"The Disease of Writing": Ganda and Nyoro Kinglists in a Newly-Literate World', *APS*, pp. 240–61.
225   Henige, David, 'Generation-Counting and Late New Kingdom Chronology', *Journal of Egyptian Archaeology*, 67, 1981, pp. 182–84.
226   Henige, David, '"In the Possession of the Author": The Problem of Source Monopoly in Oral Historiography', *International Journal of Oral History*. 1, 1980, pp. 181–94.
227   Henige, David, 'Kingship in Elmina Before 1869: A Study in "Feedback" and the Traditional Idealization of the Past', *Cahiers d'Etudes Africaines*, 14, 1974, pp. 499–520.
228   Henige, David, 'On the Contact Population of Hispaniola: History as Higher Mathematics', *Hispanic American Historical Review*, 58, 1978, pp. 217–37, 700–12.
229   Henige, David, 'The Problem of Feedback in Oral Tradition: Four Examples from the Fante Coastlands', *JAH*, 14, 1973, pp. 223–35.
230   Henige, David, 'Royal Tombs and Preternatural Ancestors: A Devil's Advocacy', *Paideuma*, 23, 1977, pp. 205–19.
231   Henige, David, 'Seniority and Succession in the Krobo Stools', *IJAHS*, 7, 1974, pp. 203–26.
232   Henige, David, 'A Snare and a Delusion (Or, Danger, Europeans at Work)', *HA*, 5, 1978, pp. 43–61.

233   Henige, David, 'Truths Yet Unborn?: Oral Tradition as A Casualty of Culture Contact'
       JAH, 23, 1982.
234   Henige, David, 'Word of Mouth: Inchoate Thoughts on the Creation and Use of Oral
       Historical Materials', in *FOAS*, pp. 103–15.
235   Hewsen, R. H., 'The *Primary History of Armenia*: An Examination of the Validity of an
       Immemorially Transmitted Historical Tradition', *HA*, 2, 1975, pp. 91–100.
236   Hicks, G. L., 'Informant Anonymity and Scientific Accuracy: The Problem of
       Pseudonyms', *Human Organization*, 36, 1977, pp. 214–20.
237   Hindley, C., 'Problems of Interviewing in Obtaining Retrospective Information', *RMSS*.
       pp. 100–14.
238   Hodgen, Margaret, *Early Anthropology in the Sixteenth and Seventeenth Centuries*, Philadelphia,
       1964.
239   Hoopes, James, *Oral History. An Introduction for Students*, Chapel Hill, 1979.
240   Hoover, J. J., '*Mythe et remous historique*: A Lunda Response to De Heusch', *HA*, 5, 1978,
       pp. 63–80.
241   Hopkins, A. G., 'Imperial Business in Africa. I. Sources', *JAH*, 17, 1976, pp. 29–48.
242   Horton, R., 'African Traditional Thought and Western Science', *Africa*, 37, 1967,
       pp. 50–71, 155–87.
243   Howard, A., 'Polynesian Origins and Migrations: A Review of Two Centuries of
       Speculation and Theory', *Polynesian Culture History*, Highland, Genevieve (ed.),
       Honolulu, 1967, pp. 45–101.
244   Howe, K. R., 'The Maori Response to Christianity in Thames-Waikato Area,
       1833–1840', *NZJH*, 7, 1973, pp. 28–46.
245   Hrdličková, K. V., 'Japanese Professional Storytellers', in *Folklore Genres*, Ben-Amos,
       Daniel (ed.), Austin, 1976, pp. 171–90.
246   Huddleston, Lee E., *Origins of the American Indians, European Concepts, 1492–1729*,
       Austin, 1967.
247   Hughes, Kathleen, *Early Christian Ireland: Introduction to the Sources*, London, 1972.
248   Hunter, C. E., 'The Delaware Nativist Revival of the Mid-Eighteenth Century',
       Ethnohistory, 18, 1971, pp. 39–49.
249   Hunter, Virginia, J., *Thucydides, the Artful Reporter*, Toronto, 1973.
250   Ibn Khaldun, *The Muqaddimah*, Rosenthal, Franz (trans.). 3 vols, London, 1967.
251   Irvine, Cecelia, *The Church of Christ in Zaire: A Handbook of Protestant Churches, Missions, and
       Communities, 1878–1978*, Indianapolis, 1978.
252   Irvine, J. T., 'When in Genealogy History? Wolof Genealogies in Comparative
       Perspective', *American Ethnologist*, 5, 1978, pp. 651–75.
253   Irwin, Paul, *Liptako Speaks. History From Oral Tradition in Africa*, Princeton, 1981.
254   *Israelite and Judaean History*, Hayes, John H., and Miller, J. Maxwell (eds), London, 1977.
255   Iyasere, S. O., 'African Oral Tradition: Criticism as a Performance' in *Myth and History*,
       Jones, Eldred D. (ed.), London, 1980, pp. 169–74 [*African Literature Today*, 11].
256   Jackson, M. D., 'Literacy, Communications, and Social Change: A Study of the
       Meaning and Effect of Literacy in Early Nineteenth-Century Maori Society', in
       Conflict and Compromise: Essays on the Maori Since Colonisation, Kawharu, I. H. (ed.),
       Wellington, 1977, pp. 27–54.
257   Jacob, C., 'The Greek Traveler's Area of Knowledge: Myth and Other Discourse in
       Pausanias' *Description of Greece*', *Rethinking History: Time, Myth, and Writing*, Logan,
       Mary-Rose, and John F., (eds), New Haven, 1980, pp. 65–85.
258   Japhet, S., 'Conquest and Settlement in Chronicles', *Journal of Biblical Literature*, 98, 1979,
       pp. 205–18.
259   *The Jesuit Relations and Allied Documents*, Thwaites, Reuben G. (ed.), 73 vols, Cleveland,
       1896–1901.
260   Johannesson, Kurt, *Saxo Grammaticus. Komposition och världsbild i Gesta Danorum*, Stockholm,
       1978.
261   Johansen, J. Prytz, *Studies in Maori Myths and Rites*, Copenhagen, 1958.
262   Johnsen, A. O., 'The Lauritz Weibull Discussion: A Norwegian Contribution',
       Mediaeval Scandinavia, 10, 1977, pp. 179–87.
263   Johnson, Allen, *The Historian and Historical Evidence*, New York, 1926.
264   Johnson, D., 'Epic and History in Early China: The Matter of Wu Tzu-hsü', *Journal of
       Asian Studies*, 40, 1981, pp. 255–71.

265   Johnson, D., 'The Wu Tzu-hsü Cults and Oral Sources of the Wu Tzu-hsü *Pien-wen*', *Harvard Journal of Asiatic Studies*, 40, 1980, pp. 465–505.

266   Johnson, J. W., 'The Scythian: His Rise and Fall', *Journal of the History of Ideas*, 20, 1959, pp. 250–57.

267   Jones, D. H., 'Problems of African Chronology', *JAH*, 11, 1970, pp. 161–76.

268   Kalin, E. R., 'Early Traditions About Mark's Gospel: Canonical Status Emerges, the Story Grows', *Currents in Theology and Mission*, 2, 1975, pp. 332–41.

269   Kashoki, M. E., 'The Foreign Researcher: Friend or Foe?' *HA*, 5, 1978, pp. 275–99.

270   Keck, L. E., 'Oral Traditional Literature and the Gospels: The Seminar', in *The Relationships Among the Gospels*, Walker, William O., jr. (ed.), San Antonio, 1978, pp. 103–22.

271   Kehoe, A. B., 'The Sacred Heart: A Case for Stimulus Diffusion', *American Ethnologist*, 6, 1979, pp. 763–71.

272   Kelber, W. H., 'Mark and Oral Tradition', *Semeia*, 16, 1979, pp. 7–55.

273   Kelleher, J. V., 'Early Irish History and Pseudo-History', *Studia Hibernica*, 3, 1963, pp. 113–37.

274   Kemler, H., 'Hegesipps römische Bischofsliste', *Vigiliae Christianae*, 25, 1971, pp. 182–96.

275   Kendall, D. G., 'The Genealogy of Genealogy: Branching Processes Before (and After) 1873', *Bulletin of the London Mathematical Society*, 7, 1975, pp. 225–53.

276   Khalidi, Tarif, *Islamic Historiography: The Histories of Masʿudi*, Albany, 1975.

277   Khan, M. S., 'The Eye-Witness Reporters of Miskawaih's Contemporary History', *Islamic Culture*, 38, 1964, pp. 295–313.

278   Khan, M. S., 'The Personal Evidence in Miskawaih's Contemporary History', *Islamic Quarterly*, 11, 1967, pp. 50–63.

279   Khoury, R. G., 'Quelques réflexions sur les citations de la Bible dans les premières générations Islamiques du premier et du deuxième siècles de l'Hegire', *d'études orientales* [Damascus], 29, 1977, pp. 269–78.

280   Kirch, P. V., 'Archaeology and the Evolution of Polynesian Culture', *Archaeology*, 32 5, Sept.-Oct. 1979, pp. 44–52.

281   Klaiber, J. L., 'The Posthumous Christianization of the Inca Empire in Colonial Peru', *Journal of the History of Ideas*, 37, 1976, pp. 507–20.

282   Klauser, T., 'Die Anfänger der römischen Bischofliste', in *Gesammelte Arbeiten zur Liturgiegeschichte, Kirchengeschichte, und christlichen Archälogie*, Münster, 1974, pp. 121–38.

283   Knott, Eleanor and Gerard Murphy, *Early Irish Literature*, New York, 1966.

284   Koestler, Arthur, *The Thirteenth Tribe*, London, 1977.

285   Kötting, B., 'Zur Frage der "Successio Apostolica" in frühkirchlicher Sicht', *Catholica*, 27, 1973, pp. 234–47.

286   Labrie-Bouthillier, V., 'Les expériences sur la transmission orale: d'un modèle individuel à un modèle collectif', *Fabula*, 18, 1977, pp. 1–17.

287   Lafaye, Jacques, *Quetzalcoatl and Guadalupe: The Formation of the Mexican National Consciousness, 1521–1815*, Chicago, 1976.

288   Lal, B. B., 'The Indo-Aryan Hypothesis Vis-à-Vis Indian Archaeology', *Journal of Central Asia*, i, 1, July, 1978, pp. 21–41.

289   Lang, A., 'The Great Gladstone Myth', in Lang, Andrew, *In the Wrong Paradise and Other Stories*, London, 1886, pp. 283–99.

290   Langlois, Charles V., and Seignobos, Charles, *Introduction aux études historiques*, Paris, 1898.

291   Law, R., 'Early Yoruba Historiography', *HA*, 3, 1976, pp. 69–89.

292   Lawal, B., 'Dating Problems at Igbo-Ukwu', *JAH*, 14, 1973, pp. 1–8.

293   Leiman, Sid Z., *The Canonization of Hebrew Scripture: The Talmudic and Midrashic Evidence*, Hamden, Conn., 1976.

294   Lichtman, Allan J., and French, Valerie, *Historians and the Living Past: Theory and Practice of Historical Study*, Arlington Hgts., Ill, 1978.

295   Lieury, Alain, *La mémoire, résultats et théories*, Brussels, 1975.

296   Little, K., 'Explanation and Individual Lives: A Reconsideration of Life Writing in Anthropology', *Dialectical Anthropology*, 5, 1980, pp. 215–26.

297   Lloyd, Alan B., Herodotus, Book II, Leiden, 1975.

298   Loftus, Elizabeth F., *Eyewitness Testimony*, Cambridge, Mass., 1979.
299   Lord, A. B., 'The Gospels as Oral Traditional Literature', in *The Relationships Among the Gospels*, Walker, William O., jr. (ed.), San Antonio, 1978, pp. 33–91.
300   Lord, A. B., 'Homer, the Trojan War, and History', *JFI*, 8, 1971, pp. 85–92.
301   Lowie, Robert H., 'Oral Tradition and History', *American Anthropologist*, 17, 1915, pp. 597–99.
302   Lowie, Robert H., 'Oral Tradition and History', *JAF*, 30, 1917, pp. 161–67.
303   Luyster, R., 'Myth and History in the Book of Exodus', *Religion*, 8, 1978, pp. 155–70.
304   Lyon, P. J., '"Early Formative Period of Coastal Ecuador": Where is the Evidence?' *Nawpa Pacha*, 10/12, 1972/74, pp. 33–48.
305   MacAirt, S., *'Filidecht* and *Coimnge'*, *Eriu*, 18, 1958, pp. 139–52.
306   Maccarrone, Michele, *Apostolicità, episcopato e primato di Pietro. Richerche e testimonianze dal II al V secolo*, Rome, 1976.
307   McDonald, W. C., 'Maximilian I of Habsburg and the Veneration of Hercules: On the Revival of Myth and the German Renaissance', *Journal of Medieval and Renaissance Studies*, 6, 1976, pp. 139–54.
308   MacGaffey, W., 'African History, Anthropology, and the Rationality of Natives', *HA*, 5, 1978, pp. 101–20.
309   MacGaffey, W., 'Oral Tradition in Central Africa', *IJAHS*, 8, 1975, pp. 417–26.
310   McGregor, D. E., 'New Guinea Myths and Scriptural Similarities', *Missiology*, 2, 1974, pp. 33–46.
311   McKay, J., 'The Coalescence of History and Archaeology', *Historical Archaeology*, 10, 1976, pp. 93–98.
312   Mackenzie, George, *A Defense of the Antiquity of the Royal Line of Scotland*, London, 1685.
313   Mahdi, Muhsin, *Ibn Khaldun's Philosophy of History*, London, 1957.
314   *Marginal Natives: Anthropologists at Work*, Freilich, Morris (ed.), New York, 1970.
315   Margolis, J., 'Remembering', *Mind*, 86, 1977, pp. 186–205.
316   Marienstras, Elise, *Les mythes fondateurs de la nation amérique*, Paris, 1976.
317   Marin, Elma, *Abu Ja'far b. Jarir al-Tabari's The Reign of al-Mu'tasim*, New Haven, 1951.
318   Marshall, I. H., 'Orthodoxy and Heresy in Earlier Christianity', *Themelios*, 2, 1976, pp. 5–14.
319   Martínez Marín, C., 'Historiograffía de la migración Méxica', *Estudios de Cultura Nahuatl*, 12, 1976, pp. 121–33.
320   Maskell, David, *The Historical Epic in France, 1500–1700*, New York, 1974.
321   al-Mas'udi, *Les prairies d'or*, 2 vols, Paris, 1962–65.
322   Mendenhall, G., 'The Hebrew Conquest of Palestine', *Biblical Archaeologist*, 25, 1962, pp. 66–87.
323   Mercer, P. M., 'Oral Tradition in the Pacific: Problems of Interpretation', *JPH*, 14, 1979, pp. 130–53.
324   Mercer, P. M., 'Tapping the Slave Narrative Collection for the Responses of Black South Carolinans to Emancipation and Reconstruction', *Australian Journal of Politics and History*, 25, 1979, pp. 358–74.
325   Metzger, B. M., 'Names for the Nameless in the New Testament: A Study in the Growth of Christian Tradition', in *Kyriakon. Festschrift Johannes Quasten*, Granfield, P., and Jungmann, J. A. (eds), 2 vols, Munich, 1970, i, pp. 79–99.
326   Meyer, E., and Olivera de Bonfil, A., 'Oral History in Mexico', *Journal of Library History*, 7, 1972, pp. 360–65.
327   Miller, J. M., 'Archaeology and the Israelite Conquest of Canaan: Some Methodological Observations', *PEQ*, 109, 1977, pp. 87–93.
328   Miller, J. C., 'The Dynamics of Oral Tradition in Africa', in *FOAS*, pp. 75–102.
329   Miller, J. C., 'The Imbangala and the Chronology of Early Central African History', *JAH*, 13, 1972, pp. 549–74.
330   Miller, J. C., 'Kings, Lists, and History in Kasanje', *HA*, 6, 1979, pp. 51–96.
331   Miller, J. C., 'Listening for the African Past', in *APS*, pp. 1–59.
332   Mills, G. B. and E. S., *'Roots* and the New "Faction": A Legitimate Tool for Clio?' *Virginia Magazine of History and Biography*, 89, 1981, pp. 3–26.
333   Mintz, S. W., 'The Anthropology Interview and Life History', *OHR*, 1979, pp. 18–26.
334   Momigliano, A., 'Tradition and the Classical Historian', *History and Theory*, 11, 1972, pp. 279–93.

335   Monberg, T., 'Informants Fire Back: A Micro-Study in Anthropological Methods', *JPS*, 84, 1975, pp. 218–24.
336   Mörner, M., 'A Reappraisal of the Sources of Inca History: The Works of Ake Wedin', *The Americas*, 25, 1968/69, pp. 174–90.
337   Morrison, K. M., 'Towards a History of Intimate Encounters: Algonkian Folklore, Jesuit Missionaries, and Kikakwe, The Cannibal Giant', *American Indian Culture and Research Journal*, 3/4, 1979, pp. 51–80.
338   Mudenge, S. I. G., 'Eighteenth-Century Portuguese Settlements on the Zambezi and the Dating of the Rhodesian Ruins: Some Reflections on the Problems of Reference Dating', *IJAHS*, 10, 1977, pp. 384–93.
339   Munz, P., 'The Purity of the Historical Method: Some Skeptical Reflections on the Current Enthusiasm for the History of Non-European Societies', *NZJH*, 5, 1971, pp. 1–17.
340   Nash, J., 'Nationalism and Fieldwork', *ARA*, 4, 1975, pp. 225–45.
341   Nelson, William, *Fact or Fiction: The Dilemma of the Renaissance Storyteller*, Cambridge, Mass., 1975.
342   Neuenschwander, J. A., 'Remembrance of Things Past: Oral Historians and Long-Term Memory', *OHR*, 1978, pp. 45–53.
343   Neville, J. W., 'Herodotus on the Trojan War', *Greece and Rome*, second ser. 24, 1977, pp. 3–12.
344   Newcomb, W. W., 'The Walam Olum of the Delaware Indians in Perspective', *Texas Journal of Science*, 7, 1955, pp. 57–63.
345   Newton, Robert R., *Medieval Chronicles and the Rotation of the Earth*, Baltimore, 1972.
346   Nieuwenhuysen, J. W. van., 'Eclipses as Omens of Death', in *Explorations in the Anthropology of Religion*, van Beek, W. E. H., and Scherer, J. H. (eds), Hague, 1975, pp. 112–20.
347   O Coileáin, S., 'Oral or Literary: Some Strands of the Argument', *Studia Hibernica*, 17/18, 1977/78, pp. 7–35.
348   Ó Cuív, B., 'Literary Creation and Irish Historical Tradition', *Proceedings of the British Academy*, 49, 1963, pp. 233–62.
349   O'Farrell, P., 'Oral History: Facts and Fiction', *Quadrant*, 23, Nov. 1979, pp. 4–8.
350   O'Gorman, E., 'El resgate de Motolinía', *Revista de Indias*, 37, 1977, pp. 375–424.
351   Opler, M. K., 'The Southern Ute of Colorado', in *Seven American Indian Tribes*, Linton, Robert (ed.), New York, 1940, pp. 119–206.
352   O'Rahilly, Thomas F., *Early Irish History and Mythology*, Dublin, 1946.
353   Orbell, M., 'The Religious Significance of Maori Migration Traditions', *JPS*, 84, 1975, pp. 341–47.
354   Ossio, J. M., 'Myth and History: the Seventeenth-Century Chronicle of Guaman Poma de Ayala', in *Text and Context: The Social Anthropology of Tradition*, Jain, Rajendra K. (ed.), Philadelphia, 1977, pp. 51–93.
355   Otto of Freising, *The Two Cities. A Chronicle of Universal History to the Year A.D. 1146*, Mierow, Charles C. (trans.), New York, 1928.
356   Owens, J., 'Religious Disputation in Whangaroa, 1823–27', *JPS*, 79, 1970, pp. 288–304.
357   Padden, R. C., 'On Diffusion and Historicity', *AHR*, 78, 1973, pp. 987–1004.
358   Page, M. E., 'Malawians and the Great War: Oral History in Reconstructing Africa's Recent Past', *OHR*, 1980, pp. 49–61.
359   Park, C. C., 'The Mother of the Muses: In Praise of Memory', *American Scholar*, 50, 1980/81, pp. 55–71.
360   Park Seong-rae, 'Portents in Korean History', *Journal of Social Sciences and Humanities* [Seoul], 47, June 1978, pp. 31–92.
361   Partner, Nancy, 'Henry of Huntingdon: Clerical Celibacy and the Writing of History', *Church History*, 42, 1973, pp. 467–75.
362   Partner, Nancy, *Serious Entertainments. The Writing of History in Twelfth-Century England*, Chicago, 1977.
363   Passin, H., 'Tarahumara Prevarication: A Problem in Field Method', *American Anthropologist*, 44, 1942, pp. 235–47.
364   Pease, Franklin, 'The Andean Creator God', *Numen*, 17, 1970, pp. 161–75.
365   Pease, Franklin, 'Etnohistoria andina: un estado de la cuestión', *Historia y Cultura* [Lima], 10, 1976/77, pp. 207–28.

366   Peires, J., 'The Lovedale Press: Literature for the Bantu Revisited', *HA*, 6, 1979, pp. 155–75.

367   Pender-Cudlip, P., 'Encyclopedic Informants and Early Interlacustrine History', *IJAHS*, 6, 1973, pp. 198–210.

368   Pentikäinen, J., 'Oral Transmission of Knowledge', in *Folklore in the Modern World*, Dorson, Richard M. (ed.), Hague, 1978, pp. 237–52.

369   Percival, J., 'Thucydides and the Uses of History', *Greece and Rome*, second ser. 18, 1971, pp. 199–212.

370   Peschel, E. R., 'Structural Parallelisms in Two Flood Myths: Noah and the Maori', *Folklore*, 82, 1971, pp. 116–23.

371   Petersen, Erling L., *ʿAli and Muʿawiya in Early Arabic Tradition*, Copenhagen, 1964.

372   Peterson, Harold, *The Man Who Invented Baseball*, New York, 1973.

373   Pinot, Virgile, *La Chine et la formation de l'esprit philosophique en France (1640–1740)*, Paris, 1932.

374   Popkin, R. H., 'The Pre-Adamite Theory in the Renaissance', in *Philosophy and Humanism*, Mahoney, Edward P. (ed.), New York, 1976, pp. 50–69.

375   Poucet, J., 'Fabius Pictor et Denys d'Halicarnasse: les enfances de Romulus et de Remus', *Historia*, 25, 1976, pp. 201–16.

376   Price, R., 'Kwasimukamba's Gambit', *Bijdragen tot de Taal-, Land-, en Volkenkunde*, 135, 1979, pp. 151–69.

377   Prins, G., 'Grist for the Mill: On Researching the History of Bulozi', *HA*, 5, 1978, pp. 311–25.

378   Rabinow, Paul, *Reflections on Fieldwork in Morocco*, Berkeley, 1977.

379   Raglan, FitzRoy Somerset, Baron, *The Hero*, London, 1949.

380   Ram, K. V., 'Survey of Canadian Protestant Missionary Archives Relating to Africa', *HA*, 7, 1980, pp. 359–68.

381   Ramsey, J., 'The Bible in Western Indian Mythology', *JAF*, 90, 1977, pp. 442–54.

382   Ranum, Orest, *Artisans of Glory: Writers and Historical Thought in Seventeenth-Century France*, Chapel Hill, 1980.

383   Raphäel, F., 'Le travail de la mémoire et les limites de l'histoire orale', *Annales: Economies, Sociétés, Civilisations*, 35, 1980, pp. 127–45.

384   Rapport, L., 'How Valid are the Federal Writers' Project Life Stories? An Iconoclast Among True Believers', *OHR*, 1979, pp. 6–17.

385   Ras, J. J., *Hikajat Bandjar: A Study in Malay Historiography*, Hague, 1968.

386   Rawlings, Hunter, *The Structure of Thucydides' History*, Princeton, 1981.

387   Ray, R. D., 'Medieval Historiography Through the Twelfth Century: Problems and Progress of Research', *Viator*, 5, 1974, pp. 33–59.

388   Rearick, Charles, *Beyond the Enlightenment: Historians and Folklore in Nineteenth-Century France*, Bloomington, 1974.

389   Renier, G. J., *History: Its Purpose and Method*, London, 1950.

390   Rioux, J.-P., 'L'histoire orale en France: orientation bibliographique', *Bulletin de l'Institut d'Histoire du Temps du Présent*, 1, 1980, pp. 27–48.

391   Rivers, W. H. R., 'History and Ethnology', *History*, 5, 1920/21, pp. 65–80.

392   Robinson, J. A., 'Personal Narratives Reconsidered', *JAF*, 94, 1981, pp. 58–85.

393   Robson, J., 'Hadith', *Encyclopaedia of Islam*, rev. ed. iii, pp. 25–28.

394   Robson, J., 'Ibn Ishaq's Use of the Isnad', *BJRUL*, 38, 1955/56, pp. 449–65.

395   Robson, J., 'Tradition: Investigation and Classification', *Muslim World*, 41, 1951, pp. 98–112.

396   Robson, J., 'Tradition: The Second Foundation of Islam', *Muslim World*, 41, 1951, pp. 22–33.

397   Romero Galván, J. R., 'Las fuentes de la diferentes historias originales del Chimalpahin', *JSA*, 64, 1977, pp. 51–56.

398   Romney, J., 'Legal Considerations in Oral History', *OHR*, 1973, pp. 66–76.

399   Romney, J., 'Oral History, Law, and Libraries', *Drexel Library Quarterly*, 15, Oct. 1979, pp. 39–49.

400   Rosenthal, Franz, *History of Muslim Historiography*, Leiden, 1952.

401   Rosenthal, Franz, *The Technique and Approach of Muslim Scholarship*, Rome, 1947.

402   Rowe, J. H., 'Religión e historia en la obra de Bernabé Cobo', *Antropología Andina*, 3, 1979, pp. 31–39.

403   Runciman, S., 'Teucri and Turci', in *Medieval and Near Eastern Studies in Honor of Aziz Suryal Atiya*, Hanna, S. A. (ed.), Leiden, 1972, pp. 344–48.
404   Ruysschaert, J., and Capitani, O., 'Apostolicità, episcopato e primato di Pietro dal II al V secolo', *Rivista di Storia della Chiesa in Italia*, 31, 1977, pp. 485–95.
405   Sabbah, Guy, *La méthode d'Ammien Marcellin*, Paris, 1978.
406   Sahlins, M., 'The Apotheosis of Captain Cook', *Kroeber Anthropological Society Papers*, 49/50, 1976/77, pp. 1–31.
407   Salamone, F. A., 'The Methodological Significance of the Lying Informant', *AQ*, 50, 1977, pp. 117–24.
408   Sankalia, H. D., 'Archaeology and Tradition', in Sankalia, H. D., *Aspects of Indian History and Archaeology*, Delhi, 1977, pp. 269–81.
409   Sawyer, J. F. A., 'Why is a Solar Eclipse Mentioned in the Passion Narrative?' *Journal of Theological Studies*, 23, 1972, pp. 124–28.
410   Saxo Grammaticus, *The First Nine Books of the Danish History of Saxo Grammaticus*, Elton, Oliver (ed.), London, 1893.
411   Saxo Grammaticus, *The History of the Danes*, Fisher, Peter (trans.) and Davidson, Hilda E. (ed.), 2 vols, London, 1979–80.
412   Schacht, Joseph *Introduction to Islamic Law*, Oxford, 1964.
413   Schacht, Joseph, 'A Revaluation of Islamic Traditions', *Journal of the Royal Asiatic Society*, 1949, pp. 143–54.
414   Scheub, Harold, *The Xhosa Ntsomi*, Oxford, 1975.
415   Schmidt, Peter R., *Historical Archaeology: A Structural Approach in an African Culture*, Westport, Conn., 1978.
416   Schmidt, Peter R., 'A New Look at Interpretations of the Early Iron Age in East Africa', *HA*, 2, 1975, pp. 127–36.
417   Schonfield, D., and Robertson, B.-A., 'Memory Storage and Aging', *Canadian Journal of Psychology*, 20, 1966, pp. 228–36.
418   Schwerin, K. H., 'The Future of Ethnohistory', *Ethnohistory*, 23, 1976, pp. 323–41.
419   Seymour, Harold, *Baseball: The Early Years*, New York, 1960.
420   Shafer, Robert J., *A Guide to Historical Method*, Homewood, Ill., 1974.
421   Shah, A. M., and Shroff, R. G., 'The Vahivanca Barots of Gujarat: A Caste of Genealogists and Mythographers', in *Traditional India: Structure and Change*, Singer, Milton (ed.), Philadelphia, 1959, pp. 40–70.
422   Sharp, Andrew, *Ancient Voyagers of the Pacific*, Wellington, 1956.
423   Sidersky, D., *Les origines des légendes musulmanes dans le Coran*, Paris, 1933.
424   Simmons, David R., *The Great New Zealand Myth. A Study of the Discovery and Origin Traditions of the Maori*, Wellington, 1976.
425   Simmons, David R., and Biggs, Bruce G., 'The Sources of the Lore of the Whare-wananga', *JPS*, 79, 1970, pp. 22–42.
426   Simonsen, J., 'A Contribution to an Analysis of the Traditions Contained in the *Futuh al-Buldan*', *Acta Orientalia* [Copenhagen], 40, 1979, pp. 73–85.
427   Skeldon, R., 'Volcanic Ash, Hailstorm, and Crops: Oral History from the Eastern Highlands', *JPS*, 86, 1977, pp. 403–10.
428   Skøvgaard-Petersen, I., 'Saxo, Historian of the Patria', *MS*, 2, 1969, pp. 54–77.
429   Slotkin, Richard, *Regeneration Through Violence*, Middletown, Conn., 1973.
430   Smithyman, K., 'Making History: John White and S. Percy Smith at Work', *JPS*, 88, 1979, pp. 375–413.
431   Snorri Sturluson, *Heimskringla. History of the Kings of Norway*, Hollander, Lee M. (ed.), Austin, 1964.
432   Soapes, T. F., 'The Federal Writers' Project Slave Interviews: Useful Data or Misleading Source?' *OHR*, 1977, pp. 33–39.
433   Sosne, E., 'Of Biases and Queens: The Shi Past Through an Androgynous Looking-Glass', *HA*, 6, 1979, pp. 225–52.
434   Spear, T., 'Oral Traditions: Whose History?' *HA*, 8, 1981, pp. 165–81.
435   Spores, R., 'New World Ethnohistory and Archaeology, 1970–1980', *ARA*, 9, 1980, pp. 575–603.
436   Spradley, James P., *The Ethnographic Interview*, New York, 1979.
437   Starr, L. M., 'Oral History: Problems and Prospects', *Advances in Librarianship*, 2, 1971, pp. 275–304.

438   Steiner, George, *After Babel. Aspects of Language and Translation*, London, 1974.
439   Stephenson, F. R., 'Astronomical Verification and Dating of Old Testament Passages
       Referring to Solar Eclipses', *PEQ*, 1975, pp. 107–20.
440   Stillingfleet, Edward, *Origines Britanniae*, London, 1685.
441   Storm-Clark, C., 'The Miners, 1870–1920: A Test Case for Oral History', *Victorian
       Studies*, 15, 1971/72, pp. 49–74.
442   Strobel, M., 'Doing Oral History as an Outsider', *Frontiers*, 2, 1977, pp. 68–72.
443   Tabari, Abu Jaᶜfar Muhammad b. Jarir al-, *Chronique de Abou-Djafar Mohammed ben Djarir
       ben Yezid Tabari*, 4 vols, Paris, 1958.
444   Talbert, C. H., 'Oral and Independent or Literary and Interdependent? A Response to
       Albert B. Lord', in *The Relationships Among the Gospels*, Walker, William O., jr. (ed.),
       San Antonio, 1978, pp. 93–102.
445   Talland, G. A., 'Age and the Span of Immediate Recall', in *Human Aging and Behavior*,
       Talland, George A. (ed.), New York, 1968, pp. 93–129.
446   Temple, Robert, *The Sirius Mystery*, New York, 1976.
447   Terwiel, B. J., 'The Origin of the T'ai Peoples Reconsidered', *Oriens Extremus*, 25, 1978,
       pp. 239–57.
448   Thapar, R., 'Origin Myths and Early Indian Historical Tradition', in *History and Society*,
       Chattopadhyaya, Debiprasad (ed.), Calcutta, 1978, pp. 271–94.
449   Thomas, C. G., 'A Dorian Invasion? The Early Literary Evidence', *Studi Micenei ed
       Egeo-Anatolici*, 19, 1978, pp. 77–87.
450   Thomas, L. L., *et al*., 'Asdiwal Crumbles: A Critique of Lévi-Straussian Myth Analysis',
       American Ethnologist, 3, 1976, pp. 147–73.
451   Thompson, Paul, 'The New Oral History in France', *Oral History*, 8, 1, Spring 1980,
       pp. 14–20.
452   Thompson, Paul, 'Problems of Method in Oral History', *Oral History*, 4, 1973, pp. 1–55.
453   Thompson, Paul, *The Voice of the Past*, London, 1978.
454   Thomson, Basil, *The Fijians*, London, 1908.
455   Thomson, D. S., 'Gaelic Learned Orders and Literati in Medieval Scotland', *Scottish
       Studies*, 12, 1968, pp. 57–78.
456   Tonkin, E., 'The Boundaries of History in Oral Performance', *HA*, 9, 1982.
457   Tosh, John, *Clan Leaders and Colonial Chiefs in Lango*, Oxford, 1978.
458   Toumanoff, Cyril, *Studies in Christian Caucasian History*, Washington, 1963.
459   Trevor-Roper, H., 'The Rise of Christian Europe', *The Listener*, 70, 1963, pp. 871–75,
       915–19, 975–79, 1019–23, 1061–65.
460   Trigger, B. F., 'Archaeology and the Image of the American Indian', *American Antiquity*,
       45, 1980, pp. 662–76.
461   Tuchman, B., 'Distinguishing the Significant from the Insignificant', *Radcliffe Quarterly*,
       56, Oct. 1972, pp. 9–10.
462   Turville-Petre, J., 'The Genealogist and History: Ari to Snorri', *Saga-Book of the Viking
       Society*, 20, 1978/79, pp. 1–23.
463   Twaddle, M., 'On Ganda Historiography', *HA*, 1, 1974, pp. 77–91.
464   Twaddle, M., 'Towards an Early History of the East African Interior', *HA*, 2, 1975,
       pp. 147–84.
465   Urbanowicz, C. F., 'Motives and Methods: Missionaries in Tonga in the Early 19th
       Century', *JPS*, 86, 1977, pp. 245–63.
466   Utley, F. L., 'The Migration of Folktales: Four Channels to the Americas', *Current
       Anthropology*, 15, 1974, pp. 5–27.
467   Uzoigwe, G. N., 'Recording the Oral History of Africa: Reflections from Field
       Experience in Bunyoro', *African Studies Review*, 16, 1973, pp. 183–201.
468   Van Kley, E. J., 'Europe's Discovery of China and the Writing of World History', *AHR*,
       76, 1971, pp. 358–85.
469   Van Noten, Francis L., *Les tombes de roi Cyirima Rujugira et de la reine Nyirayuhi Kangojera*,
       Tervuren, 1972.
470   Vansina, Jan, 'Bantu in the Crystal Ball', *HA*, 6, 1979, pp. 287–333; 7, 1980,
       pp. 293–325.
471   Vansina, Jan, 'Kuba Chronology Revisited', *Paideuma*, 21, 1975, pp. 134–50.
472   Vansina, Jan, *Le légende du passé. Traditions orales du Burundi*, Tervuren, 1972.
473   Vansina, Jan, 'Memory and Oral Tradition', in *APS*, pp. 262–79.

474   Vansina, Jan, *Oral Tradition*, Chicago, 1965.
475   Vásquez, G., 'El Popol Vuh y el Génesis: estudio comparativo', *Mysterium*, 30, 1971, pp. 3–26.
476   Vaughan, Richard, *Matthew Paris*, Cambridge, 1958.
477   Verdin, H., 'Hérodote historien? quelques interprétations récentes', *L'Antiquité Classique*, 44, 1975, pp. 668–85.
478   Vigneras, L. A., 'Saint Thomas, Apostle of America', *Hispanic American Historical Review*, 57, 1977, pp. 82–90.
479   Vitaliano, Dorothy B., *Legends of the Earth: Their Geological Origins*, Bloomington, 1973.
480   Waddell, J., 'The Invasion Hypothesis in Irish Prehistory', *Antiquity*, 52, 1978, pp. 121–28.
481   *Walam Olum or Red Score. The Migration Legend of the Lenni Lenape or Delaware Indians*, Voegelin, C. F., *et al.* (eds), Indianapolis, 1954.
482   Wallace, A. F. C., 'New Religions Among the Delaware Indians, 1600–1900', *Southwestern Journal of Anthropology*, 12, 1956, pp. 1–21.
483   Wallace, A. F. C., and Reyburn, W. D., 'Crossing the Ice: A Migration Legend of the Tuscarora Indians', *International Journal of American Linguistics*, 17, 1951, pp. 42–47.
484   Wauchope, Robert, *Lost Tribes and Sunken Continents*, Chicago, 1962.
485   Wax, Rosalie, *Doing Fieldwork*, Chicago, 1971.
486   Webster, J. B., 'Research Methods in Teso', *East African Journal*, 7, Feb. 1970, pp. 30–38.
487   Welbourn, Michael, 'The Transmission of Knowledge', *Philosophical Quarterly*, 29, 1979, pp. 1–9.
488   Weslager, C. A., *The Delaware Indians: A History*, New Brunswick, N.J., 1972.
489   Whitemen, D. L., 'The Christian Mission and Culture Change in New Guinea', *Missiology*, 2, 1974, pp. 17–32.
490   Wilken, Robert L., *The Myth of Christian Beginnings: History's Impact on Belief*, Garden City, N.Y., 1971.
491   Wilkie, James W., *Elitelore*, Los Angeles, 1973.
492   Wilks, I., 'The Transmission of Islamic Learning in the Western Sudan', in *Literacy in Traditional Societies*, Goody, Jack (ed.), Cambridge, 1969, pp. 161–97.
493   William of Malmesbury, *De gestis pontificium Anglorum*, Hamilton, N.E.S.A. (ed.), London, 1870.
494   Wiseman, Timothy P., *Clio's Cosmetics*, Leicester, 1979.
495   Wiseman, Timothy P., 'Legendary Genealogies in Late Republican Rome', *Greece and Rome*, second ser. 21, 1974/75, pp. 153–64.
496   Wivell, C. J., 'The Chinese Oral and Pseudo-Oral Narrative Traditions', *CHINOPERL News*, 5, 1975, pp. 115–25.
497   Woodward, C. V., 'History from Slave Sources', *AHR*, 79, 1974, pp. 470–81.
498   Wright, Donald R., 'Koli Tengela in Sonko Traditions of Origin: An Example of the Process of Change in Mandinka Oral Traditions', *HA*, 5, 1978, pp. 257–71.
499   Wright, Donald R., *Oral Traditions from the Gambia*, 2 vols., Athens, Ohio, 1979–80.
500   Wright, Donald R., 'Uprooting Kunta Kinte: On the Perils of Relying on Encyclopedic Informants', *HA*, 7, 1981, pp. 205–17.
501   Yetman, N. R., 'The Background of the Slave Narrative Collection', *American Quarterly*, 19, 1967, pp. 534–53.
502   Ziegler, N. P., 'The Seventeenth-Century Chronicles of Marvara: A Study in the Evolution and Use of Oral Traditions in Western India', *HA*, 3, 1976, pp. 127–53.

INDEX